Patricia Sandoval has a truly amazing story, or
also of grace and redemption. Above all, it is
God loves us, walks with us even when we stu
to the good for those who love Him." This well-written book is always engaging and has something to challenge and inspire each of us, particularly in support of God's littlest ones, the unborn.

Archbishop Salvatore Cordileone
Archdiocese of San Francisco, California

As a priest, I have read many books, but none like the tale of love between Patricia and God, her Father. While I was reading, I gave glory to God many times for his work of mercy and transforming love in his little girl. Few are the books that after turning the last page, the reader senses that he or she has grown in faith, hope, and love. This is one of those books.

It is a story that calls to mind biblical figures, little ones through whom God does great works, who because of their weakness, have let themselves be transformed by the Holy Spirit.

At the end of each chapter are a series of facts that shed light on pro-life and family values and serve as valuable information for preaching the Gospel of Life.

This book is a gift from heaven for those who believe there is no hope left for their lives, a balm of spiritual consolation for whomever is blessed to read it. It is an excellent gift for any occasion.

P. Víctor Salomón
Coordinator of Defiendelavida.org

I could not put this book down and give it an enthusiastic recommendation! This generation, so badly wounded by the sexual revolution, needs to read Patricia Sandoval's story of triumph. It is never too late to heal and to rescue the treasures of our Godly inheritance: faith, family, sanctity of life, and authentic love. Patricia is truly a light for the world, and her story will leave you speechless.

Astrid Bennett Gutierrez
EWTN Host, Executive Director of The VIDA Initiative

Mrs. Watkins' latest book, *Transfigured: Patricia Sandoval's Escape from Drugs, Homelessness, and the Back Doors of Planned Parenthood*, truly surprises the mind through a dramatic and spiritual journey that can certainly inspire parents, teachers, and teenagers. This book is a resource for the New Evangelization, bringing the joy of true conversion and the hope of a better life for everyone.

Bishop Michael C. Barber, SJ
Diocese of Oakland, California

This heart-rending testimony of Patricia will touch many souls, some who are in pain and others in confusion: those who, pushed and deceived by the culture of death and the continuous attack on life and love, are dragged to a downward path without a way out, where darkness covers life and takes possession of the soul. On the other hand, her testimony will help those who want to resist, those who fight and do not want to fall into the swamp, those who know that love is the greatest treasure that we have. It will help them draw closer to the good, opening their hearts to life, opening their hearts to the light that illuminates everything: the omnipotent Light of God.

I am so grateful to Patricia for her courage and her sharing. May this Light continue to enlighten her steps and strengthen her spirit.

Emmanuel
Renowned singer throughout Latin America

Patricia Sandoval's story is gripping and inspirational. It might be compared with the classic life histories of many of the penitent saints: Sandoval shows us that no matter where we find ourselves, no matter how dark the situation or the prospects, grace looks for us, and if we so much as begin to cooperate, it eagerly sets to work, turning sinners toward sainthood. In collaboration with Ms. Sandoval, Christine Watkins writes with admirable clarity and intelligence; she is one of the best of the new generation of Catholic writers. This book is a joy to read.

Fr. Jim Sullivan
Author of *And the Angels Sing* and *The Rosary and the Gospels*

Patricia Sandoval is a modern-day Mary Magdalene. Her testimony is raw. It is the story of a soul who hit rock bottom and looked to Jesus, the real lover of our souls. This book will inspire many to come back to God and cause others to fall more deeply in love with Jesus Christ, our hope, out of gratitude for his incredible mercy. Patricia is one of the bravest women I have ever met. She is a prophetess for such a time as this.

Jesse Romero

Catholic Evangelist and Radio Host

Transfigured is an amazing story, able to reach even the most broken people and show them there is hope. Written in a moving and compelling style, this book is exceptionally hard to put down.

John-Henry Westen
Co-Founder and Editor-in-Chief, LifeSiteNews.com

Authors Christine Watkins and Patricia Sandoval do an outstanding job of helping the reader follow each thread of Patricia Sandoval's powerful, moving, tumultuous life, as it twists into knots and circles back to find disconnected threads. Pursued and decorated by God's unrelenting mercy, the frayed and broken web of her story is untangled into a richly textured tapestry, perfectly ordered into His divine will. As Patricia comes close to Him and tries to flee His gaze, the reader will identify with the anxiety of laying down our common human fears to risk crossing the turbulent bridge of trusting God. This book is an adventure of surrender that will give you hope and reshape your ideas about what life is all about.

Dr. Theresa Burke
Author of *Forbidden Grief: The Unspoken Pain of Abortion*
Founder, Rachel's Vineyard Ministries and Grief to Grace Ministries

Patricia Sandoval was misled by this culture of lies and lived horrifying experiences—just as so many people ensnared by the same contradictions are currently doing. The victory, however, is that God's grace pulled her through to powerfully advocate against everything that almost destroyed her. As a mother and survivor of several attempts against my own prenatal life, I am so proud of Patricia's strength and choice to embrace God's mercy, as we all must do. Moods, upbringings, political agendas, personal faith experiences, and even moral issues aside, Patricia's firsthand encounter with Planned Parenthood and the insidious agenda of the Culture of Death is a game changer. The primary message of this book, which I wholeheartedly recommend, dispels the myth that abortion is a viable, or even harmless "choice." You will laugh, cry, and even question—but it will be impossible to walk away from this story unchanged.

Bridget Gabrielle Hylak
Author and Founder, Pro Good Choice, Inc.

A television broadcast DVD of *Transfigured* is available at www.QueenofPeaceMedia.com/shop—**AS SEEN ON EWTN.** Follow the remarkable journey of Patricia Sandoval—a story that has the power to radically change lives and hearts in one sitting. The DVD includes bonus features of women and men sharing their heartfelt experiences of finding healing and transformation after abortion.

To see the book trailer and for inspiring Catholic books and media: CDs, videos, blogs, prayer requests, and more, go to www.QueenofPeaceMedia.com. If you would like to keep updated with our free video content, visit our YouTube Channel, Queen of Peace Media, at bit.ly/2HDl65U, and click on "Subscribe."

Patricia Sandoval travels the world as a professional speaker in high demand. Learn more by visiting www.patriciasandoval.com.

Disponible en español:

TRANSFIGURADA

See PatriciaSandoval.com and Amazon.com

Companion Videos

This book comes with short companion videos of Patricia Sandoval speaking to the reader at various chapter intervals. When you see the words "CHAPTER VIDEO" you are invited to go to the YouTube site listed to hear a message from Ms. Sandoval that relates to the content you will have just read.

TRANSFIGURED

Patricia Sandoval's Escape from Drugs, Homelessness, and the Back Doors of Planned Parenthood

Christine Watkins & Patricia Sandoval

www.queenofpeacemedia.com
Sacramento, California

Books may be purchased in quantity by contacting the publisher directly at orders@queenofpeacemedia.com.

ISBN-13: 978-1-947701-00-7
ISBN-10: 1947701002

Contents

Foreword by Fr. Donald Calloway, MIC 11

Introduction 13

Chapter One: The Little Princess 15

Chapter Two: Where's Mom? .... **Error! Bookmark not defined.**

Chapter Three: Dangerous Intimacy 35

Chapter Four: Life or Death 42

Chapter Five: Best Mom Ever 48

Chapter Six: Don't Ever Tell 53

Chapter Seven: Living a Lie 62

Chapter Eight: Looking Up 74

Chapter Nine: Living in Two Worlds 83

Chapter Ten: The Purge 95

Chapter Eleven: A Time to Heal 113

Chapter Twelve: Serenaded 123

Chapter Thirteen: Going Home 135

Chapter Fourteen: The Utter Blindness 147

Chapter Fifteen: Across the Airwaves 156

Chapter Sixteen: The Heart of Mercy 164

Chapter Seventeen: Let Me Live 175

Chapter Eighteen: In God's Time 185

Chapter Nineteen: Flowers from Jesus 192

Chapter Twenty: Press On 204

Chapter Twenty-one: Jesus, I Trust in You! 211

Other Books by Author, Christine Watkins 225

Appendix with Endnotes 231

Foreword

Are you ready to read one of the most powerful conversion stories ever written? Seriously, are you? It's a bold and shocking claim, I admit. But the story you are about to have the pleasure of reading is so intense and brutally candid that I wouldn't be surprised if it brings you to tears multiple times and opens the door to an experience of mercy and healing. This story is made for the big screen, and I pray it makes it there someday. It's that incredible.

When my friend Christine Watkins asked me to read the manuscript for *Transfigured* and pray about writing the foreword, I had to confess to her that I had never heard of Patricia Sandoval. After Christine told me a little about Patricia and piqued my interest with the subtitle, I realized that I couldn't turn down an offer to support a work that magnifies the mercy of God, offers a journey of inner healing from one's past, holiness for the future, and exposes the inner workings of Planned Parenthood.

Christine probably thought I would identify with the story since I had undergone a radical conversion and found freedom in Jesus, Mary, and Catholicism. My hunch about that turned out to be right. But I was unprepared for the intense emotional experience I would have while reading this book.

I couldn't put the thing down! The story of "the chick from Petaluma," as Patricia calls herself, completely drew me in. I became consumed with finding out what would happen on the next page. Not knowing her personally didn't matter. I've known a thousand souls like her. I'm one of them.

What is contained in these pages is about as raw, real, and riveting as a story can get. It is filled with heartache, pain, loss, forgiveness, tears, reconciliation, and joy. It's a story of God romancing a soul. Patricia is so ruggedly honest that she even admits to falling back into the same deadly sins after receiving countless graces and mercies from Jesus and Mary. This is part of what makes her testimony so real and so apropos for our times. Modern men and women, teenage boys and girls, need this witness.

Transfigured is masterfully written too. In addition to its message of love and mercy, each chapter is packed with the heart-wrenching reality of just how evil the world has become. You might wonder, at times, if certain facts related to Patricia's experience can be verified. Those questions are answered at the end of each chapter with statistics and well-researched bits of data that expose important lies and falsehoods of our times. These eye-opening "fact sections" provide a much-needed reality check for all of us.

Chances are that, like me, you don't know Patricia personally and that your name isn't in this book. But I believe you'll find yourself here. We are all inside these pages. If you do not identify directly with Patricia, you will connect with someone else in her story, and it will cause you to come face to face with your own story of brokenness and need for mercy. The world, especially Catholics, need to know this story of redemption. Reading it was an emotional rollercoaster for me, but thanks to Patricia's courage in sharing, I have found renewed hope and healing. I believe this book can be healing for you too.

So prepare yourselves for a wild ride, my friends. You are going to witness the innocence and beauty of a woman being restored. You are going to learn how Jesus, Mary, and Catholicism have the power to transfigure any soul.

And I'll bet you're going to want to be transfigured, too.

Fr. Donald Calloway, MIC
Author of *No Turning Back: A Witness to Mercy* and
Champions of the Rosary

Introduction

When I started to write this book, no one knew of Patricia Sandoval. Her dark secrets were closely guarded, and laying bare her past was unthinkable. Yet for the sake of the Kingdom, she surrendered her story to God and began to share with me and public audiences her jaw-dropping past. God responded by writing into her life the final chapters of this book, and events unfolded that she couldn't have possibly imagined. By the time the last chapter was completed, Ms. Sandoval had become an international speaker in high demand, sharing her testimony on dozens of television shows and radio stations, in front of stadium audiences, and in schools and churches across the United States, Latin America, and Europe.

Why this explosion of interest and enthusiasm? Why has Ms. Sandoval's testimony consistently astonished, inspired, and transformed even the most confused and hardened hearts in country after country? Why is it that when she speaks, tears of healing fall, minds change, souls are saved, unborn lives are rescued, and a flurry of apostolic activity ensues? Because her story is not simply another account of someone who was healed of a drug addiction. Neither is it merely one more tale of abandonment, unhealthy relationships, and misused sexuality. Nor is it only a testimony of post-abortion healing or another indicting exposé of Planned Parenthood and the abortion industry.

This is ultimately the story of the One behind the scenes: God, who, when we stumble and get hurt, longs to pick us up, carry us home in His arms, forgive us with tears, heal our battered souls, dress us in His radiance, and place us in front of others so that they, too, might seek Him and find that He was always there.

This is what God did for Patricia Sandoval, and He is poised and ready to do the same for you. As you read forward, you are invited to pray that God will give you an encounter with Himself. God is Love and Mercy, and these, his greatest attributes, desire to lift off the following pages and manifest in your heart. He will refashion you in His image as much as you allow Him to. God is Truth, and at the end of each chapter you will find little-known facts that shatter strongholds of cultural beliefs, founded on dark lies. God's Holy Word closes each chapter section to seal your faith in His power. As the prophet Isaiah says (Is. 55:11b): "It shall not return to me empty, but shall do what pleases me, achieving the end for which I sent it."

St. Padre Pio once lamented, "The harm that comes to souls from the lack of reading holy books makes me shudder . . . What power spiritual reading has to lead to a change of course, and to make even worldly people enter into the way of perfection."

Perhaps you've been through rough patches in life and wonder how you can ever heal and find peace. Possibly you live with a private shame that gnaws at your spirit, whispering, "You're unworthy. Unlovable. Rejected. Damaged. Bad." Maybe you are young and afraid, feeling alone in a sea of negativity and peer pressure. Or you may be an educator, youth minister, parent, or priest trying to effectively teach eternal truths about the human body and the human soul. Whether you can use a large dose of God's redeeming love, or a way to share hope with those who are suffering or in doubt, or simply would enjoy reading a conversion story that will make you fall in love with God all the more, this book is for you.

The amazing life of Patricia Sandoval sends forth bright rays into a gray world. It is no wonder that God wanted her story told.

CHAPTER
ONE

The Little Princess

WHEN I WAS A TODDLER, my mother bought a large picture of the Sacred Heart of Jesus, and she hung it above the headboard in the master bedroom. In the image, which framed Jesus' head and chest, His exposed heart was wrapped in thorns and set aflame by love. He looked alive, especially His eyes. They seemed to penetrate my thoughts, my feelings. Jesus wasn't merely looking at me; He was looking through me, and followed my every move around the room. At times, I hesitated before entering my parents' bedroom, wondering if He might tilt his head my way and call out my name. Fearfully, I would crawl on the floor, hoping to avoid His all-pervasive glare.

"Who is He?" I asked my mom incessantly, wanting to hear her answer over and over again.

"This is your *Papi Dios* (Daddy God) who takes care of you in heaven. He's with the angels," she'd say. Although she never prayed or went to church, my mom's belief in Jesus was genuine. Little did she know that her words would become a reality for her little girl.

One night at age three, as I lay awake in my bed, tummy down, I somehow knew that Jesus was waiting for me just outside of a high rectangular window close to the ceiling.

For reasons beyond my understanding, I could sense His arms extend toward me, although I didn't dare look up. My heart began to beat rapidly, but I didn't want Him to know that I felt scared. After all, He was Papi Dios, and I'd been taught not to be afraid of Him.

Eventually, I mustered the courage to twist my head farther to one side and glance upward. And there was Jesus, outside my window, smiling adoringly at me, His arms reaching right through the glass toward my tiny frame.

Caught up in his loving gaze, my body began to levitate off the bed. Unable to feel my little legs touching the bedcovers, I wanted to know if this floating sensation was real; still facing downward, I lowered my chin toward my chest to see the front of my white pull-up diaper and my white T-shirt. Sure enough, my legs weren't touching the bed—nor was any other part of me. I was hovering face-down in midair. Amazed, I turned my head to the left and saw my five-year-old sister in her twin bed across the room, tossing and turning in her sleep. "Oh my gosh," I told myself, "this is real." I knew I couldn't be dreaming or outside of my physical body or my room because I was clearly still in them.

Slowly, delicately, my body began to float upward toward the window. My little palms started to sweat and my heart seemed to stop, as if I were at the crest of a roller coaster. Scared and confused, I remained face down, eyes bulging, looking at my sister, wondering why she wasn't floating too. Then my body changed to a sitting position, facing Jesus.

As I floated closer to Him, I noticed fresh wounds in the center of Jesus' upturned palms. Then I saw His gown, made of three dark, rich, and shiny colors: a magnificent gold covering His torso, an intense forest green draping around his left arm, and a dark, burgundy red swooping across His right. Last, I noticed His hair: brown, wavy, falling a little past his shoulders. Each aspect of his appearance was perfectly clear. The glass in the window had disappeared.

He didn't say a word to me, but the warm look in his eyes put me at ease. With great tenderness and compassion, He reached out his arms in anticipation of holding me, and His smile expressed His pure delight in my innocence. When I got so close as to touch Him, my arms instinctively wrapped tightly around His neck. Next to my bare arms and legs, His garments felt like silk, and His hands, which cupped my sidesaddle legs, felt strong and safe.

We took off flying full force through the sky. I could feel Jesus' hair against my right cheek and His left arm tight and secure under my knees as each cloud quickly brushed my face and the wind whipped by, tossing my hair in all directions.

My arms were gripping Him so tightly that I wondered if I might be choking Him. Finally, we stopped and hovered in midair. I let go of His neck and turned my head to the right to see what lay before us. It was a scene in shades of radiant light blue. Grand stairs, so wide they traveled sideways past my area of vision, led up to a spectacular wooden door, much like the entryway of a medieval castle. About twenty feet high and wide with an arched top, the door was fortified with rivets and metal bars and secured shut with an iron bolt.

Off slightly to the right on the top step, stood two angels, facing each other and playfully conversing. In the center of the steps, sat another angel in repose, resting his elbow on one lifted knee, his chin cupped in his right hand. All of them wore long, light-colored tunics, looked about twelve years old, and had wings rising from their thin frames. They were waiting for me to arrive.

The entire scene was suspended in midair and lasted for a blink. Jesus gave me instant knowledge that heaven was behind that door. He was going to leave me with the angels who would take me there, and I was going to have a wonderful time. I also knew I would remember little to nothing of what I was about to see.

What happened in heaven and how long I stayed, I do not know. I only recall wanting to remain there forever. My next memory is of clinging to Jesus with my arms squeezing His neck, back outside the high window.

Without talking, I communicated that I didn't want Him to leave. I knew I had been somewhere that was a lot of fun, and I wanted to stay with Him; but He let me know I had to go back into my room. And so we said our sweet good-byes without words. Then He lovingly released His arms and, touching my diapered bottom with one hand, gave me a tiny push inside. I began to float down as though an angel were tenderly and carefully carrying me in his arms. As I approached the bed while still in midair, my body was gently turned to face the window and then moved into a sitting position so that when I landed on my bed, my back rested against the cold wall. After remaining there stunned for a moment, I started yelling for my mom.

My mother has since told me that my screaming woke her up, and she took me into my parents' room to sleep in their bed. Sandwiched between them, I talked all night about how Papi Dios had taken me to heaven where I played with the angels and had so much fun. My parents kept telling me to be quiet and settle down, but I didn't sleep a wink.

In the days that followed, my parents didn't believe me. But over time, they realized that my tale never faded or changed or ceased to bring me joy. By the time I was six years old, my mother was so convinced of my story's veracity that she began asking me to share it with friends and family.

Never before or since have I had such a miraculous encounter with God, one that was not only spiritual but also tactile and embodied. I've always known that it wasn't a dream or simply my imagination. I'd never seen the movie *Peter Pan*, and floating in the air or flying without a plane had never appealed to me. Those were someone else's childhood fantasies, not mine. Throughout my life, this encounter with Jesus remained such a vivid memory that belief in Him never once left my heart. I would need this belief as time went on. Only the Good Lord knew how much.

> . . . Jesus said, "Let the children come to me, and do not prevent them; for the kingdom of heaven belongs to such as these."
> –Matthew 19:14

My father first met my mother at his sister's Christmas Eve party, when he was twenty and my mom was eighteen. My father picked up my four-month-old sister, who was playing on the floor, and said, "Who's the mom of this pretty little girl?" He was a gentleman with a reputation for being responsible and hardworking, and this attracted my mom. Two months after immigrating to the States from Mexico, she had gotten a job working at a chocolate factory earning minimum wage, where she'd burn her hands daily on the hot machines. Each morning and evening, my mom, only five feet tall, had to walk an hour across town in the snow and bitter cold Chicago wind, carrying a child in her arms. One of the first things my father told her was, "You'll never have to walk again."

When I was born, my uncle, a quasi-identical-looking, outgoing version of my dad (both of them five feet ten and handsome, with round Mexican facial features and olive skin) immediately loved me like his own. He insisted that my name be Patricia, which means "Noble One"—and I certainly felt noble. My childhood was as close to perfect as my young mind could imagine. Joy and security, adulation and admiration pervaded every day of my early upbringing.

I thought my mother was the best. She showered my older sister, younger brother, and me with tender, doting affection. In her care, our home was tidy and beautiful, and her little ones well-groomed and behaved. My mother's generous nurturing extended beyond our immediate family to my older cousin Xochil's three children, who often stayed with us when their mother went to work. My father, a stoic Mexican American man, was known for helping anyone who needed a handyman and, while less outwardly affectionate than my mom, he liked to spoil his children. He worked hard in construction to provide for the family and showed his love through material gifts and deeds. As his firstborn, I was the apple of his eye. My obedience, good grades, and openly affectionate nature toward my parents made him proud.

Dad would tuck me and my siblings into bed every night, then stand in the doorway and say a blessing over us, making the sign of the cross. In the shadow of his gesture and words, I felt protected and comforted throughout the night. In the morning, my mom would burst into my room, singing, "Who's the prettiest princess in the whole world?"

"Me—it's me!" I would respond, fully believing it.

My mother was an attractive woman who refused to buy an item of clothing on sale and insisted on high-end creams and makeup for her fine skin. "I'd rather be dead than get a wrinkle on my face by the time I'm forty," she said a couple of times, which made me fear for her life. Year after year, I would search for any ominous, death-dealing lines emerging on her face. Aging, therefore, equaled suicide. Youthful beauty was life itself.

With my mother's vanity spilling onto my childhood, I loved nothing more than to look in the mirror and admire my long, soft, straight brown hair. For hours, I'd lock myself in my mom's bathroom, surrounded by brushes and bobby pins, and stare at the mini-goddess I perceived in my reflection. My self-absorption was bolstered by a cavalcade of compliments that would tumble out of the mouths of more than fifty extended family members. Of my thirty brown-eyed Mexican American cousins, I was the only one with green eyes, inherited from my mom. Whenever I walked into a family event—dressed often in a signature pink, fluffy outfit—I stood and posed, waiting expectantly for accolades.

When it came time for my First Communion at age seven, I felt like I was marrying into royalty. My dress was an extravagant, ten-piece composite of imitation silk, white lace, and pearls with a Gone with the Wind five-foot-wide hoop skirt, three-foot-wide bow, and plenty of sparkles. I had picked it out myself, of course. On the way to the church, I barely fit into the front seat of my parents' car and couldn't see where we were going because the front of my dress covered half the windshield. As I walked down the center aisle to receive my First Holy Communion, people gasped.

I felt I was so special that the world had to see me. My dream was to be *somebody* in life, and not a doubt sullied the firm plans in my mind of being a famous actress or model. My beauty would surely get me there. Then my sister, searching for any flaw whatsoever on my body, found a couple of small brown dots on my left forearm. "They will never accept you in the modeling world because of . . . *those*!"

My entire life plan was crushed in one blow. From then on, I would shout at God, "Why did you give me this cursed defect? It has ruined my whole modeling career!" For years to come, I stared at my dots in terror, watching them grow bigger along with me. My grandmother Consuelo—my mother's mother—had the same birthmark in the same place; and to make matters worse, my relatives would sometimes comment, "You're going to look just like your grandma." For me, this was a nightmare come alive. Not only did she have "the mark," she had wrinkles and thin lips!

Even while my dreams of vainglory struggled to survive, something inside of me still knew—really knew—that I was special to God. I would talk to Papi Dios often throughout the day. In the backyard of our home in Petaluma, California, I would sit on the grass to write Him letters, tie them to a balloon, and send them up to heaven, hoping they would reach Him. For me, God was in the sky, and whenever I saw a shooting star, it was because He wanted to grant me a wish. From age five to ten, the greatest prayer of my heart was, "God, make me rich one day so I can pick up all the poor children in the world and put them in a big building and give them food and a shower—and a makeover."

> Your adornment should not be an external one: braiding the hair, wearing gold jewelry, or dressing in fine clothes, but rather the hidden character of the heart, expressed in the imperishable beauty of a gentle and calm disposition, which is precious in the sight of God.
> –1 Peter 3:3–4

There was plenty of family love to go around, not only in the United States but in Mexico as well, where we traveled at least once a year to stay at grandma's house, my father's childhood home. But there was one missing detail. Our spirituality was not rooted in the living God. We never went to church but said we were Catholic. Without our knowing it, our house was not built on the Rock. Jesus was not our Lord and King.

Danger entered our home when my mom met our new neighbor. Dolly was her name, and she suffered from depression. Often already in tears when she arrived, she would sit down with my mom in our living room and talk with her for hours. Eventually, they became good friends. Dolly would take her out for coffee with friends from Colombia and Central America. But their clique wouldn't only drink their cups of joe; they'd read each other's futures in the grounds.

Soon my mom claimed to be psychic and said she knew how to read people's palms. When word got out, almost everyone who came over wanted to know their future. She taught my siblings and me her new "art" and then sat me down to read my palm. I felt so excited to receive this special mother-daughter treat. But when she looked at my short "lifeline," she gasped, "Oh, my God, you're going to die in only two years!" I was only ten. Then she announced that the way I was going to die was in a car accident. For a couple years after that, I would look at my short little lifeline, terrified that my life would soon end. I prayed to God constantly, asking him to extend the line on my hand. As my twelfth birthday approached, I panicked. When the day passed uneventfully, I was ecstatic: *"I'm alive! I'm still alive!"*

Mom continued her antics undeterred. When she learned that Deepak Chopra, a New Age giant, was coming to California, she made someone drive her for hours in order to hear his "wisdom." She gave my sister and me books to read by Brian Weiss, who piqued my interest in reincarnation, and by Sophia Brown, the self-professed psychic healer, whose books became our bibles. My sister invited me to join her in getting a tattoo—an unsightly symbol of my zodiac sign, Virgo—saying that it would bond us as two powerful New Age women. Mom arranged slumber parties for us kids in the living room where we cuddled up in our sleeping bags, aligned our chakras, studied our auras, and fell asleep to the voice of New Age actress Shirley MacLaine. More videos arrived as we joined the search for other worlds. My mom even got to the point where she believed Jesus was an alien.

When my mother's sibling, Sister Olga, Mother Superior of the Sacred Heart of Jesus of the Blessed Sacrament, would come to visit from Mexico, she hardly knew what to think about our shenanigans. Unfamiliar with the New Age movement, she would wring her hands and say with a bewildered look, "I'm going to pray for you." Pulling me aside, she would share with me that Jesus died on the Cross for us and God was the Holy Trinity. I nodded politely without understanding.

The increasingly frequent visits to our home by my mom's friends inevitably morphed into small psychic home fairs, and there was no shortage of large New Age fairs to attend in the area. When I was fifteen, Mom took my sister and me to one where we could buy tickets for different station booths: three tickets for information about our past lives, four for palm readings, five for tarot . . . With stacks of tickets in hand, we split up and dashed to different booths. Planting myself at a past-life station, I found out I had been a princess in one life. In the next, I was a queen married to a king with seven wives—I was his favorite, of course. But I wasn't happy, so I committed suicide in a tub. I then reincarnated into a handsome, blue-eyed blond boy in France, who dressed up in leather booties and nylons, like Robin Hood. At age fourteen, when I was courageously running back and forth in the crossfire, delivering scrolls to kings, an arrow pierced my back, and I fell to the ground dead.

During a break in the fair, the three of us reconvened, and I couldn't wait to tell my mom and my sister that I not only had been a queen—I was the king's main wife. My sister was the first to speak. She looked at me and burst with excitement: "I was a queen in my last life!"

I said, "Wait, I was one, too."

And then my mom chimed in: "Oh well, so was I." Pushing probability aside, we continued to believe . . .

At the recommendation of a friend, Mom went to see a psychic who greeted her in the midst of pyramid-shaped crystals. "There are angels trapped inside of these," he said. "And one of them wants to go home with you." The crystals were three hundred to four hundred dollars each. Mom was ecstatic. Her trapped angel, he said, was named Princess Deva. After taking Mom's large wad of cash, the man performed a ritual with a piece of my mother's hair. Then he instructed her to go home and put the large pink crystal on top of her heart and surrender herself to it. That night before falling asleep, as she lay face up on her bed, she placed the pyramid on top of her chest and gave it and all its powers permission to come into her heart. The next morning, it wasn't in her bed, in her bedclothes, or under the bed. It wasn't anywhere. My brother, sister, and I hadn't come into her room, so she blamed my father, an exceedingly honest man. "Where's my princess? You took it from me!" she accused him.

Wondering about her sanity, he responded matter-of-factly, "I never touched anything." The crystal had simply disappeared.

One New Year's Day, we came home after traveling out of town to find that someone had put black salt around and inside of our home. A "friend" of my mother, we later learned, had secretly wanted my father for herself and performed a Wiccan ceremony to make her wish come true.

In the seven years following the invasion of the New Age into our home, all seemed well in the family. My siblings and I never saw our parents fight, and they loved and cared for us without reserve. But when the crystal disappeared, the darkness veiled behind the glitter of the New Age made itself known.

> Do not go to mediums or consult fortune-tellers, for you will be defiled by them. I, the LORD, am your God.
> –Leviticus 19:3

I was twelve, my brother ten, and my sister fourteen the day the ground fell from underneath our feet. Around the dinner table sat us kids on one side and my mother on the other. My dad stood off to the side, silent. My mother said few words: "We're getting a divorce." We were given a choice. We could stay in Petaluma and live with our father at our aunt and uncle's home or leave immediately for Mexico with our mother.

My brother and sister broke down crying. I started to wail. Catapulted into shock in one second and forced to make this life-changing decision in the next, I cried out, "But Mom, you don't even have any money. How are you going to take care of us?"

Before that moment, I had never challenged or questioned my mom. I had always been compliant with her desires and submitted my will to hers. Something inside my mother snapped when she heard my protest, and her eyes pierced me with a cold stare. "Okay," she said through tears, "if you're picking your dad, get out of my house."

I had not seen my parents argue even once, and now a full-scale war had erupted. I went from having what I thought was a loving, unified family to being brutally kicked out of a broken home—all within fifteen minutes. Sobbing and screaming, I was forced to grab a few belongings and get in the car with my dad. When we arrived at my aunt and uncle's home, my face was beet red, and I couldn't stop crying long enough to catch a full breath.

My mom had never raised her voice at me, never spoken harshly to me. In my estimation, she was all love. My parents had nicknamed me "The Alarm" as a baby because when I was in my mother's arms, I'd scream if someone reached out to touch me. I didn't want to be with anyone else. When she bathed me at night, she would sing songs as she scrubbed my little feet and legs. Every morning, to get us ready for school, Mom would wake up my sister, give her ten minutes of kisses, then do the same for me and for my brother. She did all the housework, cooked for us, danced with us, and showed incredible patience. She gave us special nicknames, spoke to us in both Spanish and English, sang us lullabies, and made us feel warm and safe. Her bedtime stories, created nightly by her fertile imagination, transported us to new lands. All her attention was on her children, and every day I heard her say, "You're beautiful. You're my princess." My mom was everything to me. She was my world—my joy. Where was my mommy now?

My dad sold our house, at my mother's request, and they divided the spoils fifty/fifty. We stayed at my aunt and uncle's for a week and then moved to live with my cousin. For an entire year, I had no contact with my mother, who had moved to Guadalajara. She felt betrayed, and so did we.

During that time, I would occasionally walk into my dad's room to ask him a question and find him on his knees next to his bed, with copious tears streaming down his reddened face and a deep sadness shaping his eyes. His stoic and reserved personality couldn't hide his broken heart, and he often escaped to his room to cry. I watched him wander through his days without purpose or motivation; even our trips to his hometown in Mexico, which he always used to enjoy, meant nothing to him. My father, who had been such a strong figurehead, was struggling to manage the simplest household tasks, burning his fingers while trying to cook and ruining clothes in the laundry. Never before had I seen him so vulnerable, and I didn't know how to react, except to feel compassion for him and rage against my mom, whom I blamed for everything. After all, she was the one who left.

Dreams started to trick me at night, always with the same theme: moments of joy and togetherness with the family unit I had lost. Whether my parents were visible in the dreams or not, I always sensed that they were somewhere nearby and together, keeping me safe and secure. For many years to come, these recurring dreams would haunt my psyche—sometimes weekly, sometimes monthly. They were beautiful, yet cruel, because I always had to wake up.

I had no one to talk to, no adult to comfort me after my parents' sudden separation. My dad never once asked me, "How do you feel?" To cope with my rising anxiety, I developed trichotillomania, an addictive tendency to pull my hair out. This started when a friend showed me how to find a hair, split it in two, and then yank it out from its root. Always complimented for my beautiful hair, I now found comfort in destroying it. By splitting my "perfect" hairs down the middle, then pulling them out and causing pain, my subconscious was trying to resolve the traumatic split of my parents' "perfect" marriage and my sudden and painful yank from my home: my "roots." During the day, if something stressful crossed my mind, I'd start looking for a hair, and with the snap of it coming out, my body felt a release of tension. I'd get so lost in my hair every day that for up to two hours at a time, I would lock myself in my room or the bathroom and search for strands to pull, leaving behind a small pile of hair on the floor.

As it turned out, life didn't work out so well for my mom in Mexico. Though very intelligent, she'd never learned how to pay a credit card bill or put gas in her car. After a year away, she started contacting my dad. One day, I happened to overhear him speaking on the phone with her. I hadn't seen him so happy in a long time. When he hung up, he turned to me with a big smile and said, "Your mom wants to work things out."

"Hell, no!" I retorted. I'd seen him suffer so much and was furious about what she'd done. By no means did I want to see my mom or see my parents back together. My dad tried to convince me that everything was going to be okay, but I held tightly to my grudge.

Dad went out and bought a brand-new house in Petaluma, custom made, with marble floors and grand, expansive rooms—his elaborate attempt to keep Mom happy. By nature, quiet and uncommunicative, he didn't know how to express tender affection or feelings, so he had always revealed his heart to her through material things. I was thirteen when the family got together once again, and it was like nothing had ever happened. My mom was as loving as ever, and her warmth melted my stone-cold heart. I quickly forgave her for everything, but our dance of abandonment hadn't ended. It had just begun.

So they are no longer two, but one flesh. Therefore, what God has joined together, no human being must separate.
–Matthew 19:6

Fact: Statistics on divorce in the United States consistently reveal that the children of divorced parents are more at risk for health, behavioral, learning, and emotional problems: (1) Girls tend to become more anxious, withdrawn, and sexually active at a younger age. Difficulties for both sexes also include a higher risk of too much alcohol and drug use, teen pregnancy, taking a criminal path, and suicide. Later on in life, they tend to be lonelier, unhappier, have riskier sexual relationships, and lean more toward having children outside of marriage. Religious worship often decreases or stops after the parents divorce. (2)

Popular myth has it that the divorce rate in the United States is around 50 percent. But this statistic is false. The divorce rate is only about 20 to 25 percent for first-time marriages, and among churchgoers, the rate is even lower—in the single digits or teens. (3, 4)

Chapter Two

Where's Mom?

THE NEXT FIVE YEARS passed peacefully as we enjoyed our second honeymoon as a family. Then one day, when I was eighteen, Mom started packing up her things. I was downstairs watching TV when Dad came down the stairs to say, "Your mom is leaving." I ran upstairs to see if it was true, and there Mom was in my parents' room, stuffing her suitcases full. "What's happening? What's going on?" I cried out.

"Don't talk to me," she responded coldly. "Don't get near me. Leave me alone, and let me pack my things myself."

I went back downstairs and saw my dad, sitting on a kitchen stool, bent over the counter with his head buried in his arms, dissolved in uncontrollable sobbing. My sister, in her own shock and grief, stood next to him, trying to console him. When Mom came downstairs with her luggage, we tried to hug her, but she said, "Don't touch me. Don't hug me. Don't talk to me. Let me leave."

My dad gave her one of our cars, and as she was driving away, he started running after her. When she turned the corner at the end of the block, he dropped and fell onto the concrete in the middle of the street, wailing like a child. As our neighbors, who were barbecuing on their lawns, looked on, my sister walked over to him, helped him get up, put his arm around her shoulders, and dragged him home. He could barely walk.

My mom moved to San Jose to live with a friend, but her stay didn't last long. Still unaccustomed to independence, she came back after six months to say to my father, "This house that we own is fifty/fifty, so I deserve to live here as a roommate, and I'm going to do whatever the hell I want."

Dad loved my mom and took her back; but none of us children wanted her at home anymore. My brother stayed very quiet. He bottled his emotions, except to curse women, and avoided the arguments flying around him. I'd gained a lot of weight, and he started joining others' "chunky girl" comments about my round figure, getting back at me for my taunts when he was little. My sister grew hard and tough as she strained to maintain a sense of normalcy among the scattered pieces of our family. I became overprotective of my father and didn't want my mom to hurt him, insult him, touch him, even come near him. At every turn, I defended Dad and fought my mother, throwing hurtful words her way, such as, "Why don't you just leave?"

Mom's New Age practices were in full force, as was her newfound desire to go out partying into the early morning hours with young friends from the junior college she was now attending—while Dad waited up for her on the living-room couch. She was determined to enjoy the freedom her youth never gave her. Two days before Thanksgiving, she went out; Thanksgiving morning, she still wasn't home. My sister took action, although none of us knew how to cook, including her. My brother moved methodically around the kitchen, without a word. Dad said precious little, and I watched his look of contemplative melancholy harden into a bitter stare. That evening, numb and coping, we sat around the table, staring sorrowfully at our food, trying to make the best of it as we asked the silent question, "Where's Mom?"

The next day, Mom straggled in without explanation. That's the day my dad got angry. He took the car keys away from her so she couldn't go anywhere. He pulled the phone jacks from my room to stop her from locking herself in there and talking for hours on the phone. It was war.

At this point, my mom became unrecognizable. She said things to me that were not normal. With my sister as a witness, she shouted, "You're the biggest whore in the world." Then she barged into my room and started cutting up my clothes. "If you die and you're six feet under," she snapped, "I would never go to your funeral."

One day, shaking with rage, she grabbed a huge, black animal statue from our living room and lifted it up over her head with both hands in an attempt to crash it down on top of me. I covered my head with my arms, thinking I was going to die. Dad grabbed the statue away from her and roared, "Don't you hurt my daughter!" Then my sister escorted my mom up to her room and told her she needed to pack up her things and go. Mom left. She doesn't remember any of this.

Two days later, she returned. "Get the hell out of the house!" she bellowed at me. "You'll have to live on the streets. I'm going to be in your room. Take all your crap out because you're not sleeping there. I don't care. I'm not your mother. You're not my daughter."

She walked behind me like a snowplow, pushing me around the house at a steady pace while spewing a stream of evil insults. I ran between the bathroom and my room, grabbing what I could as my dad stood passively in the hallway, saying nothing. I looked over at him helplessly. His body was frozen and pain contorted his face. Desperately, I wanted him to shout out, "No, she's not going anywhere! She's my daughter. She stays right here. This is her home!" But instead, in powerless resignation, he threw up his hands, as if to say, "What do you want me to do?"

At the risk of losing his wife, he was willing to sacrifice his daughter. My loving dad, who had always stood by me and whose side I had always taken, betrayed me with his silence.

I walked outside and looked at my car. "So this is my home now?" Filled with crashing waves of shame and sweating from shock, my mind ricocheted between scenes of homelessness and knocking at someone's door with my meager belongings. I sat down in the back seat, feeling dizzy and claustrophobic, as reality pressed in on me through the four sides of my small car. I couldn't fathom how my dad hadn't raised a hand to help me in any way, not even to make a call to find a place for me to stay. Curling into a ball, I cried myself to sleep, praying I would never wake up.

When morning came, I opened my tear-filled eyes, dreading the confirmation that yesterday's nightmare was true. Wondering how I would survive, the idea came to call my good friend Veronica, who had dropped out of high school and had a four-year-old son. Mustering the courage to dial her number, I told her through sobs what had happened. She and her mom, an angel of a woman, immediately decided to welcome me into their Petaluma home.

I went from living in a spacious house with my family to sharing a twin-sized bed with a friend. I couldn't accept the quick, one hundred and eighty-degree turn of my life. Without parents to support me anymore, I plummeted from being a straight-A student to dropping out of my last year of high school. My new motto about my parents—and life—had begun: "You don't care about me, so I'm not going to care about me either. F--- it."

One day, Veronica accompanied me to my family's home to retrieve my belongings since, in addition to the cash that my dad handed me now and again, I had only a few items of clothing. While I knocked on the front door with my fist, my mom stood inside on the stairs screaming, "You can't come in!" Veronica had been around my family for many years and had known my mom as the loving, peaceful, woman she had been—the mother who never said an unkind word.

Veronica stepped back in disbelief as my mom continued to yell, "Get out! You're not going to take anything out of this house!"

"I'm going to call the police," I told her, "and have them help me get my stuff."

"Go ahead," she said. So I did. The police arrived at the house and stood at the door, keeping guard as I walked inside, went upstairs, and grabbed my things.

That night, I silently cried myself to sleep. In between bouts of tossing and turning, I had a dream:

I am in my parents' bathroom. My mom is brushing my hair, getting me ready for school. She puts water on the brush and pulls my hair back into a side ponytail so tight that I protest. Yet at the same time, I like it because her hands make me feel loved. Walking me to the kitchen, she starts making hot chocolate and pancakes for me, like she did every morning. I eat and feel fully satisfied. As I get up from the table, she straightens my collar and kisses me gently on the forehead. Then she hands me my lunch, made up of a ham sandwich, fresh fruit, and my favorite snack: jello.

Suddenly, we're across from my elementary school where she used to drop me off. I get out of the car and walk toward my first-grade classroom. I look back to see her loving figure leaning out the window, making sure I get across the street safely, and I hear her say. "I hope you have a wonderful day, my princess."

> Can a mother forget her infant, be without tenderness for the child of her womb? Even should she forget, I will never forget you.
> –Isaiah 49:15

CHAPTER VIDEO
Patricia Sandoval Speaks to Those Who Feel Abandoned
See https://youtu.be/6uFdMyF3XB8
Or go to YouTube.com and find the video by searching
Queen of Peace Media

Veronica hung out with a bad crowd. On weekends, she would leave her little boy with her mother and go party in Los Angeles, and I decided to join her. One particular weekend, a young man offered to drive us from Petaluma to LA and to pay our way so we could party with him there. We could hardly restrain our glee. Perhaps Veronica knew, but I didn't, that he was toting several pounds of cocaine.

Partying, for me, meant dancing and getting a little buzzed, with no sex or drugs involved. I was a virgin who had never gotten high on anything. But in L.A., the devil pointed to a door I'd never noticed before and then opened it, motioning for me to walk through. It happened one evening when Veronica and I, a friend of ours named Angelina, and the young man, were lounging around in our L.A. hotel room—that he had also paid for. Angelina reached into her pocket and then laid out four lines of cocaine. I had never seen the substance in my life. As I stared at the white powder, a sudden fear seized me. The fourth line was for me.

"Oh, just try it. Don't be chicken," said Veronica. "I've done it before. It's not a big deal." After snorting their lines, they rolled up a dollar bill for me. They told me to close one nostril with my forefinger and middle finger, put the rolled bill with one end in my open nostril and the other at the beginning of the line of white powder, and then breathe in forcefully. I didn't want to take it, but with trembling hands, I followed their instructions. My nose began to burn, my throat and mouth went numb, and my heart started beating rapidly as a strong combination of anxiety and euphoria buzzed and swirled through my system.

The high didn't last long, but after I took one line, I wanted another one not more than an hour later, then soon another, and another. All night, we took lines while my mind raced with wonderful ideas for my future. Veronica and I were going to be famous Hollywood stars or models. Either one would do. We'd met a couple of well-known Mexican actors, and we figured that their fame would rub off on us. We'd been learning how to do makeovers, so we were also going to be millionaire entrepreneurs, running our own cosmetic business. Somehow, we looked better than all of the other girls in Los Angeles. Our pupils were dilated, our skin was breaking out in zits, and our lips were dry and chapped from the cocaine. But we were hot. When the drug effect died down, we thought, "Maybe not."

Off of the high, I felt exhausted, lonely, depressed, and hopeless about my life. My body collapsed, and I slept for twenty-four hours. But with the high of the next weekend, the pain went away, and all was possible again. Cocaine was the thing to do in the City of the Angels. Veronica and I would walk into bathrooms and see other girls doing lines in the stalls. The drug presented itself to us at every turn, given the company we were keeping. Each weekend, in a different hotel room, we'd take a rock of cocaine from a tiny Ziploc® bag, we'd place it on top of the night-table, pull out a Bible from the top drawer, raise it in the air above the cocaine, and smash it down forcefully on top of the rock to crush it into a powder. Then we would separate the powder into lines on top of the Holy Bible and pass it around the room for people to snort. The first time I saw a group of girls do this, I felt a terrible sense of sacrilege; but because no one cared, I began to think nothing of it.

As excited as I was to reap the drug's effects of euphoria and weight loss, I hated its aftereffects and the fact that I started pulling my hair out even more. I didn't tell anyone who didn't need to know what I was doing, and I told myself after my third weekend of snorting lines throughout the night that I wasn't going to get addicted, that it was only for fun on the weekends.

My trust still remained in New Age spirituality, despite the evidence that something was terribly amiss. One red flag stands out alongside many others. I went to see a psychic named Sonya because I had a crush on a guy who started dating my female friend instead of me, and I felt devastated by the "betrayal." Sitting behind a table covered with a purple cloth with red tassels, she read her assorted tarot cards with great concern and told me there was a block on my relationship with him. Evil had been done by my girlfriend, who had placed the block there through witchcraft. "You need to pay me two thousand dollars," she said, "because there is big witchcraft on your life. Here, put this potion on." She wanted the money in cash. Naively, I borrowed the entire sum, came back, and threw in more for the love potion, which I had to rub on my body in the shower while chanting something four or five times. It didn't work. The guy never called.

"Come back," she said. "Let's see what's going on." Sitting in front of her trusted cards, she chanted, "Oh, this is getting complicated. This is stronger than I thought. I'm going to have to do a ritual tonight, and I need four hundred dollars to buy special candles because it's really powerful." I gave her the money, and she supposedly did a ritual on her own. Still the guy didn't call me! Days went by and I didn't hear anything from the guy or from her so I called her to see what was going on. "Your friend is doing a bigger ritual against us now and putting up an even bigger block," she warned, "so I'll need another $400 to do an even bigger ritual back." I gave her the money, and he never called. After a time, she wanted even more money. Only then did I realize it was all baloney.

My most dangerous dabbling in the New Age occurred around the Ouija board. When I was only eight, a friend walked me down into the basement of her home to introduce me to the "game." She explained that we could call upon the spiritual world to give us answers to our questions. Printed on a rectangular board were the letters of the alphabet, zero, the numerals one through nine, and the words, "YES," "NO," "HELLO," and "GOODBYE." Placing on the board a triangular marker with a round clear plastic window through which the markings on the board could be seen, my friend lowered her voice to a hush. "See, this glides by itself just with a light touch of my fingertips. It's moved by the spirits of the dead. They're going to give us answers."

Ten years after my first introduction to the "game," I still put my faith in it when friends and I would sit around a table, asking questions of dead people and unknown spirits, to the smooth sound of the zigzagging marker. "Is my boyfriend cheating behind my back?" "Will I meet someone cute?" When my turn came to touch the glass marker, a sense of anxious excitement would shiver down my spine because I knew I wasn't moving the triangle with my hand. Underneath my fingertips, the marker would start to vibrate, then glide in a particular direction, land for a second or two on a letter, and then ricochet onto another and another, pausing once a word was formed. The marker would form perfectly spelled words and correct sentences and seemed to gain momentum the more the Ouija board was used and believed in. Sometimes the answers turned out to be right. Sometimes they were wrong. At times, I feared, "What if it tells everyone I've been taking cocaine?"

Little did I know, I was courting demons.

> Let there not be found among you anyone who immolates his son or daughter in the fire, nor a fortune-teller, soothsayer, charmer, diviner, or caster of spells, nor one who consults ghosts and spirits or seeks oracles from the dead. Anyone who does such things is an abomination to the LORD.
> –Deuteronomy 18:10–12b

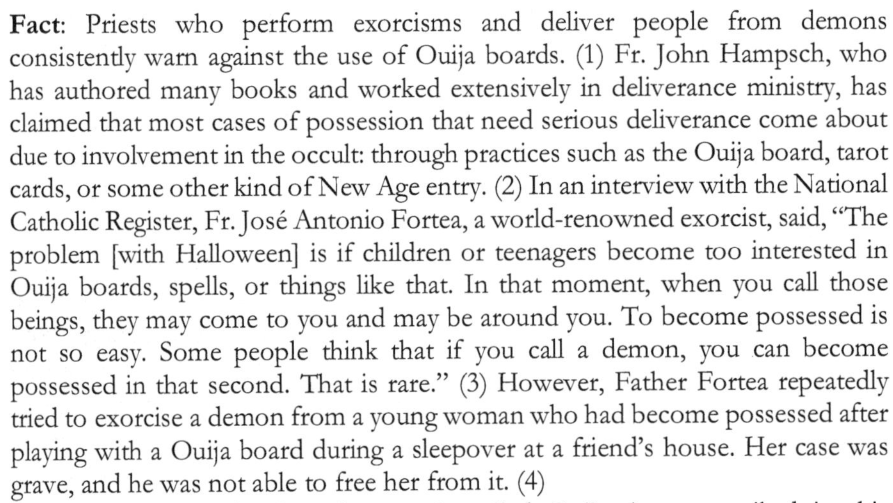

Fact: Priests who perform exorcisms and deliver people from demons consistently warn against the use of Ouija boards. (1) Fr. John Hampsch, who has authored many books and worked extensively in deliverance ministry, has claimed that most cases of possession that need serious deliverance come about due to involvement in the occult: through practices such as the Ouija board, tarot cards, or some other kind of New Age entry. (2) In an interview with the National Catholic Register, Fr. José Antonio Fortea, a world-renowned exorcist, said, "The problem [with Halloween] is if children or teenagers become too interested in Ouija boards, spells, or things like that. In that moment, when you call those beings, they may come to you and may be around you. To become possessed is not so easy. Some people think that if you call a demon, you can become possessed in that second. That is rare." (3) However, Father Fortea repeatedly tried to exorcise a demon from a young woman who had become possessed after playing with a Ouija board during a sleepover at a friend's house. Her case was grave, and he was not able to free her from it. (4)

After Hollywood released a movie called Ouija, interest spiked in this dangerous game. Internet searches for Ouija boards went up by 300 percent, according to the search-engine giant, Google. (5) Despite the dangers, Ouija boards continue to fascinate and to be sold openly in stores.

CHAPTER THREE

Dangerous Intimacy

AROUND THIS TIME, I started to work as a secretary in a medical office and to date a guy named Ozzie, a broke and unemployed twenty-year-old who was perpetually high on speed and neglected his two kids. He had been an addict since age fourteen. When I first met him, he showed great interest in me, and I didn't like him at all. But when he stopped coming around, I began to miss him. Veronica warned me repeatedly that he was an irresponsible loser, but his humor and affectionate attention attracted me, so I started to call him, and he came back into my life.

We started to flirt with each other, and one night, even though I had purposefully waited years for the perfect moment with that special someone, I decided to give away my virginity. I knew I was offering Ozzie something so valuable, a precious part of myself, and I imagined our union would be magical and meaningful, especially for him. The experience was nothing like what I expected. Eighteen and nervous, I didn't know what I was doing and didn't enjoy it. Something so sacred, something I had saved for the one I would love, was given away haphazardly, and my heart felt that Ozzie didn't even value it. What hurt most was that I sensed I had lost a part of myself I could never get back.

Shortly afterward, Ozzie started seeing his ex-girlfriend on the side—the mother of his kids. Veronica counseled him while we were all high on drugs as to how and why he should change and treat me well, and I put my hope in her "sessions." But Ozzie finally left me to return to his ex, and I was left feeling lonely and used.

Not long after that, my father phoned unexpectedly to let me know that my mom had left, that divorce proceedings had begun, and the house I had named "the hell hole" had been sold. He had wanted to keep the property for the family and pay Mom out, but she didn't want any of us to have the home or live in it. Dad said to me, "I now have an apartment, and if you want to live here with me and your brother, you are welcome."

Over time, my initial fury toward my dad had melted into pity as I realized that he had thrown up his hands and abandoned me not from lack of love, but out of human weakness and the desire not to lose his wife again. Not knowing how to show emotional support, he had expressed his continued care by calling me, gifting me with a new car, teaching me how to drive, and stopping by to hand over money not only to me but to Veronica's mother as well. I felt happy and relieved to get my dad's call and accepted his offer immediately. Yet how, I wondered, would I be able to maintain my party lifestyle and live with him? I craved his approval and felt I could never openly bring shame upon him. I decided I would move in but live a lie. I would play the role of the good daughter.

I transferred my few belongings to my dad's new apartment, and we quickly became each other's best friend. When I wasn't out partying on weekends or working as a medical receptionist, I was with him: eating, shopping, cleaning, watching TV, or hanging out doing little nothings. His spirits lifted when I came home from work, and so did mine. Unfortunately, however, the only person he would go out with was me. If Dad knew that one of his brothers or cousins was getting married or celebrating a baptism, he purposely turned off his phone and refused to go. Shrinking into a thinning frame and hiding behind gloomy eyes, he spent an entire decade numb and depressed and became somewhat of a recluse.

In my recurring dreams, though, things were different . . .

My immediate family sits down to eat dinner in the dining room. I look around and think of how much I love my family. Their faces appear beautiful and content. My mom starts to serve the food, like she always did. "Everybody is here, and we are back together!" I exclaim. "I can't believe how wonderful this is! I thought I had lost you all."

But it was nothing more than a dream. I did have my father with me, but living so close to him, I soon learned that he was a master of emotional punishment, something my mother had undoubtedly experienced. If he was unhappy with me, he took away possessions, stopped paying for things, and became mute, refusing to tell me what was wrong. I'd have no recourse, or even any way of knowing why I was being punished. In response to any questioning, he would fume, "I don't want to talk because I don't want to talk!"

At those times, I really missed my mom. I couldn't turn to my poor, fourteen-year-old brother, who was escaping into marijuana, and though I didn't want to see or talk to my mom because I felt she deserved my distance, deep down, I wanted her back. I wanted everything to be exactly the way it was. My parents had protected me to the point where I didn't know the world could be unsafe.

My mother had even saved my life. It happened when I was age four, playing poolside with my favorite cousin, Camila, who was like a twin sister to me. The two of us would share secret tea parties, dress alike whenever we could, seek each other out as soon as we were up and about in the morning, and ride our bikes around town together. One day, we decided it would be cool to jump in the pool wearing only one flotation armband. While our mothers sat on the opposite side of the pool, chatting nonchalantly under a sun umbrella, I remember drinking gulps of water and gasping for air as we pushed each other's heads down and looked over at our parents, who were unaware. Wanting to scream, we could only gasp, gag, and swallow. Our bodies descended toward the bottom of the pool, and before we lost consciousness, our mothers' hands grabbed our pigtails and pulled us out of the water. Lying on the cement, gasping, I looked up at my mother's concerned eyes and knew that everything would be okay.

But now, looking into the shattered mirror of a perfect past, my spirit oscillated between depression and fear. When anxious sadness swelled within me to a crescendo, my hands would reach for my hair and begin pulling. Little Patricia, who felt so secure and cherished, had died long ago. The insecure princess who evolved in her place, however, remained very much alive: an insatiable people-pleaser, yearning for someone to notice her, to say she was beautiful, to say she was strong, to let her know that she was the most special one of all.

> Charm is deceptive and beauty fleeting; the woman who fears the LORD is to be praised.
> –Proverbs 31:30

One night when I was eighteen, the limelight fell on me. While dancing in a Mexican night club in Vallejo, California, my eyes caught sight of an attractive twenty-four-year-old dancing with a girl. Taken by his outfit, his moves, his smile, I thought, "Whoah, he's hot. I need to get him away from her." Characteristically shy, I managed to get up the courage to smile at him flirtatiously and make eye contact.

He approached me, and we danced into the late hours, falling for each other immediately. His name was Saul, and he called me the next day to ask me out. Dinner dates turned quickly into a serious relationship. He was generous, kind, courteous, and adoring—an attentive boyfriend who opened car doors for me, never allowed me to pay for anything, and showered me with compliments. In his presence and with his closely knit family, I felt the safety, comfort, and attention that my soul was craving.

Meanwhile, I kept my cocaine use in the shadows. I had kept up my friendship with Veronica, although Saul felt suspicious of her influence on me. As my drug use became more consistent, clues began to emerge. I started breaking out in acne, dropping weight rapidly, losing sleep, and functioning poorly at my work as a medical receptionist, so I made the decision to quit cocaine and stop hanging out with Veronica before my secret could be discovered.

Only one month into my relationship with Saul, I announced to my father that I would always be away on weekends with friends, while in reality, those weekends were slotted for clubs and for Saul. Every Saturday night, Saul and I threw away our religious heritage of saving sex for marriage. To us, it was an outdated and irrelevant Mexican custom, stuck in the minds of grandmothers. We thought nothing of hopping into bed. "We love each other. We're faithful. Everything is fine."

Yet all was far from fine. Intercourse fell into the category of people-pleasing, and I never truly enjoyed it. I had learned from the world that the way to show my boyfriend my love was to have sex with him—just be sure to use a condom. I'd been taught that sex was an important way to satisfy a man, the necessary means to sustain a relationship, the ultimate expression of love, a normal act of intimacy—and I hardly wanted to be seen as abnormal. So even though the act was a painful chore, not to mention the multiple bladder infections and rounds of antibiotics I endured, I pushed myself to do it. I can only assume that Saul's libido overrode his concern for my welfare. Five years my senior, he had more experience sexually than I and was not an advocate of abstinence or the consistent practice of "safe" sex. Three or four times, I ran to get Plan B pills, which contributed to my physical symptoms and my mental agony. Sex was truly an ungodly martyrdom for me.

All of my antibiotics, condoms, birth control and Plan B pills were doled out free by Planned Parenthood. "These people are my saviors!" I thought. "I don't have to tell my dad anything. I don't have to spend money. They make things so easy!" Their large clinic, extensive hold times on the phone, long lines—a wait of at least thirty minutes at any hour of the day when they were open—impressed me. "This is success," I thought to myself as I reclined in their cushioned waiting-room chairs. Yet the chairs could hardly make me comfortable. My eyes would dart around, fearful of seeing a familiar face, and my skin would flush involuntarily. As soon as my name was called, a wave of embarrassment pushed me quickly through the door to the examining rooms.

The same feeling seized me every Sunday morning as I embarked upon my walk of shame—leaving Saul's apartment in an evening dress and stilettos as the sun began to rise, then furtively entering my father's house and dashing into my room before I could get caught in the lie that we both pretended he didn't know.

Five months into my relationship with Saul, what I somehow thought was impossible happened. I started to feel nauseated and tired. I couldn't eat much and collapsed on the couch to sleep for hours each day after work. "What is wrong with me?" I wondered. "I can't be pregnant. We used a condom. Shouldn't that have worked?" Not knowing where to turn, I frantically called my cousin Camila.

She quickly came over with a home pregnancy test. Together we stared at the test applicator in a deafening silence. As the pink line appeared, she started screaming and crying, and I immediately followed suit. My very first thought filled me with unattenuated horror: "Oh no, I'm going to get fat again!" Fears, fears, and more agonizing fears ripped through me in rapid succession. "My life is over" . . . "I'm stuck with this guy forever!" While I loved Saul, I felt too young, too unsure if he was "the one." "And I'll never have a career," I lamented, although I didn't know exactly what that career would be. Yet my biggest fear by far was my father's reaction. I would bring shame and dishonor to him and our whole family. In the Mexican Hispanic culture, if you're not married in the Church, or if you get pregnant before wedlock, people judge you and discuss your condition incessantly. Gossip that begins in the United States travels south like lightning, and it knows no ends or bounds below the border.

We sat in my room, bawling, and I asked Camila, "What do you think I should do?"

Calming herself, she said matter-of-factly and with good intentions, "What I think you should do is have an abortion. Learn your lesson and focus on your life goals."

When I heard her say the word "abortion," my insides grew cold. I could barely believe that I'd put myself in this situation. Somehow, I had separated sex from pregnancy, while the truth was that women got pregnant on birth control all the time. I'd told myself that if I ever got pregnant, I would never abort a baby. Freely, openly, and confidently, I had spoken against abortion and thought women who went through the procedure were wicked.

But now I didn't know if I wanted to keep the baby or not. Confused and distressed, I called Saul that night, searching for an answer. Although I knew he felt so in love with me that he would have married me in a heartbeat, I didn't know how he'd react to a pregnancy. When I told him, his voice brimmed with such excitement that he began to laugh as he spoke. He chimed about how happy he was for us, how thrilled he felt to be a father. He told me not to worry, that he would support me in every way he could. His joy and support made me want to keep the baby. Accepting our situation resignedly, I sighed, "Oh well, I'm going to end up with this guy, and I'm too young; but it's not the end of the world."

One month into the pregnancy, I started taking prenatal pills. At two months and again at two and a half months, I had ultrasounds and began to rub my tummy and talk to my child. During the second ultrasound, Saul held my hand as we stared at the screen. With stunning clarity, we saw our baby's head and arms moving quickly and his or her little heart beating full force. It was a moment of awe. I wanted to cry. For the first time in my pregnancy, I felt excited.

One morning around this time, I woke up, looked over at my boyfriend, and started crying. "I had this dream . . . My mom called me to apologize and tell me she missed me." My heart flowed with joy and seized up with pain all at once because the closeness I felt to her in the dream plunged my soul into longing. As I was telling Saul the dream, my cell phone rang, and the screen registered "Mom." After two years of no contact whatsoever, she apologized in tears for hurting me in any way and said she wanted to have a relationship with me again. Layers of anger and pain buried themselves underneath my consciousness. I wanted my mommy. I wanted her back exactly how she was when I was a little girl. Sobbing from happiness, I immediately forgave her.

With this monumental healing, God was paving the way for me to be a mother, to marry a good man from a good family, to be rid of drugs and lies, and to care for the beautiful life he had just brought into the world. I had always loved children and imagined I'd be a great mom. But I didn't know God.

> Before I formed you in the womb I knew you . . .
> –Jeremiah 1:5a

Fact: Carol Everett, a former abortion clinic owner, stated, "We had a whole plan to sell abortions, called 'sex education': break down their natural modesty, separate them from their parents and their values, and become the sex expert in their lives so they'd turn to us, and we'd give them a low-dose birth control that they'd get pregnant on, or a defective condom, because we didn't buy the most expensive condoms, we bought the cheapest condoms. Our goal was three to five abortions from every girl between the ages of thirteen and eighteen." See Ms. Everett interviewed in the documentary Blood Money. (1)

Planned Parenthood Federation of America (PPFA), the largest provider of abortion services in the United States, offers three types of condoms for free. According to Consumer Reports, two of those three have poor ratings in terms of strength and reliability. (2)

For kindergarteners through college age youth, Planned Parenthood promotes sexual rights and freedoms. PPFA argues that an introduction to homosexuality and all its variations must start in kindergarten. For teens, the organization promotes dangerous sexual acts such as anal sex and fisting, bondage, and sadomasochistic sex practices. In one of their educational videos, a teen girl shares tips on how to engage in S&M. (3) Planned Parenthood receives hundreds of millions of government and taxpayer dollars for their comprehensive sex education programs.

The International Planned Parenthood Federation argues against laws requiring people who are HIV positive to disclose information to sex partners regarding this potentially lethal infection because doing so violates the sexual rights of the HIV-infected person. In the opinion of the executive director of American Life League, Paul E. Rondeau, "One thing is for sure: to Planned Parenthood, sexual pleasure is more important than life itself." (4)

Chapter Four

Life or Death

At age nineteen and three months pregnant, I went to a birthday party along with a few girlfriends. They cornered me as soon as we got there: "We think you're too young to be a mom. Are you sure you want to have this baby?" All of them felt terribly unhappy about my pregnancy and collectively probed me for any misgivings while putting fearful thoughts in my head. I left the party feeling confused, upset, and offended.

One of those friends, Naomi, called me a month later to ask if I would accompany her to get a tarot card reading by a psychic. She was feeling devastated over a break up and wanted help. I agreed to go with her, but when we arrived, I felt an eerie hesitation. The path to the psychic's small, white house was flanked by two giant pillars; each supported a large, ugly, stone lion with its mouth open in a roar.

I pushed past my uncertainty. When we reached the house, a joyless, wrinkled lady, who looked at least ninety years old, flung open the door to welcome us. My initial reluctance mushroomed when I saw her one lazy eye with a white pupil and its lid draped down halfway and a big, bent sixth toe with a long yellow nail, pointy and dirty like the rest, emerging from the top of her sandaled foot.

Motioning for us to follow her, she led us through a sliding door into an additional indoor patio attached to the back of her home. She sat down in a chair, looking bent and sad. Behind her, rose two towering life-size statues of angels—black ones. Lit candles were scattered all around, but their light was hardly comforting.

As she began to speak, my attention couldn't help but focus on her monstrous toe, which seemed demonic as it poked out of her sandals.

When she finished Naomi's reading, she turned to me and asked, "Do you want me to do yours?"

Still a believer in readings, I cast aside my disgust and said, "Okay."

The psychic shuffled her cards and laid them out in front of me. Her eyes darted in different directions as she sat deep in thought. Then she looked at me seriously through her little, white pupil and said, "You are going to receive a very important letter tomorrow, and you must pay attention to it." My friend began to cry uncontrollably. I didn't know why.

When I got home from work the next day, there was a letter for me in the mail. It was from Naomi. She had written, "Your pregnancy is a big mistake. You are far too young to be a mother. You have so much to look forward to. If you have this baby, you will be ruining your life. The best thing for you to do is have an abortion." The letter continued in a desperate tone, begging me not to have my child. Lacking the courage to tell me in person how she felt about my pregnancy, she had written me a few days before we saw the psychic, but had not told her about it.

I wondered if Naomi had been chosen to be spokesperson for my other friends. We were a closely knit group, so I initiated a conference call and asked them to tell me the truth. As one united voice they chanted, "You should have an abortion." I was too young, they said; I needed to have the procedure urgently—now—because I was four months pregnant, and soon I wouldn't be able to have one. "Hurry!" they urged.

All the joy I had felt about the pregnancy vanished. I made the decision to abort my baby the moment I hung up the phone. Ripped apart by panic and grief, I cried, "They're right. If I don't do this now, I won't be able to." Like the rush of a broken dam, plans poured into my head. "Okay, I can't tell Saul I'm going to have an abortion. He's not going to accept it, so I have to come up with a lie. When I'm in a delicate state right after the abortion, I will say I had a miscarriage." But I knew what I was doing, and I knew it was wrong. "How can I suddenly go from imagining my child smiling in my arms to strategizing how to kill it?" Ignoring my conscience, I continued to form my game plan. Then I looked down at my tummy and felt like a traitor.

From that moment on, I shut my thoughts away from the life within me. I wouldn't rub my tummy. I wouldn't imagine my child. Instead, I conjured up thoughts of relief over not having to get "fat" and forged ahead, making an appointment at an abortion center. As the day of my procedure approached, I thought, "There's a baby in my stomach, and it's not going to be there anymore." Feelings of selfishness crippled me with guilt, but I brushed them aside for "a better future."

One of my friends accompanied me to the clinic where I was one of their first morning appointments. Glancing around furtively, I was taken aback to see a wide array of girls in the waiting room, all of them staring at the floor, avoiding eye contact with one another. They looked so frightened and sad. Feeling the same way, I sat down with them. Eventually, the nurse called my name and took me into a back room. I lay down on the cold, sanitized paper covering the examining table. After squeezing gel onto my lower abdomen, the nurse placed what looked like a computer mouse, a device called a transducer, on top of the gel and looked at a screen displaying an ultrasound picture of my baby.

"Can I see the screen?" I asked her.

She wouldn't let me. "No, it's not something you need to see. There's nothing really there."

"Am I too far along?" I asked her nervously. "Is my baby too developed to have this abortion? Is the baby going to be hurt?"

Staring at me blankly, she said, "It's not a child. It's a sac."

I had seen my last ultrasound two months previously, and even then, I was able to see my baby's head and limbs move, not to mention his or her beating heart, so I knew that the nurse was lying to my face. Even so, I wanted to believe her.

She then guided me into the procedure room, where a female doctor could see that I was shaking. I felt horrified by the thought of the procedure, so she tried to calm me down by saying, "I've had one abortion, and my daughter has had two abortions. In fact, I even performed the abortions on my own daughter." Putting her hand on her heart, she added, "I'm okay. My daughter is okay. Nothing happened to me, nothing happened to her, and nothing's going to happen to you. You're going to be fine."

[CAUTION TO THE READER: PLEASE SKIP THE NEXT TWO PARAGRAPHS IF YOU WOULD PREFER NOT TO READ THE DETAILS OF AN ABORTION.]

Her words put me at ease. She was a doctor, an expert in her field, so I trusted her. "Besides, it will only take five minutes," she assured me, "so you will be out of here soon." She reached down to insert a clamp to open up my cervix, and then she showed me a huge needle, about the length from my elbow to the tip of my middle finger. "There will be seven injections," she said and proceeded to insert the huge needle into my vagina. I tried with all my might to look strong, to hide my terror by appearing as though I were mastering the procedure and it was no big deal.

After the doctor made seven injections into my cervix, and my insides grew numb, she turned on a machine that sounded like a vacuum cleaner.

I then felt a hose press into me, causing tremendous cramping as she began to suck my baby out. At the same time, I sensed my own life being pulled out of me and the specter of death entering in. I felt like a killer. "Wasn't it only a few days ago when I had been rubbing my belly with joy?" And now it was empty. My mind raced. "I've ripped my baby out!" "I'm so selfish, so selfish!" The staff saw that my body was still shaking and that guilt was writing painful lines on my face. The nurse and the doctor kept telling me I wasn't doing anything wrong at all, that it wasn't a child . . . *it wasn't a child.* It was nothing more than a lifeless mass of tissue . . . meanwhile, pictures of my ultrasound flashed through my mind. I tried to calm myself. "Wow, you're not even moving," said the doctor. "You're one of our best patients."

Finally, the sucking noise of the machine went silent. "You're so brave. You did such a good job." Part of me, the people-pleaser, felt proud that I had endured the procedure without screaming aloud. I even thanked the doctor. But when she walked out of the room, and I sat up on the table in my own blood and closed my legs, a shameful, empty feeling, worse than death, shuddered through me. It was mixed with a sense of relief. "Now I'm not going to get fat," I thought to myself, "and I can go back to the gym."

From there, I was led to an incubation room where I sat in surgical socks and a surgical gown, surrounded by crying. I remember, in particular, a young couple, both of them no older than sixteen, sitting across from me and weeping bitterly. No one looked each other in the face.

Before I walked out the clinic's back door, the doctor handed me a big, brown bag of contraceptives and a lecture: "Since you don't know how to use a condom properly, here are also some birth control pills so that this won't occur again."

"Thank you," I said, shrinking from embarrassment. Walking toward my car, I thought, "I got out of this car pregnant, and I'm getting back in it without my baby. I can't believe I'm now part of the statistics of women who've had an abortion." Everything felt terribly strange and amiss. "Didn't I just possess a child? Now all I have is a black hole."

That night I called my boyfriend to tell him that I was bleeding and cramping and worried that something was wrong with my pregnancy. Then I lied again and claimed I was going to see my doctor the next morning for a checkup. At noon the following day, he called to ask if I'd seen the doctor, and I feigned devastation as I told him about my "miscarriage." Never had I heard him sound so sad. The next morning, his pillow was wet from his sobbing throughout the night. "How come he's crying, and I can't?" I wondered, unaware that my trauma had been quickly repressed. "I feel absolutely nothing. Is there something wrong with me?"

In the days that followed, Saul looked for a reason why he might have caused the miscarriage and apologized for not taking as good care of me as he should have. To deflect my shame over his sadness, I used it to my advantage and let him sink in his guilt and take the blame. "Yeah, you shouldn't argue with me that often. Maybe it happened because I was stressed out."

After that, my friends who had been so concerned about me before my abortion slowly faded out of my life, one by one. They never once asked, "How do you feel?" They acted like they didn't want to know. My wellbeing and my future were suddenly no longer their concern. And I, being so ashamed, embarrassed, and disturbed over having aborted a four-month-old, and fearful of their gossip, never dared to mention the abortion again.

> You wearied yourself with many consultations, at which you toiled from your youth; Let the astrologers stand forth to save you, the stargazers who forecast at each new moon what would happen to you. Lo, they are like stubble, fire consumes them; They cannot save themselves from the spreading flames. This is no warming ember, no fire to sit before. Thus do your wizards serve you with whom you have toiled from your youth; Each wanders his own way, with none to save you.
> –Isaiah 47:13–15

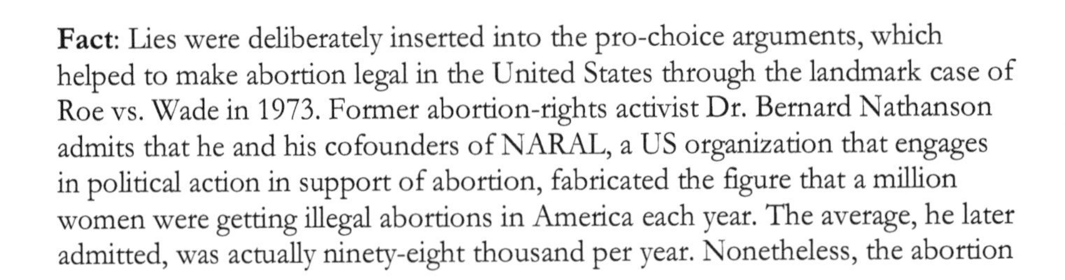

Fact: Lies were deliberately inserted into the pro-choice arguments, which helped to make abortion legal in the United States through the landmark case of Roe vs. Wade in 1973. Former abortion-rights activist Dr. Bernard Nathanson admits that he and his cofounders of NARAL, a US organization that engages in political action in support of abortion, fabricated the figure that a million women were getting illegal abortions in America each year. The average, he later admitted, was actually ninety-eight thousand per year. Nonetheless, the abortion advocates fed their concocted figures to the media, which eagerly disseminated the false information.

Research, though, confirmed that the actual number of abortion deaths in the twenty-five years prior to 1973 averaged 250 a year. Nathan said of his made-up numbers, "It was always '5,000 to 10,000 deaths a year.' I confess that I knew the figures were totally false, and I suppose the others did too, if they stopped to think of it. But in the 'morality' of our revolution, it was a useful figure, widely accepted, so why go out of our way to correct it with honest statistics? The overriding concern was to get the laws [against abortion] eliminated, and anything within reason that had to be done was permissible." (1)

CHAPTER

FIVE

Best Mom Ever

I'M WALKING ACROSS *the living-room floor toward the kitchen, holding my baby brother in my wobbly arms. Then I sit him down in his highchair and lock the plastic tray in place. He's one year old; I'm five, and I'm feeling quite proud of my accomplishment. I attempt to feed him breakfast and watch as his chubby hands with dimples for knuckles shove half of his Cheerios in his mouth and half onto the floor. "This is fun," I say to myself. "I'm gonna be the best mom ever."*

In time, my conscience dimmed, and I simply felt relieved not to be pregnant anymore. Now I could go out, be with my friends, and pursue my goals—or at least figure out what they were. In my mind and memory, my pregnancy was no longer a blessing. It was a problem I'd gotten rid of.

But my problems, in fact, had merely begun. After the abortion, every destructive habit and negative thought pattern I'd acquired thus far in life began to flourish while any peace or happiness I'd enjoyed disappeared. Violent thoughts would scrape through my mind—ideas such as going into the kitchen and grabbing a knife and stabbing myself. My personality was changing into one of little control.

The attraction and chemistry I had felt for my boyfriend vanished, and I began to question whether he was the person I wanted to be with. His presence irked me and reminded me of what I'd done. Two months after "the miscarriage," he said, "I think we would have had a little girl." He had seen her in a dream and began to describe her to me: "She had straight brown hair and big, beautiful eyes . . ." Each word out of his mouth was a shot of guilt, and I stopped him from describing her further.

Saul was falling more in love with me as my heart was falling away. Nevertheless, I continued to spend weekend nights with him, popping birth control pills and having sex simply out of habit.

Not five months after my abortion, the foods that I loved started to sicken me, and the symptoms of nausea, breast tenderness, and physical fatigue drove me hurriedly to the drug store. With trembling hands, I took a home pregnancy test, and when it came out positive, my anger toward myself exploded: "Damn, Patricia! You put yourself in this position *again*! And weren't these stupid pills supposed to work?" My mind bucked and reeled. "Hell, no," I thought. "I'm not keeping it. I don't want to marry Saul, and I refuse to get fat. Right then and there I knew I was not going to have the baby. "I'm going to have an abortion before it even turns into a fetus . . . while it's still a sac." This time I wouldn't have to tell anyone. This time it would be easier to go through with it because I already knew what to expect . . . This time I had no emotion at all.

Not wanting to go to the same private clinic for fear they'd have a low opinion of me and think I was using abortion as birth control, I went to Planned Parenthood instead and sat down nervously in their waiting room. I knew that an acquaintance of mine, whom I had met through clubbing, worked as a receptionist there, and my ardent prayer to God on the day of my abortion was to not run into her. The many other times I'd walked into Planned Parenthood for birth control or antibiotics for bladder infections, I ran into people I knew all the time. But today was different. I was afraid to look up. When I did, I saw a row of young couples all silently crying with their heads bowed low, avoiding eye contact, even with their partners. My name was finally called, and with a sigh of relief, I escaped the public eye. With my feelings shoved behind a callous wall, I told the intake nurse I was having my first abortion. Then a "counselor" explained the procedure in one sentence and told me that afterward, I would feel some slight cramping and would be ready to go back to work the next day. "Take some aspirin, if you need it."

She made it sound so easy! I felt grateful.

The memories that still flicker are the chill in the clinic, the long needle, the scraping of the instruments, the sucking of the vacuum, and my firm determination to be even stronger than the last time—less flinching, less fear. I could master this. In the recovery room, the staff lay me down with hot blankets and fuzzy socks, a cup of water, and two aspirin. They comforted me with words—"Honey, take your time"—and nurtured me with touch, checking my forehead for any rise in temperature and rubbing my back. With special care and attention, they gave me a consoling drop of the love for which I yearned.

Before I opened my car door to drive home, I noticed my reflection in the window on the driver's side. My image stared back at me as if to say, "You are a woman who has had two abortions. You are marked for life. This can never be erased."

After my second abortion, more lies and more guilt fueled my sense of disconnection from Saul. The more my heart turned away from him, the more he clung to me, and the more I felt repulsed. Intellectually, my mind found him very attractive and sweet; but I could no longer stomach any kissing or sexual activity whatsoever, and I didn't know that this was an effect from abortion. Even a peck on the cheek felt invasive and uncomfortable, and he could tell something was wrong. Yet I kept myself in the relationship and forced myself to be sexually active because I felt badly for him. He treated me well and loved me so much that I couldn't imagine leaving him.

Five months after my second abortion, I started to feel sick again. Sensing that I was going to throw up, I thought, "God, no!" and then, "I'm not going to lie anymore." So I made Saul stop with me at a pharmacy. The person ringing up the pregnancy test smiled and said, "Good luck!"

"Oh no, don't wish me luck," I mumbled. We got back in Saul's car to return to his place, and I made him pull over at a gas station, so eager was I to know the results. The pink line began to form. Positive. Again.

"F---!" I screamed. I felt irresponsible and furious with myself. Then and there, in the gas station bathroom, I decided: "I need to get another abortion, stop this, and leave him because this is too much." Numb to the idea of another procedure, I got into the car and in a tone of disappointment, told him the test was positive. He was happy but worried about my reaction. Then out came more lies. Not wanting to go to the clinic alone, I convinced him that I didn't *want* an abortion, but said that because I wanted to marry him and get married in the Church—and because I certainly didn't want to disappoint my dad—we should go get the abortion and then do things the right way.

I forced him to go to a clinic with me, called—a different one, due to my overwhelming embarrassment. The clinic name, Common Women's Health, made me believe that they cared about my health. Candles and scented oils permeated the place while New Age music wafted through the air, setting a romantic atmosphere. They preferred cash.

The pre-procedure instructions were given to everyone in a group, followed by breathing exercises we women were to do with our partners. We were told this would help us to relax and bond as sisters in support of one another and go through the procedure in the healthiest way. Afterward, they said, we would only have slight cramping and bleeding. "Take an aspirin and go to work tomorrow. No problem."

I remember looking at a Hispanic woman who was alone and appeared terrorized. She understood nothing and seemed unable even to hold her trembling body up to stand. Wanting to be helpful, I translated for her, but she half-dismissed my help, perhaps not wanting to be recognized, perhaps not wanting to hear what I was saying. Meanwhile, an unspoken dialogue passed between me and the woman and Saul: "Why are you here? This goes against everything our culture believes in." As I watched sweat pour down her anguished face, I wondered, once again, if there was something wrong with me. This would be my third abortion within a year and a half, and I couldn't understand her emotions. "Why is she so terribly afraid?"

The only moment I remember from the procedure itself was of looking up at Saul and seeing a river of tears running down his face. Frightened for me, he squeezed my hand tightly, and when the vacuum sound began, horror covered his face. "I've already killed two of his children," I thought to myself, "and he thinks this is the first." That is when I felt truly evil—wicked—like an assassin. "Not a single soul will ever know," I decided. "I will take these abortions to my tomb."

After that, I didn't want Saul near me. I recoiled at his touch, and the mere thought of kissing him made me want to throw up. Sensing my repugnance, he would cling to me and act needy: "What's wrong? Don't you find me attractive anymore?" In my eyes, he had turned from a strong, confident, handsome young man into a little leech.

Our relationship lasted only two weeks after that abortion. My mind doesn't recall how I broke up with Saul, but his devastation remains etched in my memory. I could see the pain in his face, but I didn't care. He was telling me he was suicidal; he called me, crying, day and night. Once, when he had waited for me outside of my house, I got out of my car and snapped, "What are you doing here? You're stalking me. You need to leave me alone!" As I turned around to walk away, he dropped to his knees and grabbed my legs, begging me not to leave him. I walked into the house and shut the door with a cold slam.

After that, he got angry. In a virulent phone call, he said he was going to tell my dad that I had been pregnant, and he threatened to put the ultrasound of our baby on my dad's windshield. That ignited my ultimate fear, so I packed up and left Petaluma to escape from him. But even in a new city, Saul showed up a couple of times at my doorstep. Repelled by his presence, I asserted myself callously, giving him one final, crushing blow: "I don't love you anymore." I never saw him again.

> Now the works of the flesh are obvious: immorality, impurity, licentiousness, idolatry, sorcery, hatreds, rivalry, jealousy, outbursts of fury, acts of selfishness, dissensions, factions, occasions of envy, drinking bouts, orgies, and the like. I warn you, as I warned you before, that those who do such things will not inherit the kingdom of God.
> –Galatians 5:19–21

CHAPTER VIDEO
Patricia Sandoval Speaks to Those Considering Abortion
See https://youtu.be/-NnlDZ_idT8
Or go to YouTube.com and find the video by searching

Queen of Peace Media

Fact: By age forty-five, about one-third (three in ten) of all North American women will have had at least one abortion. (1) Of those women who get an abortion, about one half go on to have another one. (2) Of women in the United States who have abortions:

- 54 percent were using a contraceptive method (usually the condom or the pill) (3)
- 38 percent have no religious affiliation (4)
- 30 percent identify as Protestant
- 24 percent identify as Catholic (5)
- 85 percent are unmarried (6)
- 56 percent are unmarried and not cohabiting
- 58 percent are in their twenties
- 61 percent have one or more children
- 75 percent are poor or low income (4)

In contemporary abortion practice, gender discrimination against men is normative. By law, fathers are excluded from participating in the abortion decision, which means that a husband or partner who wants his child to live has no right to prevent his wife or partner from aborting his child—or all of his children. Following an abortion, men typically grieve in a private way. When men do express their grief, they usually try to do so in culturally prescribed "masculine" ways—for example, anger, aggressiveness, or control. (7)

CHAPTER SIX

Don't Ever Tell

MY COUSIN CAMILA had recently lost a roommate when I called her in distress to tell her I needed to get away quickly, and she immediately invited me to move into her apartment in Sacramento. At age twenty, I was determined to begin a new and better life. In need of a job, I began thumbing through the *Sacramento Bee* newspaper, and my eye caught sight of an ad for Planned Parenthood, which urgently desired a Spanish-speaking staff person since an overflow of Latina women needed "services." My spirits lifted with the thought of working for them because they had been so nice to me during and after my abortions and so generous in giving me free contraceptives. I felt like I owed them a favor.

Shortly after I phoned them to express my interest, the manager called me for an interview and told me to come in through the back door of the clinic since protestors were lined up in the front. Walking by the protestors to get to the back of the building, I felt a little ashamed and didn't want to look up at their signs or listen to what they were saying. By this time, I had become very pro-choice and thought to myself, "Those people are crazy. It's a woman's body. She can do with it whatever she wants."

One of the first questions asked of me in the interview was, "Do you have a problem with abortion?"

"No," I responded confidently, "I don't have any problem with abortion at all. I've actually had one myself."

"So you have no problem with seeing a massive amount of blood?"

"No."

"Because here we have abortions twice a week on Wednesdays and Fridays, and we're dealing with at least twenty a day. A lot of Hispanic women are coming in, and we need someone who can speak Spanish with them."

She hired me right on the spot. I would start on Monday. My experience in the medical field had always been in the front office, but now I would work in the back office, assisting the doctors. I felt that I was moving up in the world.

When Monday came, the manager, cold and brusque, took me by the hand and walked me into to her office to go over a few preliminary matters. Her first words to me were, "Don't ever call it a 'baby,' a 'he,' or a 'she.' You call it an 'it' or a 'sac.' Today, you will be giving consultations to women before their appointments, and if you see that a woman is having doubts about getting her abortion, you have to do everything in your will to get her to come in for that appointment."

I was shocked. I thought, "I can't believe they're telling me to do this. This is what they did to me." But since I was pro-choice, I went along with it.

Throughout the day, I "counseled" women, one of whom I remember well. Bawling hysterically and grabbing her womb, she asked me over and over, "Is my baby going to feel? Is my baby going to be in pain?"

With confidence, I told her over and over, "It's not a baby. It's a sac."

Trying to put her at ease in the same way the abortion doctor had consoled me, I repeated, "I had an abortion, and I'm fine. Nothing happened to me." She still wasn't convinced. There was no peace in her heart.

On Tuesdays and Thursdays, the women who wanted to keep their babies were seen in the clinic. They were filled with the hope of giving birth, and the staff would joyfully call the "sac" a baby. The mothers-to-be were allowed to see the ultrasound screen and talk about the baby's heartbeat, his five little toes, her developing organs. On Tuesdays and Thursdays, the staff spoke passionately to these women about their pregnancies: "Look at your growing belly!" . . . "Your baby is so beautiful!" . . . "Here, look at the screen!" . . . "You can see her heart beating. She's so alive and precious! Can you believe it?"

On Mondays, the staff would perform ultrasounds on the women planning to abort, but not let them see the screen. Employees would call the babies "blobs," "cells," "clusters," "tissue," "sacs" and "its," but never "babies" or "children." Abortions were encouraged but alternatives were never explained or offered. Wednesdays and Fridays were abortion days for the clinic—totaling forty-five to fifty abortions each week. The women were moved quickly into surgery, with any emotional, psychological or spiritual risks denied or left unmentioned. The staff would push aside the "obstacles" of the women's doubts and trepidation and assure the conflicted that everything would be just fine.

That's when their hypocrisy sunk in. My thoughts ricocheted between what I had believed as a child and what I had learned from the culture as I grew older. Until my teenage years, I had automatically assumed that if you're pregnant, you have a baby, and that's it. But then I heard, "It's a bunch of cells, an embryo, a fetus, a product of conception"—anything but a baby or someone's child. Even now, I felt confused and didn't know what to think. I wanted to impress the staff, so I hid my upset over their duplicity. I wanted them to like me and see that I could do my job well.

Wednesday came—an abortion day. I peered into the waiting room, stunned to see the number of African American and Latina women filing into the clinic. I reeled. "This is not a part of our culture." My manager took me into her office to tell me the day would be busy, and I had to work quickly because they wanted the doctor to bounce between two operating rooms.

Then she looked me in the eye and said, "Don't ever, ever tell anybody—not even your friends or relatives—about what you see there in the back." Using the prohibited words—mother, father, and baby—she continued, "Never tell the mothers and never tell the fathers who are sitting out in the waiting room what you see behind those closed doors. If the women who come into the clinic ask you what we do with the babies, never tell them that we basically throw them in the garbage."

Thus began my first day of horror. Amidst intermittent eruptions of women weeping and screaming, the doctor jumped from one room to the other, back and forth, spending only five minutes in each and whistling in between the cries from each abortion. Some of the women emerged from their procedure room wailing, some had silent tears running down their cheeks, some walked down the hall with blank stares. Not one looked happy or relieved. I felt like I'd entered a slaughter house.

The first few days of my job, I would hold the hands of women during their abortions. Then trying to be strong while also giving in to curiosity, I stood back to witness an abortion from behind the doctor's shoulder. Two clamps opened up the vagina, and again I saw that big needle, the length of a forearm, and the doctor injecting the woman's cervix repeatedly with it. After a short lapse of time while the anesthesia took effect, I watched the doctor take a canula (a long, thin metal stick, attached to the end of a long hose) and plunge it in and out of the woman's cervix, with blood pouring out from the sides. It was invasive, gruesome, and awful. The doctor couldn't see inside the small, dark opening of the cervix, which was covered with clamps and blood. With his arm swinging back and forth violently, the doctor couldn't see at all! "This is a blind man's surgery," I thought to myself. "How does he know how far to push? How is he not destroying this woman's insides?" The only indicator telling the doctor when to stop was the volume of blood being expelled into a glass cylinder nearby.

After that abortion, the girl training me grabbed the bag with the bloody contents in it, and we went into a back room. "We need to find five parts, and we need to find them fast because the patient can't leave the room until we do. Then we can tell the doctor that the abortion was successful." On top of the counter lay a huge petri dish. As my trainer opened the bag and emptied out the contents onto the container, blood splashed around us and on us. A horrendous smell filled the room. I wanted to vomit.

"This is the placenta," she told me, pointing to a glob of tissue. Then, with a pair of tweezers, she navigated through the body parts, lifted up an arm, and held it up to the light. Terror seeped into me as I stared at the hand, its knuckles, the lines on its palm, and its tiny-nailed fingers spreading out. "Here's part number one," she said mechanically. Pushing it aside, she clamped her tweezers around the belly with the umbilical cord still connected and a leg dangling in the air beneath it, with knees and toes intact. I could see the little hairs on the skin, the nails on the toes. "This is the second part." Then she looked for the second arm and held it up, exposing an upper arm, elbow, and forearm. "Number three." She set it down, and her tweezers squeezed another leg: "Number four." Then she found the head and lifted it up in the air. I could see the eyes, the eyelashes, the nose, even the eyebrows that had begun to form. The mouth was hanging wide open. "Part number five. Success."

I was aghast. Agonizing thoughts blew through my mind faster than I could suppress them. This was actually a human being. This abortion had been done at three-and-a-half-months' gestation. My first abortion had happened at four. What startled me even more was seeing that the human being in front of me had no emotion. While sorting through body parts, the other women in the clinic also wore blank, robotic faces and discussed what they were going to have for lunch. Meanwhile, the doctor would bounce in and out of the room in a jolly mood. "What the f---- is wrong with these people?" I wondered as I looked around. "Why am I the only one horrified by what is going on?"

I searched for the parts of more than twenty babies that day. Some of the body pieces were very small, some very big, and some were huge, the size of a baby born premature. Most of them were well formed. All the while, the staff acted like all this was normal, even cool, and I felt like I was contributing to a holocaust.

The parts of the many babies were thrown into one large, red biohazard garbage bag, which was placed in a freezer along with other bags of about twenty tiny people. At the end of the month, a biohazard unit would pick up this "trash": compact collections of body parts, iced and with dates on them, ready to be dumped.

Every morning, I felt sick when I thought about having to go to work. After the first day, the job equaled torture for me, but I didn't want to be a quitter. I tried to rally myself by focusing on the idea that perhaps this was a good chance for me to learn about injections and taking vitals. Yet the days were so long and my devastation so complete that I had to face the reality that I had been placed in Planned Parenthood for a reason—to face my own sin. I had thought that I had done nothing wrong, and now I saw the truth for what it really was: I had killed my children.

Now, in a professional workplace, I was being trained to lie and deceive—and to help kill. Come Wednesdays and Fridays, I couldn't eat. During lunch, I would sit in my car and cry.

Two weeks into the job, I walked into work and found my manager smiling broadly and in a great mood; and that woman never smiled. She introduced me to a sixteen-year-old girl and said I would be assisting in her abortion. I looked down at the girl's belly, which was huge. More than five and a half, almost six, months pregnant with twins, she was going to have her procedure after lunch. The clinic made big money on second-trimester abortions, and twins were a bonus on top of that. Now I knew why the manager was so happy. Escaping the clinic to catch a breath of fresh air, I thought about her babies. "How is she going to murder her two kids? It's not only one . . . it's two." I knew I would be handed the bag of the babies' body parts to look through after lunch.

At lunchtime, I got into the car and wept. "I don't want to look at those dismembered babies. I don't want to!" Terrified to see how big they would be—to see twins—I wondered what to do. I knew I was doing something terribly wrong and that my family would be mortified if they discovered where I was employed. Sitting in the driver's seat with my forehead bent over on the steering wheel, I lifted my cell phone to my ear and called Camila. Through uncontrollable sobs, I told her of the nightmare I was witnessing and said, "I can't take this anymore. I don't want to see this girl get an abortion."

"Just leave that place," Camila said. "Come home." I drove off and never went back.

> You shall not kill.
> –Exodus 20:13

When I stopped working at Planned Parenthood, my descent into a darkness as opaque as a starless sky began. I'd seen the truth, faced my sin and, for a time, felt abhorrence toward my three abortions and my workplace. But now I wanted to forget that any of it ever happened. I stuffed my emotions into deep inner caverns and unconsciously hid those parts of my past from myself and from others. Burying everything, however, helped nothing.

As a child, I hadn't been able to stop looking at myself; but now the mirror became my utmost enemy. In my reflection, I saw the parts of my own body as distorted, ugly, fat—even horrifying—while my conscious mind forgot the dismembered body parts of babies. My self-esteem plummeted toward the bottom of a trash barrel, and my heart weighed heavy with sadness and grief. Yet due to my repression and denial, I had no idea where these feelings were coming from.

I continued to live with Camila, who was nineteen at the time, a year younger than I. Studious and responsible, she was paying her bills, maintaining her own apartment, and studying criminal justice at Sacramento State University to reach her goal of being a cop—while I began to tumble precipitously in the opposite direction.

Around this time, my first fling, Ozzie, started looking for me. He had moved only a half hour away to Woodland, California, a town riddled with drug activity. When he came around again, my eyes saw him differently. Gone was the irresponsible loser. In his place was a witty, silly, altogether loveable, attractive, tall, dark-skinned Mexican American with big, beautiful eyelashes. Showing me tender physical affection, he swept me into his web, and I fell swiftly in love because he made me laugh. And I needed to laugh.

Soon we were hanging out every day and going to parties with about ten addicts in a home where Ozzie would smoke methamphetamines and search for coke to give to me. Grateful to have the attention and something to make me feel better, I started using cocaine again on the weekends, still with the mindset that I wouldn't get addicted.

Each time I showed up in a home to do drugs, people stared at me in disbelief. I didn't have the "look." Their expressions and whispers revealed their thoughts: "She's so prissy and dressed up. What is she doing here? And what is she doing with *him*?"

Ozzie never asked me to be his girlfriend, but at some point, when he began introducing me to all his friends, we knew we were a couple. I figured I could change him . . . that if I were good enough, if he loved me enough, he would get off the drugs. But everything happened in reverse. Pulling me into his den of darkness, he ended up changing me.

As cocaine started to become much more than a weekend affair for me, Ozzie noticed I was getting frequent nosebleeds and said I was going to ruin the cartilage in my nose. He seemed to know because his was already ruined. "Why don't you just smoke the meth?" he suggested. "You get the same high without the stinging and burning sensations in your nose or the nasty aftertaste going down your throat."

I decided to try it, and since I didn't know how to smoke properly from a pipe, Ozzie would inhale it and then blow the smoke into my mouth. Soon I not only learned to smoke meth by myself right out of the pipe, but I became so good at it that I received the dubious title, "The Dragon." My lungs could inhale copious amounts of smoke in one hit, more than those who had been smoking methamphetamines for a couple of decades. In the act of inhaling, my body would become invigorated with the rush of adrenalin; in the exhale, I enjoyed a short-lived release of depression, stress, and pain as I watched the smoke billowing from my mouth. For a brief moment, I could blow away a cloud of worry. There was nothing about meth that I didn't like. Nothing. I loved the smell of it, even its grisly aftertaste. On meth, I felt on top of the world.

But then the high would end. Plunged into earthly reality and deprived of chemical happiness, I would feel much worse than before I took a hit. Demoted from the top of life to the bottom, my mind spiraled downward into twisted, suicidal thoughts, which condemned me as the worst person on earth. My hair-pulling addiction grew worse, creating small patches of baldness on my scalp. It was nothing that a cute hat or scarf couldn't hide; but my drop in weight could be seen by all. People began to comment that

I was getting too thin, yet when I looked in the mirror, I couldn't see my weight loss at all. I was obsessively worried about my body image, and thin was never enough. "I can always lose more," I thought, "and then I'll be happy. *Then* I'll be happy."

Camila saw the changes in me. She also knew that Ozzie was a drug addict and noted that I was starting to lock my bedroom door. One day, as I was walking out the front door, I saw her sitting on the couch with tears rolling down her face. Trying to act stern, she mustered the courage to say, "If you continue to do drugs in my house, and if you continue to have Ozzie over, I can't have you here. I love you, and I want you to be with me. I don't want you to leave, I just want you to change . . ." I didn't let the conversation last more than five minutes. She started to sob from her heart as mine hardened. I was offended, indignant, and full of pride—while in my depths, I felt bitterly ashamed because I knew she was right. "Right or not, how dare she confront me! How dare she ask me to leave!" I got my stuff immediately and stormed out, never to come back.

> Pride goes before disaster, and a haughty spirit before a fall.
> –Proverbs 16:18

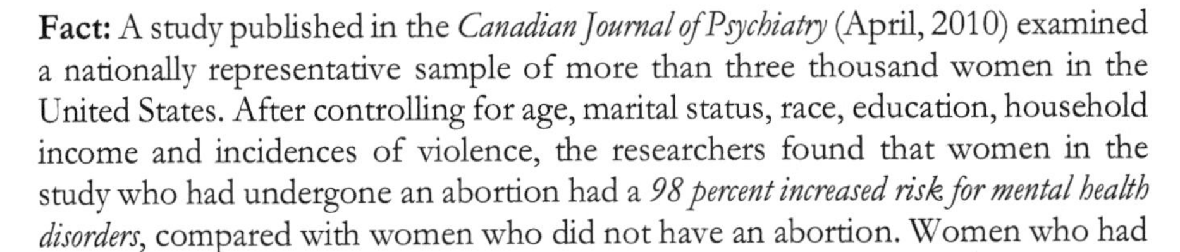

Fact: A study published in the *Canadian Journal of Psychiatry* (April, 2010) examined a nationally representative sample of more than three thousand women in the United States. After controlling for age, marital status, race, education, household income and incidences of violence, the researchers found that women in the study who had undergone an abortion had a *98 percent increased risk for mental health disorders*, compared with women who did not have an abortion. Women who had abortions also had:

59 percent increased risk for suicidal thoughts
61 percent increased risk for mood disorders
61 percent increased risk for social anxiety disorders
261 percent increased risk for alcohol abuse
313 percent increased risk for drug abuse
280 percent increased risk for any substance use disorder

It is statistically probable that 25 percent of cases of drug use in the United States are related to abortion. (1)

These findings affirm the results of hundreds of other studies published in major medical and psychology journals throughout the world (2, 3), proving the connection between abortion and mental health problems, as well as the fact that abortion can be a causal factor in breast cancer, miscarriage, infertility, ectopic pregnancies, and other physical health complications. As one of the single most common surgical procedures in the United States, more common than biopsies and three times as frequent as tonsillectomies (4), abortion remains the only procedure about which the patient is never warned of the risks involved. In fact, the risks are flatly denied by abortion providers, as though they did not exist. (5) Planned Parenthood continues to assert in its literature, for instance: "A woman with an unwanted pregnancy is as likely to have mental health problems from abortion as she is from giving birth." (6)

Chapter Seven

Living a Lie

THE WORLD OF A DRUG ADDICT is dark. You don't worry about bills, mortgages, car payments, or even your own health. Your primary concerns are the answers to these questions: Where can I get drugs? Where can I crash to sleep and do drugs? What can I steal and then sell to buy more drugs? Whom can I call to smoke me out? Paranoia invades your twisted mind and trust is futile because your friends will steal anything—your CDs, makeup, shoes, jewelry, clothes—to buy their next high. From sun up to sundown, the earth turns as if on a different axis, in a different dimension, in a universe of no responsibilities.

You love the energy of the high. Your mind races with positive thoughts and the goals you will accomplish in life. Yet you never actually implement any of them. Your primary fear in life is that you will run out of drugs, and your sole preoccupation is how to get them. You "bust missions" all day long, mapping out a strategy each morning, reviewing your possible rides, hangouts, contacts, and whoever isn't currently broke. As you scavenge for more, you smoke more. Pipes and lighters become your lifeline. You keep them on your body and feel scared to lend them out. What if you didn't get them back and couldn't get high immediately? Then where would you be? If your stash of drugs gets low, extreme anxiety grips and cripples you; and if you run out, complete desperation engulfs you. You're on a mission. You are determined to make sure you have enough to smoke. There is no other goal, no other point to life. In every moment, you live a lie.

In this altered reality, there are different portals of surmounting danger you can walk through. I had already entered deep into the antechambers of the drug world, but now I was perched at the entryway of complete chaos and madness, which leads to the inner chambers where one thing after another after another is taken away, the end result being the stripping away of life itself.

Aware of the precipice before me and wondering where to turn for a place to stay, I thought of my mom. Our checkered past still pierced us with sharp thorns, and neither of us could keep from exploding when the subject of our shared history arose, but I felt I could turn to her. Since our reconciliation a couple years earlier, she had been motherly, sweet, and generous toward me.

By this time, Mom had been in a two-year relationship with a Honduran man. At our first introduction, I got an eerie feeling from him, and goosebumps covered my skin. After Mom let me move in, I did my best to maintain the careful balance, tense as it was, of avoiding him, pleasing her, and hiding my habit. After only a few weeks, without giving any reason, Mom unexpectedly announced to me and Ozzie that she was moving to Mexico, and her boyfriend was going with her. "You can have this house," she said. "It's furnished. You can pay the mortgage, which is really reasonable. It's all yours." My mom knew that Ozzie drank a lot and did drugs, so she made a stipulation that drugs wouldn't be tolerated in her home. Looking Ozzie in the eye, she added, "You need to man up. I'm giving you a chance to take care of my daughter."

As Mom left, she said these parting words to me, which I will never forget: "Be careful. Don't fall into his world. Don't get into that whole drug scene—because once you start getting into drugs, you lose everything."

With fake confidence, I responded, "Mom, you don't have to worry about anything."

Soon after she left, the house turned into a drug resort. For the first three or four months, Ozzie and I celebrated our newfound freedom in what became known as "The Dream Home" to druggies from Ozzie's hometown. A constant stream of methamphetamines, alcohol, and pot trickled in, as addicts accustomed to being crammed into small rooms, crack houses, ghetto cars, and sidewalks stayed for days in the comfort of their own rooms, replete with a full bath and access to a kitchen and backyard. Drugs were used around the clock, and all of Ozzie's druggie friends quickly became mine.

To pay the mortgage, I started doing administrative work at temp jobs where I also took it upon myself to passionately preach my New Age beliefs, making sure my coworkers were convinced. But there were also days when I couldn't function. After twenty-four hours without sleep, a crippling mix of anxiety, depression, and grogginess would shut down my ability to cope, and I would call in sick.

In a short time, methamphetamines spread like a menacing shadow over every aspect of my life. Only four months after I switched from coke to meth, I couldn't picture my life without it. My very cells craved the drug twenty-four/seven, and I couldn't function with or without it. I began to lose my jobs because I simply wouldn't show up. Mortgage payments and bills were piling up unpaid. Day and night, cars pulled into my driveway, lights clicked on, and music blared. When I was coming off a high, confusion wracked my brain, and the fear of being ratted out by neighbors frayed my nerves.

A month after Ozzie and I took over Mom's house, he started leaving for a week or two at a time to see his ex-girlfriend. Predictably, she'd kick him out after a few days, and he'd come back to me, ingratiating himself with his charm. I took him back every time, wanting to believe his animated lies: "I really love you. I don't even love her. The only reason I go back is to see my kids because I miss them." I felt bad for his children. If he was going in order to see his kids, I didn't want to intrude. I would tell him of my hurt feelings but never picked a fight or caused any drama. I had been a people-pleaser all my life, especially with my dad, and that trait wasn't changing, even when I was high on drugs.

When Ozzie and I were together, we were attached at the hip. If we were in the same room, he would sit next to me; when we had food, we would share it; in private and in public, he would reach out to hold my hand. I never understood how Ozzie could leave me over and over again.

My hope was in him, and my self-esteem had bottomed out. Drugs were emotionally numbing, so it was hard to cry, but I suffered an internal nightmare. When Ozzie was away, I felt bitter loneliness. When he returned, he was as attached as he had been before and full of apologies, but I knew he would leave again. His ping-pong game with me lasted for two and half years. Wasn't I pretty enough or good enough for him to stay?

One night during a week when I had Ozzie to myself, I had a dream in which my mom showed up unexpectedly from Mexico because I hadn't been making the mortgage payments. The following evening, when Ozzie and I were alone in the house, shut up in my mother's master bedroom and getting high, I told Ozzie about my dream. "Wouldn't that be awful?" I said.

We both rolled with laughter. Ozzie took another hit from the pipe and said, "That would be bad if it really happened." Just then, we heard knocking at the front door, and a key turned the lock. A voice yelled, "Patricia! Patricia! It's your mom. I'm here!"

Ozzie and I looked at each other in wide-eyed panic, and he dropped his pipe, which was unheard of. I quickly locked the door, we grabbed our jackets, threw a few clothes and our drugs into a bag, and ran out the sliding back door.

That's when my life of being a homeless drug addict began.

> Lost sheep were my people, their shepherds misled them, straggling on the mountains; From mountain to hill they wandered, losing the way to their fold. Whoever came upon them devoured them . . .
> –Jeremiah 50:6–7b

For the next three years, I spent each day taking speed every two hours, never knowing where I would sleep at night. Crack houses, hotel rooms, and the street were my transitory homes. Ozzie was at the helm of our pointless voyage, seeking refuge for us among his spun-out friends. When the night shadows arrived and no friendly invitation to do drugs—which implicitly meant having a place to crash—had come our way, Ozzie would find sidewalk space in front of a friend's home and encourage me to smoke all night with him to stay awake. Sometimes, our hits kept us so high that time moved at warp speed: days and nights became one, and sleep would elude us for three or four days in a row. When my body finally got the chance to tell me it needed rest, I would doze off for two or three hours and then wake up to have speed for breakfast, preferring drugs to food.

Since I was the only person among our group of friends "responsible" enough to possess a driver's license, and because our illicit activities looked less suspicious to the police if a girl was at the wheel, I drove people around much of the day in a never-ending game of search-and-locate. If we couldn't get drugs in Woodland, we'd find them in Santa Rosa, and vice versa. For the three years that I was on the streets, I never stole, begged for, or purchased a crumb of meth. My friends "smoked me out," giving me drugs in return for rides. Because I still valued drug addicts as people and treated them well, and they in turn, liked me for my friendly personality, they simply handed me drugs.

My food came from addicts as well. Druggies don't like to smoke alone and know where to find one another in a chaotic exchange of help and harm. Ozzie, too, came up with money for my meager meals since he was stealing to support his habit and was a wanna-be drug dealer who sold little ounces of speed here and there, thinking he was big-time. The act of selling was his security blanket because it assured him that the drug would always be in his possession, which meant he would never have to go too long without a high. If his stash ran out, he would call as many as thirty people in rapid succession and have me drive for hours in hot pursuit of a short fix from a small pipeful.

Within a community bonded by addiction, dealers and designated drivers are highly esteemed. So are the glassblowers, I learned, since cocaine and meth addicts make their own pipes. Fascinated, I watched as my friends took a fire torch to a small glass tube of perfume and blew into it to make a perfect methamphetamine or crack pipe. They knew the exact moment to blow and the precise amount of air pressure needed to pop open the other end of the glass tube, making a perfect hole. This art, which they had mastered over time, surpassed the skill of even some of the most gifted glassblowers.

To clean the pipe, we would grab a soda can, place it on a surface face-down, then pour a bit of alcohol or perfume onto the bottom, which was now the top. Applying our lighters to the liquid, which ignited a small fire, we would grab our dirty, black pipes and place them amidst the flames, where they became transparent glass—clean and sparkling. These were the activities of our lives. Not much more.

After about two years of using, the pipe was barely affecting me. For three or four months, I smoked without getting any hint of a buzz. As with all addicts, in the passage of time, my body naturally adapted to my drug of choice, developing a tolerance; so instead of pleasure, my usual dosage could only offer me the avoidance of crippling withdrawal symptoms, fierce cravings, and dependence.

More and more speed was needed to achieve the same chemical effect in my system, so I graduated to bongs, which engulfed half of my face when I inhaled and spun me out with an incredible high. Excited, I thanked "the universe" that something could give me a feeling of euphoria again.

My family knew I was alive because of my occasional calls to my brother, but they didn't know of my addiction. Then a year and a half into my absence, when I was twenty-one, I knocked on my brother's door to ask if I could sleep in his car. When he saw me, he looked deeply pained, about to cry. Now he knew. I felt so embarrassed that I began to cry too. He said, "I never thought you would ask me for this type of favor. I didn't think that things could get this low for you. I don't want this life for you." He was very kind, and he did his best to help me. He gave Ozzie and me the keys to his car, and we slept in the back seat.

That night I had a dream:

It's Christmastime. We're decorating the tree—my brother, sister, and I. I pick up a colorful ornament and attach it to a branch in what I think is the perfect place. My body relaxes in the warm and cozy glow of the Christmas lights. Seeing my dad on the couch, I curl up next to him. He places his arm around me, and I feel like the most special little girl in the whole world.

Days later I heard from my brother that my dad was feeling utterly disgraced and disappointed in me. "Dad is upset," he told me over the phone, "and he doesn't even want you in the house." Those words engulfed me with a scorching sense of shame. Dad had been my best friend, and I had been his princess. His reaction made me want to stay as far away from my family as possible. Yet I wasn't angry. I knew it was my fault.

But nothing could keep me away from seeking the high—not the pain and dishonor I was inflicting on my family and myself, not the prospect of serious harm, not the fear of jail, not even the threat of losing my own life. Several harrowing incidents proved this to be the unfortunate truth. One of them happened when I was hanging out with a dealer friend of mine, an addict from a very young age, whose nickname was Julie Pipes. On one of my visits to her, we were alone in her bedroom around midday, smoking speed. She was lying on her bed, sharing her distress over losing custody of her son a couple years earlier, and I was doing my drugged-out best to listen as I lay comfortably on my side across from her. Directly behind me was a sliding glass door, covered by closed curtains, which led to her backyard.

I didn't have a devotion to the Blessed Mother at the time, nor did I ever pray to her; yet in my wallet, somehow, was a picture of Our Lady of Guadalupe. Handing it to Julie without forethought, I said, "Here, take this and read the prayer on the back of the card. Maybe she can help you."

A split second later, within a few short feet of us, we heard a gunshot coming from the other side of the sliding glass door, followed by a man's loud and painful scream. Julie jumped up and opened the curtains, then the door. A drug dealer whom she owed money to was on the ground, holding his leg, a bullet lodged in his inner thigh.

Possessing a fully loaded gun, he had come to kill her. After hearing the voice of his intended target, he started shooting without seeing and had planned to keep firing. The only things between me and that weapon were the glass doors and a thin curtain. Lying sideways, with my whole body exposed, I'd been a full target. If his first shot hadn't ricocheted off the metal frame of the doors and then hit him instead, those bullets would have entered me.

Spun off drugs, I remember nothing after that.

Another fateful day, I drove with Ozzie to Santa Rosa so that we could replenish our depleted drug stash and he could see his two boys, ages five and three. As I pulled up and parked a block away from his ex-girlfriend's home, he leaned over to give me a goodbye peck on the cheek. Before he could get out of the car, his ex-girlfriend ran toward us, wielding a hammer. In a blind rage, she began to smash the front windshield of my car. Glass shattered onto my face and arms and cut into the skin of my hands. Then she ran over to the driver's side where I was sitting and crashed the hammer through my side window, nearly hitting my face with it—but Ozzie grabbed me and quickly pulled me onto his lap on the passenger's side. Then he jumped out of the car to restrain her as she screamed, "You f---- bitch! I'm going to kill you!"

A couple of people scurried out of her house and pulled her back inside. I sat on the sidewalk next to shards of glass, rocking slightly back and forth in a silent state of trauma. Ozzie saw my tears but showed no compassion. A warrant was out for his arrest—I don't remember for what—and he didn't want more drama. He wanted to hop in the car and flee the scene, but we couldn't risk driving with a shattered window and windshield. The vehicle was soon towed, but we had no money to retrieve it, so I lost my car that day.

Yet the most degrading and harrowing incident for me, by far, involved the police. It happened at night when I was lounging in a motel room, smoking with a couple of girls and three guys, including a dealer named Eddy. One of us happened to look out the window and saw cops running up the stairs to the second floor, on their way to bust into our room and arrest us. Eddy grabbed a rock of meth the size of a five-pound sack of flour and threw it out the back window. (That rock probably cost around six thousand dollars.) Then he jumped out of the second-story window onto the ground.

Six police officers burst through the door, handcuffed all of us, and marched our sorry crew down to the parking lot for questioning. Meanwhile, a couple of cops had gone on a hunt for Eddy, who ended up in jail. As I stood in a suspect line, handcuffed next to eight police cars, my only thought was, "My dad . . . My dad's going to kill me! He's going to have to bail me out of jail. This will be the biggest disgrace of his life."

One of the cops looked at me and asked, "Why are you here?"

Quivering, I responded, "I'm hanging out with my boyfriend."

"You look like a nice young girl," he said with the concerned look of a good father. "You're very young. Your boyfriend is a loser. A nice girl like you shouldn't be hanging around these people."

That day, everyone was taken into custody except for me, since I was the only person without a record. The cop looked at me intensely, one last time, as if to impress his words upon me, and then he let me go.

Escaping prison was like winning the lottery. The world lifted off my shoulders. But to be jostled into handcuffs had been mortifying. What was my life turning out to be? Never had I imagined that I would be known as a drug addict, a homeless person, a lowlife. Humiliation over what my immediate and extended family must be thinking consumed me. Everyone had expected so much more of me. But now my respectability was lost, like a sunken ship in a sea of poor choices. "What happened? I, Patricia Sandoval, was supposed to have been somebody."

> Be not wicked to excess, and be not foolish. Why should you die before your time?
> –Ecclesiastes 7:17

For the first two years of my life as an addict, I had looked presentable, even healthy and genteel, but as I entered my third year of drugging myself, my body finally wore my sickness: my ribs and collar bones protruded outward, my face was gaunt and pale, dark half-circles cupped my eyes, my wrinkled clothes hung clumsily around my toothpick frame, and my uncovered head revealed small patches of scalp due to my trichotillomania, which was only growing worse.

I lived in constant fear. Streams of questions wracked my mind as I tried desperately to stave off a somber tomorrow: "Where was I going to sleep? Where could I take a shower? Would I eat? Could I get enough drugs?" I never knew how bad things were going to get, how much worse I would become, or where I would eventually end up.

Law enforcement became a hated, frightening enemy. Living with people who despised cops, who were forever watching out for and running from them, had multiplied the police in my mind. I saw them everywhere. I was paranoid in their presence and cursed their existence. After I lost my own wheels, I almost fainted for fear of getting pulled over because I had to drive someone else's piece-of-junk car with obvious druggies as passengers or ride with a drug dealer whose vehicle was far too expensive and flashy for his age and income. My worst nightmare was of making a collect call to my parents from prison.

Paranoia seeped into other areas of my mind as well. Greedy and possessive of my stash, I began hiding my bags of meth from friends and locking myself in a room to smoke, telling them I didn't have any drugs. I trusted no one, yet sometimes for good reason. My meager belongings were frequently snitched by my "closest friends"—clothes, jewelry, watches, purses—though I never stole from others. Even Ozzie had robbed me. Once, when I'd noticed some of my jewelry items missing from places only Ozzie was privy to, friends shared with me that he had sold them for drugs. He, of course, flatly denied it with a coy smile and told me how pretty I was.

My third year on the streets, the line between friend and foe grew thin and more permeable. One day, my cell phone kept ringing with an unknown number. I didn't respond to it until the third or fourth call. "Hello?" I finally answered.

"It's Sandra." It was Ozzie's ex. Ozzie's ex? Our last encounter had involved a hammer crashing through glass toward my head, Yet I was hardly surprised that she'd gotten my number. She, too, was part of the Santa Rosa drug ring in which information ignores boundaries.

"Yes," I answered with trepidation.

"I need to talk to Ozzie. Is he with you? Do you know where he is?"

"I haven't seen him for three days," I said, which was true. Ozzie would sometimes disappear, leaving no trace.

"I need his help. My . . . our kids have no food. They don't even have any milk."

My chilly heart quickly melted. "No milk?"

"Nothing."

Unable to bear the thought of her children having no milk, I said, "I'll come over right now and help you." In desperation, she agreed. So I pocketed the little money I had, hopped into a friend's lemon of a car, purchased some food, and drove to her home. The door was answered by a completely different Sandra—a shy and beautiful young woman, who reminded me of pictures of Pocahontas, and whom I later learned had been a straight-A student in college on her way to a bright future—that is, before she met Ozzie. In time, we would become good friends.

Radical relationship reversals were a confounding yet somehow normal part of my life as an addict. Another unexpected day of reversals happened when I was looking for a break from too many drugs and sleepless nights. I was tired of bouncing around—sleeping in cars, motels, or not at all—and wandering along countless sidewalks. I craved a cozy bed, a shower, and a place to relax. Ozzie didn't think he could provide such a spot, so I said, "Ozzie, take me to my sister's house. I want to see if I can sleep there, at least for one night."

I started to think of how much I missed my niece, who was eight by now, and my nephew, now five. In the past, I had been my sister's babysitter for years, never denying her requests to care for them from the moment they were born. When she worked two jobs, I would stay in her home for weeks, changing their diapers, playing with them, getting up at one a.m. to feed them. My sister's kids meant the world to me, and they had looked up to their "cool" aunt all their lives.

When my sister and I were growing up, I had done everything possible to please her and be in her good graces. I cherished her approval and friendship and had even gone so far, as a teenager, to get my unlovely tattoo because she insisted it would bond us as two powerful New Age women. Despite my precipitate fall into ignominy, I hoped that if my sister saw me this vulnerable, she would want to help me and, in her heart, she would feel love.

As Ozzie drove off toward her apartment in Santa Rosa, my frayed nerves couldn't keep my exhausted body awake any longer. With my head resting against the passenger window, I drifted into sleep:

I am sitting in the dirty laundry basket giggling. I hear my sister's voice: ". . . eight, nine, ten. I'm gonna get you! I'm gonna find you!"

"She'll never find me here," I think to myself. Then I realize my hiding place doesn't smell too good, and I start to hope that she'll find me soon.

"Gotcha!" she shouts, grabbing my shoulders, and I scream with delight.

A hand was tugging at my shoulder, and I heard Ozzie's voice ringing in my ear: "Patricia, wake up. We're here." He had parked the car strategically, slightly out of view of my sister's second-story apartment. "I'll wait here for you to give me the signal that you're going in."

"Okay, okay," I mumbled, disoriented and half-awake. Struggling to keep my eyelids open, I looked around at the many people barbequing on their front balconies. It was the Fourth of July. Everyone looked so normal and happy. Sighing deeply, I got out of the car, walked past the family celebrations and up the apartment stairs, and knocked on my sister's door. When she opened it, her kids were at her side, looking overjoyed to see me. Then in front of her children and all of her neighbors, she screamed at the top of her lungs, "You piece of shit! You drug addict! Get the hell out of my house, and stay the hell away from my children! You're a f---ing loser!" I started to cry and tried to tell her that I was asking for help, but she snapped her fingers at me and shoved me away from the door. My eyes made contact with my niece, who stared at me in wide-eyed shock. Then the door was slammed shut. I wanted to vanish into nothingness. While the neighbors looked on in stunned silence, I slowly turned around and began my painful walk back to Ozzie.

I couldn't imagine sinking much lower. One might wonder what hope I had in life, why I slunk forward day after day and didn't look for ways to lie down and die. The entire time I was on the streets, I carried one small torch of hope; one faint light that spurred me on. It was the belief that I could change my boyfriend, that by having climbed into his hole with him, we would somehow both get out of it together. He would love me and care about me so much that he would do anything to become a better person, to change and to make our relationship work. I looked forward to the fairy-tale ending when Ozzie and I would get off of drugs, when he would have a job, when we would get married, have children, and live happily ever after—laughing all the way.

> How long will you people mock my honor
> love what is worthless,
> chase after lies?
> Know that the LORD works wonders for the faithful;
> the LORD hears when I call out.
> –Psalm 4:3-4

Fact: Living together is not a trial of marriage but rather a training for divorce. More than eight out of ten couples who live together will break up either before the wedding or afterward in divorce. (1)

Chapter Eight

Looking Up

OZZIE AND I NEVER FOUGHT. When he hurt me, I told him so, and if I felt down, he always tried to cheer me up. From the time I fell in love with him, I gave him my heart, my body, my sobriety, my soul. Though I lived with a broken heart, his wit, looks, and passionate embrace—all topped with a high—could always soothe my shattered nerves, at least temporarily.

The only time in three years that we argued happened one late morning when we were stuffed into a small, musty hotel room in Santa Rosa, California, along with four friends. Food had been scarce, and we were running out of drugs. In search of more speed, our friends wanted to go to Woodland, but I preferred to stay put. I made a comment that irritated Ozzie. With uncharacteristic anger, he berated me in front of everyone and then yelled, "Why don't you get out! Just leave!" He'd never raised his voice at me, not even once. Startled and humiliated, I walked out. No one stopped me. No one came to my defense. Certainly, I thought, Ozzie would run after me and apologize. But he didn't; he just watched me go.

As soon as I walked out of the building and sat in the parking lot, I saw Ozzie and his buddies get into a car and drive off. I was stunned. Left with nothing and no one—not even a dime for a call and no one to call if I'd had one—I sat and cried for over an hour, hoping he'd come back and get me. "This isn't happening," I thought to myself. "This can't be true. I'm thirsty and can't even buy myself a bottle of water." My fear of reproach was so crushing that I didn't dare call my family, and I refused to become a beggar in my own eyes. Thinking of other friends I could turn to, I realized in a flash: "I don't have any." The ones who had driven off without me were more Ozzie's than mine, and in the artificial world of substances—but no substance—friends were simply people seeking the same thing you were. All that we had in common were broken families and an aim to get high.

"Ozzie will come back for me," I cried. "I gave him my virginity. I gave him my sobriety. I got into this life for him."

Time passed . . . and more time passed . . . but Ozzie wasn't coming. I couldn't believe how his heart had immediately turned cold. An hour and a half went by as I sat on the curb, riddled with crippling fears: "He's probably already in Sacramento . . . Does he even care? . . . Am I going to turn into someone who asks for money on the street?" I started to bawl. My chest heaved, cutting off my breath in an uncontrollable eruption of pain that lasted minutes but felt like hours.

Suddenly and undeniably, I felt a strong presence in the heavens looking down on me. My sobs subsided, and I looked up. The sky was bright blue with billowing clouds. I don't know how I sensed this, but I knew that the presence was God the Father, watching me at that very moment.

I reverted instantly to the faith I had as a child. Staring into the clouds, I said, "You are all that I have in life at this very moment. I've hit rock bottom. I have nothing: no friends, no money, no drugs, no family. I've ruined my life. I don't know how I let myself get to this point, but I know that You exist, and I know You're listening to me." Then something within me, in a moment of grace, made me want to praise Him. I exclaimed aloud, "I want to thank You for all the many blessings you have given me in my life. You gave me a beautiful childhood, a wonderful family, and I want to thank You for all of that. But now, I've ruined my life. I've ruined it all."

I pulled my knees to my forehead, clutching my legs, and sobbed with piercing regret. Two minutes later, I felt someone kneel directly behind me and embrace me. My eyes looked up through tears to see a pretty blond woman, about my age, twenty-three, giving me a beautiful, broad smile. The nametag on her brown uniform read "Bonnie." Staring at me with great tenderness, she said, "Jesus loves you."

I looked at her in confusion. "What did you say?"

"Jesus loves you. I am a waitress at that restaurant," she said, pointing to a building on the corner. "I was taking an order when the Lord spoke to my heart and told me, "Put down your notepad, look out that window, and tell that young lady who is sitting on the curb that even if her mother or father should abandon her, I will never abandon or forsake her. I will be with her until the end of time."

I was in awe. The Author of those words knew me, and He had answered my prayer immediately, for I had barely finished talking to Him. Then Bonnie, still smiling, said, "I'm going to take you into the restaurant.

My shift is almost over, so I'm going to feed you and then take you to wherever home is." Her face was warm and welcoming, and the love in her voice . . . it was real. It was God. She didn't view me as a worthless human being on the street. I could see in her eyes and heart that I possessed dignity and value. Sweet, polite, and well mannered, she made it seem as though plucking me off the street was so easy—like nothing, really—and that catering to me posed no burden for her at all.

Tossing a lunch menu over to me once we were inside, she said, "I'm glad that I met you, because there's a man who roams around that parking lot and picks up young girls to prostitute them, and I'm just trying to protect you." She pointed to the menu. "You can have whatever you want."

I couldn't help but notice that Bonnie appeared very whole as a person. She had her job and looked responsible. As I marveled at her smile and the happiness and charity it expressed, a thought crossed my mind: "This is what I was supposed to be."

Bonnie served me a three-course meal, and I, trying my best to appear normal and put-together—fooling no one—felt overcome with both gratitude and embarrassment. I was never one to like to ask for anything, and Bonnie's co-workers, who had seen her pull off the street a girl with swollen eyes, couldn't help but throw curious peeks my way. Yet Bonnie's very presence put me at ease.

When she took me to her car, I stopped in my tracks. "This is the same car I used to have," I stammered. It was the exact model, year, and color as the one I had lost. We climbed in, and I could see she was determined. "I'm going to take you to where home is," she stated. "You're going home." She gave me no choice. We drove the fifteen minutes to Petaluma, and when I got out of the car and thanked her, she told me she was Christian and the daughter of a pastor. We embraced, and she drove off with a friendly wave.

I was left standing at the curbside of my father's house. The twenty feet leading to his doorstep may as well have been a steep, treacherous climb leading to the edge of a sharp cliff. Standing at the entrance of his home was like preparing to jump off a precipice without knowing what lay below. As my knuckles rapped on Dad's door, my body felt the terror of falling as the fate of my future resounded in my knocking.

Dad opened the door, and there I was, a walking dead person: five feet and five inches, a frail ninety pounds, with little hair and worn-out clothes, exhausted from this life. My father's eyes filled with deep sorrow. I threw myself at his feet and sobbed, asking him to forgive me. Unable to hold back tears, he picked me up from the ground and took me into his bedroom. He didn't care about the shame I'd brought to the family, or that I'd abandoned him. At that moment, he only cared about me. With my head on his knee as he sat on the edge of the bed, together we cried. The only other time I'd seen him cry was when my mom left. His tears felt like merciful rain falling on my parched soul. We stayed there a good long hour, both of us sobbing as he caressed my hair, telling me many times that he loved me and that everything was going to be okay.

> If a man has a hundred sheep and one of them goes astray, will he not leave the ninety-nine in the hills and go in search of the stray? And if he finds it, amen, I say to you, he rejoices more over it than over the ninety-nine that did not stray. In just the same way, it is not the will of your heavenly Father that one of these little ones be lost.
> –Matthew 18:12–14

My father had welcomed home a shell of the daughter he knew. I was sick in mind and body, still addicted and barely clinging to sanity. I didn't want to leave my room. I felt so weak, depressed, and wracked by shame that entire days passed with my head barely leaving my pillow. I would cry, then pass out, then wake up on the brink of tears, thinking, "Life sucks," and then pass out again. "You are a complete failure," my thoughts repeated. "What will come of your life now?"

At times, my body would tremble and break out in sweat. When my withdrawal symptoms were severe, temptations tormented me—desires to return my friends' calls or go out looking for Ozzie. I never wanted to open the door when the doorbell rang and said cursory hellos to company before retreating. With bald areas on my scalp, I shuddered at the thought of anyone seeing me. While I still felt I could lose a couple more pounds, people would comment that my ribcage was sticking out and my collarbones were caving in. I thought they were simply exaggerating. But then I tried on my old clothes, they literally fell off of me. Maybe, just maybe, there was something to what people were saying.

My father had taken me back lovingly and without reservation, but his stoic personality proved unequipped to handle a Patricia who was weak, frail, crying, and in need. After long hours at work, he'd come home tired and say precious few words. On the rare occasion when he opened my door to peek in, he'd toss me a cursory "Hi," like a bone, which left me feeling more ashamed. I withdrew, and he grew cold. To those in the outside world who asked, "How is your daughter doing?" he tried to give good news; but he couldn't hide his disappointment from me. My father shut down. I felt like he was mad at me, and I became scared of him.

My brother, who lived at home, also welcomed me back. Like my father, he didn't know what to do or say; but underneath our awkwardness lay a deep, unspoken love between us that time and tragedy hadn't stolen. I adored and cherished my brother, and he knew that.

Living with two men who were unable to address things "touchy-feely," I had no one to talk to. But outside of home, I did have my mom, who, unbeknownst to me, had reconverted to Catholicism less than a year earlier. Her embrace of the Catholic faith began when she was working at Hewlett-Packard, and one of the technicians, who happened to also be a Christian pastor, looked at her straight in the eye and asked, "Do you read the Bible?"

She laughed at the question and responded, "I don't believe in that book; it's an ordinary book, like any other book full of stories."

"But do you have a Bible?" he asked, undaunted.

"Yes. It's somewhere, stashed away in a drawer."

"If your own father wrote you letters of love, would you store them away without reading them, or would you read them and then safely put them away?"

"Of course I would read them first."

"The letters you have stashed away are love letters from your Heavenly Father, and He is waiting with immense love for you to read His letters to you.'"

My mom felt a tender love penetrating her heart. Surprised by her own reaction, she looked at the technician and said, "I promise you I will look for my Bible and read it tonight."

He looked up toward heaven and whispered, "Thank God."

That evening when my mother got home from work, the first thing she did was look for her Bible. Sitting at her dining table alone, she randomly opened to Isaiah 49:15-16a and read, *"Can a mother forget her infant, be without tenderness for the child of her womb? Even should she forget, I will never forget you. See, upon the palms of my hands I have written your name . . ."* For the first time in her life, my mother felt that she had a Father who loved her. Something inside her soul believed that she was engraved in the palms of her Father's hands and that she was finally safe. Closing the Bible, she thought, "I don't know if this is truly the Word of God, but I know I felt something beautiful in my heart." In the days that followed, she started reading little pieces of the Bible daily—her love letters.

Then she was invited by an old friend to attend a daylong retreat. Mom did not want to go, but the friend twisted her arm. Hispanic retreats tend to include applauding, dancing, singing, and praising—nothing my mom was interested in. During the entire retreat, she felt antsy and agitated. As various priests gave talks and praise music was played, her primary prayer was that the day would soon be over. Then one of the priests exposed the Blessed Sacrament.

Mom didn't fully understand who was present in the form of the Blessed Sacrament, but following the movements of those around her, she bowed her head and looked at the floor in front of her chair. At once, she saw Jesus' feet on the ground facing her own. She could make out His sandals, His ankles, His shins, and His cloak—the same shade of brown as that of a Franciscan friar. Her soul felt vulnerable and transparent. The choir sang the words:

"He said, 'I do not like you [as you are].'
I am going to break you
and transform you
into a new vessel.
But in the process,
I'm going to make you cry
because I'm going to make you
pass through fire." (1)

Jesus stared right through her, revealing to her a heart made of stone. She gasped. "Lord, change my heart. Change my heart!" Within seconds, her heart started to feel as though it were breaking into pieces and shattering within her. Acute emotional, spiritual, and physical pain emanated from the center of her chest. Then the vision disappeared, leaving her crying for hours.

A week later, she attended a retreat miles away in Calistoga, California, where for the first time in over thirty years, she felt safe enough to expose her sins and release them in the Sacrament of Reconciliation. Drawn to the Church, like the prodigal son who longed for the comforts of his father's home, she returned to practice the faith of her childhood. Only then, when she had the nourishment of the sacraments to sustain her and faith to guide her, did she learn through the grapevine that her daughter was not only in the streets but also addicted to drugs.

Mom became depressed and worried; she hardly slept or ate and got very thin. But with the help of new friends, she turned her pain into prayer. She prayed Rosaries for me, went to Mass for me, fell to her knees in Adoration of the Blessed Sacrament on my behalf. On top of her heartbreak, she felt tremendous guilt: "If only I had taught Patricia the faith, this would never have happened to her."

One day, while sitting at Mass in front of a statue of Our Lady of Guadalupe, she pleaded repeatedly, "Oh, Holy Mother, help my daughter. Heal her!"

Our Lady spoke to my mother's heart in return, saying, "You are not praying correctly."

Surprised, my mother requested, "Holy Mother, teach me, then, how to pray correctly."

Our Lady told her, "Surrender your daughter to my Son."

"I already did."

"No, you haven't. When you start glorifying my Son by sleeping, eating, and doing away with your sadness, then you will have truly surrendered your daughter to my Son."

Hearing these words from the Blessed Mother, my mom began to trust in God, to praise Him with joy—and to expect a miracle.

With renewed confidence, she became bold in her prayers and put Satan on notice: "Mas de valio no tocas unos de mis hijos," which meant, in essence, "Don't you dare lay a hand on one of my children."

So when my mother came back into my life, she was ready to minister to me. In fact, the only comfort and consolation I received were her calls. She prayed with me deeply and soulfully on the phone every day and told me she loved me. She talked about Jesus and quoted Scripture, assuring me that God would carry me through. She told me of His promises and sent up words of petition and thanksgiving to the Father, Son, and Holy Spirit, Whom she'd come to know. Somehow, and despite my foray into the New Age and drugs, I still knew that Jesus was real. His appearance to me when I was a toddler had imprinted itself in my memory, and His words to me through Bonnie, the waitress, still echoed in the chambers of my heart: "I love you. Even if your mother or father should abandon you, I will never abandon or forsake you. I will be with you until the end of time."

I also knew from my childhood that Jesus was in the Catholic Church, and I wanted to be close to Him there. Slowly, tentatively, I began to come out of my room more often, and from there, I ventured outside to walk to the local church for Mass. Each morning, I'd sit in the same back pew, eagerly listening to the same priest who had given me my First Communion. When it came time for the Liturgy of the Eucharist, I was painfully aware that I couldn't yet receive the Body and Blood of Christ because I hadn't yet gone to Confession. But the poison of my shame was preventing me from going.

Whenever the priest's hands raised the Host in the air, followed by the Precious Blood, I felt the physical sensations of hunger and thirst. *"This is the Lamb of God who takes away the sins of the world,"* he would proclaim. With my eyes fixed on the Bread of Life, raised high, I yearned to receive Jesus into my body and my soul and cried out for healing and wholeness. The priest continued, *"Happy are those who are called to the Supper of the Lamb."* At the sound of those words, I would cringe. They stung because I wasn't one of those people. Ashamed and sorrowful to be the only one remaining in a pew while the others walked forward to receive the Lord, I would ask Jesus for a spiritual communion with Him and, many times, a beautiful peace would blanket my heart. In church, I felt like I was home, even more than in my earthly father's house. In church, the Father's love was stronger than my pain.

While God was clearly pleased with my attendance at Mass, the devil revealed that *he* was not. Enraged by my return to the Church, he mounted a spiritual attack on the day I first went to Mass. It began when I was dozing off to sleep, lying face up, and I sensed a negative presence in my room on the right side of my bed. Without warning, the presence leapt on top of me, immobilizing my body and my voice. My hands, my torso, my legs—everything but my mouth was completely paralyzed. I couldn't even scream to ask for help. Finally, after about twenty minutes of strife, the presence released its grip.

After that, every three hours throughout the night, and sometimes during the day when I would take naps or watch TV, this ominous, suffocating presence bore down on me for twenty minutes at a time. Lacking any knowledge or understanding of spiritual warfare, I thought I had to win this battle on my own. I struggled fiercely to move and to speak.

Worn out by the fight, I grew even more weak and frail. Yet for some reason, I wasn't scared. I knew God was with me.

> Fear not, you shall not be put to shame; you need not blush, for you shall not be disgraced. The shame of your youth you shall forget, the reproach of your widowhood no longer remember. For he who has become your husband is your Maker; his name is the LORD of hosts; Your redeemer is the Holy One of Israel, called God of all the earth. The LORD calls you back, like a wife forsaken and grieved in spirit, a wife married in youth and then cast off, says your God.
> –Isaiah 54:4–6

Fact: According to a nationwide poll conducted by the U.S. Religious Knowledge Survey in 2010, 45 percent of Catholics in the United States do not know that their Church teaches that the bread and wine used in Communion do not merely symbolize, but actually become, the Body and Blood of Christ. Among the American public overall, 52 percent say, incorrectly, that Catholicism teaches that the bread and wine used for Communion are simply symbols of the Body and Blood of Jesus. (2)

A survey conducted a year later in 2011 by the National Catholic Reporter stated that as many as 50 percent of adult Catholics do not know the Church's teaching regarding the Real Presence of Jesus in the Eucharist. (3)

Chapter Nine

Living in Two Worlds

ALTHOUGH FEEBLE IN BODY and mentally tired from the spiritual conflict, I was healing. Small sprouts of the old me began to grow, and some even blossomed. My father noticed the change, and his cold exterior thawed to reveal his softer side, which would converse with me. But I still looked like a Holocaust survivor. When one of my aunts came over to visit, she left concerned and called my mother: "Your daughter's ribs are protruding. She doesn't look at all well."

My mom called from her home in Sacramento that same day. She had avoided the hour-and-a-half drive to see me on the off chance of running into my father, but now she pushed through her resistance and said, "I think it's best that I pick you up tomorrow. That way you can rest with me, and I'll take care of you. I think it's important for you to have good nutrition. You're weak and need help, Patricia. Your father is too busy working, and it's hard for him to properly attend to you. Come stay with me, and tomorrow we'll visit the National Shrine of Our Lady of Guadalupe in Sacramento, where I've always wanted to go."

I hung up the phone, grateful and giddy. I would have my mom near me again! Years of childhood happiness with her flooded my memory, like a warm rain on cracked desert soil.

The enemy was not at all pleased with my mother's invitation. That night, fierce anxiety seized me, pulling my will toward the recent past. Sweating from temptation, I wanted to run outside and get high to calm the fire in my nerves. Now that I knew God, I was aware of what was at stake, and I refused to budge. The strength I was receiving from daily Mass kept me under the bed covers and in my pajamas while a tempest raged inside of me.

I could hear my brother in the next room, playing video games with his friends, and my father watching TV downstairs. After an hour of relentless fear and cravings, my will had weakened to the point of despair. Closing my eyes tightly and gripping my hands together in prayer, I called out, "Lord, you have to help me because I can't do this anymore. I have no strength left. This temptation is so strong that I have to give it to you."

All at once, my field of vision turned black and white. Like the screen of an old television set with broken antennae, everything began to move from side to side in waves, blurring and swaying into a memory or dream state, as if I were traveling into a different dimension. I had been off methamphetamines for a month now, and even when higher than a jet stream, I never experienced such a phenomenon. A minute later, the waves disappeared and my vision returned to normal, except that everything remained in black and white.

I felt compelled to look to my left. There beside me, in my own room, sat a little girl, about age twelve, with dark curly hair down to her shoulders. Her head was topped with a big, wide-brimmed hat that sprouted a large feather; her long dress had white ruffles around the wrists and neckline; and the short cloak adorning her chest and shoulders looked like that of an ancient pilgrim, priest, or pope.

"Oh, no! I'm seeing a ghost! All these years of taking drugs, and now it's my day to completely lose it." All I knew was that I was fully awake because I could still hear video-game sounds, coming from my brother's room and my dad's favorite Mexican soap opera blaring downstairs. Nevertheless, I wanted more proof, so I pinched myself as hard as I could on my left forearm, slapped my cheeks, and called out for my brother. But he ignored my cries; he hadn't finished his game. I screamed for my dad, but he was too absorbed in his soap opera to respond.

I turned my head left again. "Darn." There she was, and she wasn't going away. She was clearly alive and looked somber and serious. I stared at her, and she stared intently back at me. "This must be a ghost," I thought. "Perhaps this little girl died in this house before my dad moved in."

After a few minutes of this uncomfortable contest, I joked with her, like a playful mom might do with her daughter in a game of hide-and-seek. "I can seeee you!" I clowned. All of a sudden, she broke down and began to sob. Covering her face in her hands, she bowed forward in her chair, but I could still see her chest heaving, and heaving with sadness. After a couple of minutes passed, she picked up her head to look at me again, this time with a pained expression of heartbreak, then bent forward again and cried some more.

I pulled the covers over my head, half-hoping, half-expecting this girl to vanish. But when I took them off again, there she was. I tried this several times as she cried off and on between stares. Still there. "Strange thing," I mused. "I was terrified by my sister's stories of ghosts when I was growing up, but I'm not terrified as I'm staring straight at one? If this is a ghost, why do I feel the presence of peace in my heart?"

Finally, I said to myself, "My brain is tired. I don't know what's going on, and whatever this is isn't going away. I can't explain it or deal with it, so I'm going to bed." I grabbed the sheets, turned away from the girl, and fell asleep.

The next morning, my field of vision was completely normal. Colors were back, and the girl was gone. Bouncing out of bed and running to my dad, I exclaimed, "I saw a little girl, a ghost, in my room last night. I think she might have passed away in this home . . . or perhaps something happened to her here."

Gazing at me wearily, he heaved a big sigh and shook his head. The look on his face—a mix of exasperation and pity—left me feeling embarrassed, alone, and irrelevant. After collecting my remaining scraps of self-worth, I told him that I was going to live with my mom and try to heal some more. He said that would be fine. I studied his eyes in search of any feelings, and a pang of love passed between us.

The next day, as I began to pack my things, my feelings of unease quickly faded. My yearning to be loved and nurtured was going to be fulfilled again! When I saw my mom pull her car up in front of the house, my heart started to dance. I knew she wouldn't ring the doorbell to avoid running into my father, so I hugged my brother, kissed my dad, and walked outside into my mother's embrace.

Both Mom and I had looked forward to this day of reunion. As promised, our first stop was the National Shrine of Our Lady of Guadalupe, where our senses delighted in the architecture and style of our heritage—even the smell of the church's wood was Mexican. Sensitively sculpted statues lined the walls, and as Mom and I passed from one saint to another, we came to a four-foot plaster image of a young girl seated in a chair with her arms extending forward in a gesture of welcome. The figure wore a long, gray-blue dress with ruffles around the wrists and the neck, and a short red-brown cape fell around her shoulders. Dark-brown hair framed her cherubic face and came down to her shoulders, and on her head was a wide-brimmed hat sporting a plume.

"This little . . . this girl . . ." my mother stammered, "she appeared to me in a vision and said she was going to heal you from drugs!"

"Mom! This little girl appeared to me last night in my room!'

At that moment, a priest who was walking by said, "This is not a little girl. This is the Child Jesus of Atocha, *El Santo Niño de Atocha*. He's very miraculous. He prays and He cries for the youth who are lost." Then he walked off. Our jaws dropped.

My mom and I felt so giddy about our mutual miracle that as soon as we got to her house, we immediately called my aunt in Guadalajara, Sister Olga, to tell her what had happened. Bursting with joy, she exclaimed, "I can't believe what you're saying. Only last night, I put Patricia's picture next to the Child Jesus of Atocha, and I entrusted her to Him, asking Him to heal her from drugs!" Mom and I looked at one another, speechless.

These confirmations of the miraculous visitation of the Child Jesus of Atocha marked the beginning of many days of grace spent with my mother. When I stepped into her Sacramento home, the same house Ozzie and I had defiled, I walked into a place of prayer. Every room was now beautiful and blessed. Mom had been working as a part-time teacher's assistant, and her relationship with her Honduran boyfriend was more long distance than immediate, so I only needed to endure his visits for a few days every month or two. With all the free time she had, my mom turned her attention on me, nurturing my body through healthy food and my soul through prayer. This new Catholic mother was vastly different from the angry New Age mother, even from the doting mother of my youth. She expressed even more love, exhibited a saintly patience, and gave me all she had, freely and generously from her heart. Sometimes I barely recognized her.

Living with this new mom meant that the Catholic television channel EWTN was left on throughout the day. A gentle reminder of the Lord's presence, it was quiet and unobtrusive, catechizing me without bending my will, since I was never forced to watch it. In fact, that station was the only thing capable of quelling my anxiety. Everything shown on EWTN brought me peace: the recitation of the Rosary, the Divine Mercy Chaplet, the Mass, and the wide variety of other religious programs. It was my pacifier and my companion, and I got hooked. Each day, Catholic prayers and Catholic teachings played in the background, and each night, I fell asleep alongside Mother Angelica, the foundress of the network, whose motherly nature and quirky humor kept my soul company. I didn't know how or why, but as I sat in front of the TV, I often felt that I would be on EWTN one day.

My mom was determined to heal and save me. Leaving nothing to chance, she quickly garnered her gray-haired army of Hispanic, Catholic grandmothers, who descended upon me like "praying" vultures and carried me off to charismatic groups. These compulsory kidnappings, three times a week, would have been tolerable for thirty minutes at a time. But I was held hostage for three hours, sitting in a circle with six to ten strangers who prayed for their families, then prayed for the world, then for each other, then over each other, then prayed in tongues, then sang worship song after worship song after worship song after worship song. This, to me, was a time-bound practice for eternal suffering. Just when I thought it would end, someone would pipe up, "Now, let's pray another Rosary!" or "One more song for Jesus!" I wanted to add, "Kill me now!" My feet would have hit the ground running if I hadn't been trapped with nowhere else to go. Yet, I had to admit to myself that when these strangers laid their hands on me, I felt grateful for their genuine care, and the darkness and agitation within me faded away.

One of my mom's most endearing prayer buddies was Grandma Yolanda, a sweet, blind woman with pronounced spiritual gifts. The first time she laid her hands upon my head, she began to prophesy. Catching me entirely off guard, these words came out of her mouth: "*'My ways are not your ways, and my thoughts are not your thoughts.'* The Lord wants you for Himself. He is going to use you, and you will travel across nations."

"What!" That seemed like too much of a mission for the likes of me. I was just a drug addict. And surrender my entire self? Be wholly God's? That seemed unattractive and boring. I dismissed her words as farfetched and irrelevant—except, perhaps, for the travelling part, which I liked. Yet I could never forget them completely . . .

I wanted my transition into Catholicism to happen slowly. In my warped image of the faithful, I believed that if I became a "Super Catholic," I would have a dreadfully humdrum life and morph into a dull, drab person who wore—God forbid it—plain clothes. I'd either be alone and miserable with only a geriatric posse for company, or marry a dork because no cute guy would be turned on by a daily Mass-goer. My club-hopping days would be over, and my prayer-group-hopping days would continue forever. At twenty-three, I couldn't think of one girl my age—much less one guy—who was into religion. As I saw it, anything but the most perfunctory Catholicism would interfere with my desire to go to bars with my girlfriends, my love of Mexican hip-hop music with drug-cartel lyrics, and my dream of being a sexy fashion queen again. With looks, makeup, and nice clothes holding my fragile ego together, I could at least put up a front to show the world I was somewhat successful, even if I felt like a failure. Unwilling to bend, I vowed to walk forward with one foot in each world.

One day, when my mom and I were sitting in her car at a stoplight on our way home from the store, I couldn't help but notice the car that had pulled up next to us: a 1980 Thunderbird that was in shambles. Dirty, ragged tape held its windows in place, and black exhaust spewed from the tailpipe. The car shook so badly as it idled that it rattled; its paint was more like rust; and the body was smashed in on all sides. The vehicle looked like a time bomb ready to explode. Sitting in the driver's seat was an African American girl, about twenty years of age, playing a worship song full blast. With her left elbow swinging wildly outside the window, she was clapping her hands and singing the name of Jesus loudly with great love and joy in her voice. I looked at her, incredulous. "She doesn't seem to care what anyone thinks," I marveled. Doesn't she notice all the heads turning in the cars surrounding her? Doesn't it bother her to look so absurd? I could never be like that. She's gone way overboard."

I couldn't bear anyone labeling me the way I was labeling her. I wanted to appear cool and collected. No, I would love Jesus silently without causing a disturbance or looking like a fool. Yet I couldn't take my eyes off of her. Tears glistened in my eyes, and my heart began to ache in my chest. Underneath my judgment, I admired her terribly because she was *free*.

A few days later, I dipped into a depression and cried all day. I thought of all the dreams I had coveted as a child. I had been so popular, such a good student, adored by relatives and the apple of my dad's eye. Now I was a loser—an ex-drug addict with no job, no hair, and no true friends. The fake ones I did have were druggies. The chasm between who I was and who I wanted to be seemed unbreachable. And I missed Ozzie. I wanted him to want me, to come find me and confess his wrongdoing. Meanwhile, my mom had been praying that he'd stay far away.

As day turned to night and I hadn't budged from my bed, Mom came into my room. She had just donned her pajamas, and I'd never taken mine off. Seeing my hopeless expression as I sat slumped on the bed, she plopped down next to me and asked, "What's wrong? Are you okay?"

"No, I'm not," I answered in tears. "I feel worthless, like a nobody. I'm a complete failure. I feel like I don't have anything."

I expected my mom to say, "It's okay. We all make mistakes" or "You're so pretty. You're smart. Everything will be fine." Instead, she grabbed one of my arms firmly and looked directly into my eyes. With uncharacteristic authority and power, she said: *"This is not who you are.* This is not Patricia Sandoval. You are not valuable because of the friends you've had, or the car or the clothes you possess. Those things do not define you. People may judge and criticize you within our family, but what they say is not the truth of who you are either. The choices you have made in life do not identify you. They are things that you did, but they are not you.

With great zeal and passion, she proclaimed, "You are a daughter of a King. *You are the daughter of the most High God."* This stunned me. There was so much worth in that title. It was the first time I had ever heard such words. I had lived my life believing whatever people said about me. My entire identity was summed up in the opinions of others. "The only reason you are worthy," my mom continued, "is because Christ shed his blood for you on the Cross. You are worth the price of his blood."

I had no idea until that moment that I possessed an entirely different identity in Christ. I listened, aware that the Holy Spirit had seized my mom, for I had never heard her speak like this. "Our Heavenly Father loves you, and I'm going to tell you what He thinks of you and who you are." Taking a Bible into her hand, she read aloud. As she spoke, the Spirit pierced my heart, and I truly received God's Word:

> Can a mother forget her infant,
> be without tenderness for the child of her womb?
> Even should she forget,
> I will never forget you.
> See, upon the palms of my hands I have written your name;
> your walls are ever before me.
> Your rebuilders make haste,
> as those who tore you down and laid you waste
> go forth from you.
> –Isaiah 49:15–17

Come Saturday, my mom must have known that a First Reconciliation service was happening at St. Hilary's Church in Tiburon, California, although she told me only that we were going to a Mass. I climbed into the car, and we drove for over an hour on the highway, then along a scenic road up a hill to the front terrace of the church, which overlooked a picturesque view of the San Francisco Bay. Entering St. Hilary's, we saw a cluster of diminutive "sheep" shuffling around in front of the altar, performing a play. The ninety-nine—well, at least nine—sheep began to sing about how the Good Shepherd wanted to find his one lost sheep—a little girl sitting in the corner, bundled up in a white, fluffy car-seat cover—in order to carry her back home in His arms.

While I stood at the church entrance, struck by the cuteness of the scene and wondering how the Good Shepherd would pull this off (he was half the size of the lost sheep), some of the seven-year-olds began to shed their costumes and line up along one of the side aisles of the church. I watched as the parish priest grabbed a kindergarten chair and sat down, his knees almost touching his chin. Bending over to accommodate to their size as best he could, he motioned for the fidgeting line to come forward, one at a time, to whisper their sins into his ear. One of the ladies of the parish who knew my story—most everyone there did, grabbed my hand and said, "C'mon, you're going to go to Confession."

"Now? Here!?" I hadn't been to Confession since my First Reconciliation at age seven, and I certainly didn't want to go now, but I wasn't about to make a scene in church. Forcefully, she marched me up to the line and deposited me there. She must have been Mom's cohort, and now I was trapped. If my mom had been the one to invite me to go to Confession, I would have declined out of fear and disgrace; yet in truth, I desperately longed to go so I could finally receive the Eucharist.

Standing in line with a row of cuddly sinners, like Will Ferrell in the movie *Elf*, I imagined that all eyes were turned curiously my way. When it got close to my turn, I could hear the kids' confessions in front of me: "I let my hamster go free, and now we can't find him. It's all my fault." "I was mad at my sister, so I put gum in her hair." "I used a bad word. I called my brother a bad meanie butt-face."

Now it was my turn. I walked forward and nervously knelt down close to the priest's ear: "Forgive me, Father, for I have sinned." I paused, cringing from remorse and humiliation. "I've had three abortions. I was a crack addict"—the priest moved closer, his ear practically touching my mouth—"and I have a lot of sexual sins." He sat back in his chair and showed me through his concerned expression and a slow nodding of his head that what I had just done was extremely important. He encouraged me to live a new life, free of the serious trespasses that had hurt me and others, and he thanked me for a good confession. I sensed he would have said more but for the little ears around us. My penance was simply to pray one Our Father and three Hail Mary's. The priest absolved me from my sins, and I stood up and stepped away feeling free, happy, and clean, as though twenty pounds of accumulated garbage in my soul simply wasn't there anymore. How easy and wonderful it had been! So much sin, so much darkness—absolved in a couple of minutes! Filled with praise, I marveled at the extraordinary mercy of God.

The next day, I practically ran into our hometown church and anxiously awaited Communion, like a bride reuniting with her groom after a long-distance exchange of love letters. When I walked forward to receive the Body of Christ, I felt as special as on the day of my First Communion when I wore my miniature pink ball gown and paraded like a prom queen down the center aisle. But this time, I had no need of public adulation. My soul knew the source of its worth. It came only from Him. In the succeeding days, I sat in the very first row of the church to be the very first one to receive the One whom I knew couldn't wait to give Himself fully to me, again and again.

With the Lord newly in my soul, I developed an insatiable hunger to know my faith. I pored through much of the Bible, studied the lives of the saints, and became intrigued by Mother Mary, the model disciple, the greatest follower of Jesus on earth. When I learned that she'd appeared on earth many times, I devoured what I could find about her apparitions. But I stopped short while reading some of her words during her appearances in Fatima in 1920, and my soul filled with doubt. "The sins that lead more souls to hell are the sins of the flesh," Our Lady had said. "Styles will come that will offend Our Lord very much. Persons who serve God should not follow the styles. The Church does not have styles. Our Lord is always the same."

Her words shattered my confidence, and I called out to God, "Help me! Heal me! I'm not strong enough for this kind of life!" It didn't help that my view of holiness still consisted of colorless piety without fashion sense or fun. But the Lord heard my prayer, and one of the ways He sought to answer it was through my mother's promptings.

"There's a retreat you have to go on. It's called Rachel's Vineyard."

"Okay, what's it for?"

"Healing."

"What kind of healing?"

"Post-abortion healing."

Dead silence.

No way. I wasn't going to that. I'd never told her about my abortions, and I never would. "How could she have found out?"

After three months of living with my mom and EWTN, she gathered me and her prayer posse and told us excitedly that a young priest from Croatia with the gifts of bilocation, prophecy, reading souls, and the stigmata—among others—was coming to town. His name was Father Zlatko Sudac, and he was thirty-three. In a rare visit to the United States, he was coming to Sacramento to give a two-day conference in a large arena. Mom's cohorts would have jumped up and down with glee were it not for their arthritis.

On a Saturday morning, we piled into Mom's car to drive to the conference. I enjoyed Fr. Sudac's piercing talks and loving presence; he was the closest I'd seen to how I imagined Jesus. But after seven or eight hours of talks, interspersed with prayer, cheesy music, and enthusiastic clapping, I grew increasingly agitated inside. "Are these my weekends now? Is this my life? Is this what it means to be a Super-Catholic?" I'd had more than enough for one day, and I wanted to go home. "I am *not* coming tomorrow," I vowed to myself.

The next morning, full of anxiety but feigning extreme tiredness, I announced in a fake-scratchy voice that I needed to rest due to sudden, inexplicable weakness. Ignoring my pleas, my mom barged cheerfully into my room, trailed by blind Grandma Yolanda. "Come on, get ready. We're going to the conference."

"I'm tired and my head hurts," I complained. The happy-go-lucky expression on my mother's face devolved into a scowl that wasn't about to take no for an answer. "C'mon, you're going. You need healing."

Angry, I said defiantly, "No, I'm *not* going!"

"Oh, yes you are!" my mom shouted. "I'm not leaving you here alone. I'm your mother, and that's that!" Infuriated, I ran past my mom, skirted around Grandma Yolanda, and locked myself in the bathroom. I felt tired and exasperated from having no autonomy, no freedom or free will, and being forced into one spiritual event after another.

The two prayer warriors took up their battle arms, literally, and began banging on the bathroom door. "Open the door, Patricia. *Open this door!*" Mom screamed in a fury while Yolanda repeated, "Sweetie, God loves. you." Overriding her gentle voice, my mom yelled, "This is Satan's work! He doesn't want you to go to the conference!"

My anxiety shot through the bathroom ceiling. "They're friggin' fanatics," I decided. "I am done with their little conspiracies. No more 'Let's take her here!' 'Let's take her there!' From now on, I am going to do what *I* want." I knew that they didn't want to be late to the conference and miss a single thing, so I rode out their banging and pleading, figuring they would eventually give up and leave me alone. All the while, my angst was becoming unbearable. I needed something to calm the typhoon that was whipping up in my soul. "That's it. I've had it," I resolved. "As soon as they leave," I'm going to pack my stuff, call one of my old friends, and have someone pick me up ASAP. I'm going back to my old life. It's time for revenge. I'm going to show them that by pushing me, they pushed me right back into drugs."

> Amen, amen, I say to you, when you were younger, you used to dress yourself and go where you wanted; but when you grow old, you will stretch out your hands, and someone else will dress you and lead you where you do not want to go.
> –John 21:18

Fact: Most Catholics go to their First Reconciliation as children and never return to the Sacrament as a spiritual practice. In a study conducted by the Center for Applied Research in the Apostolate at Georgetown University in Washington, three-quarters of Catholics reported that they never participate in the Sacrament of Reconciliation, or they do so less than once a year. (1)

Beginning with the onset of the Jubilee Year of Mercy on December 8, 2015, Pope Francis made God's forgiveness for the sins of abortion and of close cooperation with abortion more accessible to people throughout the world through the Sacrament of Reconciliation. The following is the full statement from Pope Francis regarding the easement of forgiveness for abortion:

One of the serious problems of our time is clearly the changed relationship with respect to life. A widespread and insensitive mentality has led to the loss of the proper personal and social sensitivity to welcome new life. The tragedy of abortion is experienced by some with a superficial awareness, as if not realizing the extreme harm that such an act entails. Many others, on the other hand, although experiencing this moment as a defeat, believe they have no other option. I think in particular of all the women who have resorted to abortion. I am well aware of the pressure that has led them to this decision. I know that it is an existential and moral ordeal. I have met so many women who bear in their heart the scar of this agonizing and painful decision. What has happened is profoundly unjust; yet only understanding the truth of it can enable one not to lose hope. The forgiveness of God cannot be denied to one who has repented, especially when that person approaches the Sacrament of Confession with a sincere heart in order to obtain reconciliation with the Father. For this reason, too, I have decided, notwithstanding anything to the contrary, to concede to all priests for the Jubilee Year the discretion to absolve of the sin of abortion those who have procured it and who, with contrite heart, seek forgiveness for it. May priests fulfill this great task by expressing words of genuine welcome combined with a reflection that explains the gravity of the sin committed, besides indicating a path of authentic conversion by which to obtain the true and generous forgiveness of the Father who renews all with His presence.

Chapter Ten

The Purge

I DOVE RIGHT BACK INTO THE DRUG world, highlighted this time by a newfound friendship with Ozzie's ex, the woman who had tried to kill me with a hammer. I wanted nothing to do with Ozzie, who came around acting cute and funny in his attempts to get back together with me, so I felt more free to get to know Sandra, who was a natural crack-up. She and I quickly bonded over drugs and therapeutic Ozzie-mocking.

Our humor was as twisted as our minds. One day, I grabbed three thousand dollars' worth of methamphetamines and went over to Sandra's house to present it as a gift. When she opened the front door, I stepped in, dangling the bag of rocks before her eyes. *"Yeah!"* she exclaimed, clapping her hands like a small child. We sat down at her kitchen table and proceeded to fly high while mimicking the tone and mannerisms of Ozzie's most animated lies. "It's you I *really* love, Patricia," I hammed. "I don't love Sandra. The only reason I go back is to see my kids because I miss them so much."

Assuming Ozzie's casual, carefree posture, Sandra shot back, "Don't worry about a thing, Babe. I'm just using Patricia because she has the house and the car." Uproarious laughter ensued and didn't stop there. Whenever Sandra mentioned wanting to go somewhere, I'd jump at my chance to say, "Oh, I'd take you, but I don't happen to have a car anymore." And we'd crack up all over again.

Ozzie quickly discovered that he couldn't play his back-and-forth game with us. Sandra and I got along so well that we preferred our friendship to Ozzie's attention. "I'm actually really glad that I met you," she told me. "I wish I would have known you before Ozzie." Meanwhile, my heart continued to break for her and her two cute but hyper little boys. Those poor kids were so confused. At first, they were supposed to hate daddy's other girlfriend and want her to get away from them and their dad. But now they were supposed to like daddy's girlfriend, welcome her in, and hate their dad.

Around that time, Sandra got pregnant by a guy who had recently gotten out of jail. When I visited her one morning, she told me nonchalantly that she was about to get an abortion and that she'd already been through multiple ones. The words rolled off her tongue as though signifying nothing, and I recoiled in disgust, repulsed by her. I wasn't thinking of my own abortions in that moment—nor did I ever think of them, much less my work at Planned Parenthood. But my revulsion quickly retreated into its usual state of repression, and I showed my support by borrowing a car in order to pick her up from the clinic. I believed I was being a very good friend and doing something truly helpful.

But in the days that followed, my times with Sandra simply weren't that fun anymore and, after three months back on the streets, I realized that neither were my highs. Methamphetamines were still taking away my depression and anxiety—but never my nagging conscience. The drug that used to be my best friend and had catapulted me to the top of the world was now dropping me into the middle of a battlefield I didn't understand—a battle for my soul.

I knew I needed my mom. Nervously, I picked up the phone to call her, but when I heard her soft, pleading voice, I felt relieved, even in my embarrassment. "Come home, my daughter," was all she said, revealing none of the anger and worry she must have been feeling.

"Okay, Mom," I said. "I'll be right there."

> Do not be led astray: "Bad company corrupts good morals."
> Become sober as you ought and stop sinning.
> –1 Corinthians 15:33–34a

Because I was doing their bidding, the demons that had previously assailed me stopped putting up a fight during my relapse. But as soon as I returned to my mother's home, their assaults not only resumed, they became more frequent. Things reached a peak when my mom made an appointment for me to go to the Sacrament of Reconciliation. I had resubmitted myself to her wishes and resigned myself to attending prayer groups with the elderlies (I had to admit that fighting these well-meaning women was detrimental as well as useless). But during the week before my appointment, the attacks continued relentlessly, allowing me little sleep. Every half hour or so throughout the night, I was pinned to my bed as my oppressors strangled my throat, cutting off my airway to the point that I could hardly breathe, move, or think. Those demons did not want me to go to Confession. Too much was at stake.

The night before my appointment, a familiar presence of darkness came into my room and stood at the right side of my bed. It possessed powers of fear and sought to terrorize me. Chills scurried up and down my spine, but by the grace and power of God, the fear never became mine. Suddenly, the demonic presence leapt on top of me. I put up a fight to try to move, or even breathe, but found that I couldn't force either. Compressed and motionless, my body felt as though it were tied up and drowning at sea, descending slowly into deep waters. Calling out to God, I gasped, "Jesus! Jesus!" wondering why He didn't immediately intervene to help me.

After five or ten minutes of violent struggle, my airway started to open up, and I was able to move my hands a little, though the rest of my body remained paralyzed. I began to applaud Jesus and to sing a worship song I liked called *"Dios está aquí"*—"God is here." "Any minute now He'll be here," I reassured myself. But my confidence quickly devolved into pleas: "Where *are* You? You've gotta come back me up!"

Finally, my oppressor came off me and went to stand in the entrance to my room. He appeared in silhouette form—a black shadow more than six feet tall. My spirit identified him immediately. It was Satan himself. As I looked at him and he looked back at me, communication between us happened at the level of the soul, beyond the five senses, and was perfectly clear. "You know what?" he said. "Your little worship song doesn't scare me. I happen to know the song too." Then he started clapping right along with me, becoming my evil backup singer. Laughing and singing obnoxiously loud, he tried to override my voice. Searching my mind for another worship song, I switched tunes, thinking a new song might have power over him, but he simply followed suit: "I know this song too." Feeling helpless and frustrated, I continued to sing, wondering why God wasn't showing up. "I know any song you can come up with," the devil mocked, "but you don't know one verse from the whole Bible. Not one!" Putting both hands up above his ears like moose antlers, he wiggled his fingers and stuck his tongue out at me. Then he disappeared.

I ran to my mom to tell her what happened, and she said, "The Bible, that's your sword! Remember, when Jesus was tempted in the desert by Satan, He quoted the Scriptures to fend off the devil by saying, '*As it is written . . .*' followed by lines from His own book!" She reached for her Bible and read Hebrews 4:12a: *"Indeed, the word of God is living and effective, sharper than any two-edged sword . . ."*

"Why," I wondered, "did Satan give me a clue about the Bible? Did God force those words from his mouth?" I began to open my Bible every day. Now I was armed. The next time Satan came, I had my favorite quotes prepared and, sure enough, the recitation of—even the mere thought of—verses from Scripture weakened his grip on me. My favorite battle cry became a variation of 1 John 4:4b: *"Greater is He who is in me than he who is in the world!"*

The next morning, Mom took me to St. Hilary's Church to see the same priest who had heard my confession in between second graders. He had been so nice and soft-spoken that I immediately felt at ease with him. But when I shared that I had relapsed and gone back to drugs, he looked me dead in the eye and admonished me with great strength and fervor—almost to the point of yelling. "Now you listen to me. You stop those drugs! You do not play games with God. Do you understand that if you go back to drugs and you die in your sins, you could go to hell? And that is not a place where you want to end up."

He was angry, and I got scared. But I remained glued to my seat since my mom told me he had knowledge of spiritual warfare and could help me. I mustered the courage to tell him in detail about my spiritual attacks. He explained to me that since I had been living in a demonic atmosphere with drug addicts and spiritual contaminations of all sorts, the demons that were now oppressing me couldn't stand my going to Confession and taking the Eucharist so they were waging a spiritual war against me. In a retaliatory effort, they were trying dissuade me from receiving the sacraments and from continuing my walk toward Christ—and if that didn't work, the most they could do was try to make my spiritual journey miserable.

"You're not crazy," he said. "Many, many saints have experienced similar, unwelcome visits from the devil and his helpers—saints such as St. Gemma Galgani, St. Padre Pio, St. Faustina Kowalska, St. Teresa of Avila . . . Be sure to always stay close to the sacraments and call on the saints to help you. And if you want peace and strength in your soul, pray often in Adoration before the Blessed Sacrament." I thanked the priest and left the confessional feeling both fortified and mortified. The encounter was great for my soul but devastating for my ego.

My mother continued to do everything in her power to make me physically, emotionally, and spiritually well. "*Mi hija* (my daughter), I don't have enough money to take you to a doctor, a psychiatrist, or a psychologist, but you have something much better than all that—the Eucharist. The Eucharist is the same Jesus who healed people in the Gospels . . . the same Jesus who cured the leper, gave sight to the blind, and raised Lazarus from the dead. You consume Him at every Mass, and He is alive in you."

With my mother's encouragement, I decided to follow the priest's advice, and I found a church close to our home that offered Adoration of the Blessed Sacrament. Sitting in a small side chapel, I stared for some time at the Host, the Body of Christ in the appearance of a thin, circular wafer of bread. It was the presence of Jesus, Himself, displayed within a monstrance: a golden holder in the shape of the sun, supported by a vertical stand placed on top of the altar. Yet as I stared and prayed, doubts of Jesus' Real Presence in the form of that little, round wafer began to flood my mind: "Is this really God? Is that really You, Jesus?" I didn't doubt His Presence at Mass, but here in Adoration, I struggled to believe.

That night, I had a dream, realistic and in full color:

I was standing in front of an old cathedral with numerous cement steps leading up to it, and I turned around to my right to see a woman sitting on one of the steps. "Do you want me to read your palms?" she asked me.

"No," I responded emphatically.

Then thousands upon thousands of people began to approach this woman to have their palms read and receive tarot card readings. Offended that the woman was doing this in front of a house of God, I began to yell at the crowd, "No! This is false power! This is not true power!" Pointing to the entrance of the church, I shouted, "True power is inside that church! The Truth is inside that church!" But no one listened.

Feeling terribly impotent, I watched as the woman laid out her cards on the steps, and the enthralled crowd gathered round her, attracted like canines to a bone.

I wanted to console God, so I turned around and ran into the church. Inside, I noticed that the walls practically glowed in a radiant white, and the black-and-white, checkered floor looked so clean that it sparkled. Nothing filled the church but an altar, and exposed on the altar was the Blessed Sacrament in a grand and gleaming gold monstrance. I walked forward to stand in front of Jesus, my Lord, feeling heartbroken that He was completely alone on the altar with no one to adore Him. Through tears, I said, "Lord, all those people are out there following a lie, but I'm here to worship You, and I will sing and praise and honor You." To console Him, I started singing aloud, dancing in a circle—jumping, applauding, and clapping like a child—extolling His love and mercy to make up for the thousands outside.

Unexpectedly, Jesus Himself came out of the Blessed Sacrament and appeared behind the altar, standing in His human form. He wore a luminous, white garment, and His features reflected the image of Divine Mercy. Stunned, I immediately stopped singing and dancing and stood facing Him, unable to move or speak. He was looking at me with great tenderness, filling my soul with feelings of such worth! With His gaze never leaving me, He walked around the left side of the altar and descended the two stairs in front of it toward me. My pulse began to quicken, and my heart swelled with awe and disbelief. He had come solely for me! When He got so close as to be able to touch me, I felt I might faint from joy and longing. The overwhelming love radiating from His Being pierced me with ecstasy. Then with a voice of great caring mixed with powerful authority, He said to me in Spanish: "Get down on your knees, Patricia, because I am going to anoint your head." I dropped to my knees with my head bowed toward the floor. Laying His hands on me with gentleness, He said, "I'm going to purify you."

While I stared at his bare feet, Jesus prayed for me fervently in heavenly tongues, which I didn't understand. I told myself, "I'm dreaming. This isn't real." Aware that Jesus had read my heart, I felt Him purposefully press down upon my head, so that I could physically feel the strength and pressure of His hands. In my spirit, I knew He was communicating to me, "This is true, Patricia. This is real. Do not doubt Me. I am here with you, and I am here for you, and I have a plan . . ."

In the morning, I joyfully sprung out of bed and continued to jump up and down in my room, remembering every detail of the dream. I had gotten to see Him and to feel Him! All of my doubts concerning Jesus' Real Presence in the Blessed Sacrament vanished, and through the anointing of His hands, I was left with a strong sense that He had chosen me for a mission in life. But what was it?

> Hear now my words: If there be a prophet among you, I the Lord will make myself known unto him in a vision, and will speak unto him in a dream.
> –Numbers 12:6

One day, my mom said to me, out of the blue, "You've got to go on the retreat."

"What retreat?"

"Rachel's Vineyard."

I didn't respond. Why did she have to keep bringing that up? I'd hoped she'd just drop it. No way was I going. Abortion was my well-kept, locked-up secret, and I saw no point in taking it out of the closet. I had gone to Confession, so I hardly needed a retreat, and besides, it was for women and men who were suffering. I was fine. In fact, for five years my abortions had hardly ever crossed my mind, and I had forgotten entirely that I ever worked at Planned Parenthood. Case closed. Change the subject.

I had a knack for brushing away important messages if they didn't suit me. Another one came the day I met one of my mom's neighbors, a friendly thirty-year-old woman, about six years older than I. As my mom introduced me to her, saying, "This is my daughter, Patricia," she shook my hand, looked at me, and turned pale. She didn't utter a word. "What a strange encounter," I pondered as Mom and I walked away.

Over time, the woman and I became good friends, and one day she said to me, "I need to tell you something, something I've been afraid to say. I don't understand this, but at the moment I shook your hand when I met you, I had a vision—at least, I think it was a vision because nothing like this has ever happened to me." She paused, fearing I might question her mental health. "What I saw was in black and white, like a movie. On a stage was a man in a dark blue suit, a well-known man of God, speaking to thousands of youth. I saw what he looked like—tall and handsome. And you were down below in the audience, standing in front of him. He reached his hands down, placed them on your head and said, 'God bless and protect my wife and my children.' Who knows what this means? But that's what I saw. I don't know—maybe you're going to marry a Catholic man. Oh, and he was Hispanic. Anyway, that's why I froze and couldn't speak. You must have thought I was nuts."

Caught up in the web of my people-pleasing and materialistic nature, the first thing I thought of was, "How boring. A preacher-type? He doesn't even have a real job. This is a guy who wouldn't be able to support me."

The only thing I liked were his words, spoken in front of everyone, "God bless and protect my wife and my children." The acknowledgment, the protection, the love, and the children were consoling, but my imagination turned my mood to dismay. "I'd be some starving chick with a Bible. No, thanks!"

God had good things in store for me, but I still had one foot in the world and two serious sins on my soul: materialism and people-pleasing—my gateway to fornication and other troubles. God had shown me a man worth the wait. Yet I wasn't holy enough to understand what an enormous blessing it would be to wed a servant of God. I pictured this gift through eyes stained by the world and thoughts riddled with fear and judgment, therefore the vision didn't take hold.

My mom was still dating the Honduran man, who turned out to be a wolf wearing a sheep's mask. She trusted him because he put on a good front of being a holy man and supported her in many ways. To me, they never looked like they fit together as a couple. My mom was beautiful and intelligent and carried herself with an air of elegance, while his facial features twisted into a lascivious smirk. When he came to visit, his intrusive stare forced me to leave the room, sometimes the house, to escape its range.

After about a year of my living with Mom, his invasive behavior became too much for me. I realized I had to tell my mom about some of the things he was doing that he was hiding from her; but I didn't want to. I was still a weak person, recently off drugs, and I finally had a home where I felt loved and safe. Now this sick man was threatening to shatter everything. If I told my mom and she didn't believe me, she might abandon me all over again. I would lose my safe haven and my own mother—the only person in the world who nurtured and knew me.

One day, I mustered the courage to tell my mom the unfortunate news. Shaking with fright, I said in a trembling voice, "Mom, your boyfriend has been calling me . . ."

Mayhem erupted. "What are you doing to provoke this?" "Are you lying to me?"

"Why would I lie over something like this?"

"Well, I'm going to talk to him." An argument so painful and blistering ensued that I ended it with the words, "I'm leaving. I'm going back with my dad." And we were both fine with that decision.

But really, I wasn't fine. Mom didn't talk to me for a month, and I cried myself to sleep every night, tortured by the thought of losing her again.

One day, she phoned me. When I saw her number, I rejoiced, believing that she was calling to make up. But her tone was heated. She had just gotten into a fight with her boyfriend. "Look, Patricia. I need to know the truth. He's saying that what you're accusing him of didn't happen.

"Mom," I said, "why would I lie? Why don't you believe me?"

"He told me that *you* were lying and trying to separate him and me to break off our relationship," she responded.

I pleaded with her, using every piece of logic I could think of. "I gain nothing by making this up . . . I want to be with you . . . I want peace . . . I simply wanted you to know the truth."

The next words she spoke engraved themselves upon my soul, like a knife wound from a dirty blade.

"Listen to me . . . *I do not believe you.*"

I was standing in my dad's kitchen, my eyes cast down at the floor. The pain in my heart was so crippling that I could do nothing more than hang up the phone. The next thing I heard about my mom was that she had sold her house and moved away to North Carolina. I didn't know if I would ever hear from her again.

That night, I cried myself to sleep and dreamt of times past:

I'm lying in the middle of a gigantic bed alongside my sister and brother. I'm wearing my pink flowered pajamas, my sister is in her fuzzy, purple pair, and my brother is sporting his blue favorites. My mom comes into the room and lies down next to us. She hugs us together tightly, gives us each a kiss on the cheek, and begins to sing us made up songs, as she did every morning. "You're the best alarm ever," I say to her, throwing my arms around her neck to give her a big hug in return. She laughs and sings a special song to me: "Wake up, my little princess, be on your way. God's going to give you a beautiful day . . ."

"I'll get up, Mom, I promise," I say to her. "But let me stay here for just one more minute . . ." To clarify my request, I hold up my forefinger in front of my nose. My brother and sister disappear from the room as I stretch out my arms in a yawn and nestle comfortably in the crook of Mom's soft arm, enjoying the warmth and safety of her body.

Groaning, I reached out my hand to stop the clang of my alarm clock. Feeling too devastated and abandoned to get out of bed, I stayed under the covers and began to reflect on my mom's history to try and fathom how she could flee with no notice, without so much as a good-bye.

I knew that Mom's childhood had been difficult, at times, even traumatic. To understand and sympathize with her, it helped me to wonder what it must have been like for her to grow up with my Grandma Consuelo for a mother. I thought back to what I knew of Grandma—a single mom who raised nine children and wore a pistol in her bra. This hardened old woman, who scoffed at superfluous emotions, smoked a cigar, and played cards with the men at our family gatherings, hadn't always been that way.

Grandma Consuelo had grown tough and bitter after the unimaginable happened: her husband, the first and only love of her life was shot and killed. They'd had five children together (my mom's older brothers and sisters); they'd escaped poverty together; and they'd built a cheese business empire from nothing in their poor home town of Zacatecas, Mexico. Holding up her callused hands, she used to say to me, "These are the wrists of a woman who knows how to milk a cow."

During preparations for her husband's funeral service, grandma was nearly catatonic with grief. Her relatives by marriage had never liked her and didn't want her to inherit any of the money or extensive property that were rightly hers. Holding yet another legal paper before her uneducated eyes, they lied and said, "Sign here so we can put him in a casket." She didn't so much as glance at the papers, and with one sweep of the pen, signed everything away. Her relatives had left her and her five young children, including my aunt, Sister Olga, with absolutely nothing. I found this so horrible and hard to believe that I once asked Sister Olga if it was true, and she confirmed that it was.

Only days after Consuelo had to bury her husband, she was thrown into homelessness. With no money to even feed her children, she had to beg for scraps. Someone allowed her and the children to sleep in a barn for a month; but after the barn came the streets. For the next couple of years, she leaned on a married man for her children's survival and a roof over their heads, and he fathered my mother and another boy. Even though only a toddler, my mom remembers him stopping by weekly with bags of food and clothing for her and her siblings. As soon as grandma earned enough money as a seamstress to leave the affair, she did, and then later fell into the arms of an alcoholic who fathered her two youngest children.

So my mom grew up in an unsafe environment, scarce in love and filled with abuse—in a home where she had to cook, clean, iron, and bathe and feed her younger siblings. People considered her a bastard child and her mother a harlot. She knew this because people spoke that way, openly.

Grandma Consuelo eventually kicked out the alcoholic, but he refused to leave her alone and came around to visit her when drunk. One particular day when he staggered in, Consuelo, fearful over what he might do to her and her kids, ran to her bedroom and grabbed her gun, which she kept under her pillow next to her image of Our Lady of the Miraculous Medal—*La Milagrosa.* Taking the pistol in both hands, she cocked it, aimed to scare, and started shooting. Grandma told me that was simply the way people in her small town of Florencia, Mexico used to solve their differences. Needless to say, he never came back.

Grandma had a strict nature and a crazy temper. When you hit her wall, there was no going past it. As soon as my mom turned sixteen, grandma told her, "If you come back late, past my curfew, I'm not going to let you into the house." Well, my mom knocked on the door late one night, and grandma didn't let her in. With nowhere to go, Mom started to live with her boyfriend and ended up marrying him—all because of that strict curfew. At seventeen, my mom got pregnant; but her new husband was an alcoholic, a drug addict, and was physically and verbally abusive to her, even during her pregnancy. One day, when they got into an argument, he threw something at their baby's crib. Fearing for her child, my mom grabbed the baby (my older sister), ran to grandma's house, and locked the door from inside. Soon they heard scuffling just outside, along with the muted voices of my mom's husband and mother-in-law. Putting their ears to the front door, they heard the mother-in-law say, "Take the child from her."

Grandma Consuelo took action. She didn't want my mom to get back with her husband, but neither did she want her back home with the child—I guess she felt she had enough babies of her own. So she sent Mom away before he could find her and said, "I've arranged for you to work in the United States. You'll be staying at your sister's house in Chicago." My mom didn't have a moment to think about it. Grandma Consuelo had made arrangements with coyotes, men and women who take people illegally across the border. She had to leave the next day. For three perilous days and nights, my seventeen-year-old mom had to put her life in the hands of strangers, sleep in deplorable conditions, walk briskly for miles, and cross freeways and highways with a two-month-old baby in her arms, on a journey that some don't survive.

Could this be why my mom kept running?

> As soon as they had brought them outside, they said: "Flee for your life! Do not look back or stop anywhere on the Plain. Flee to the hills at once, or you will be swept away."
> –Genesis 19:17

It wasn't the first time my mom had fled, and it wouldn't be the last. Eventually, she did come back to northern California, leaving the Honduran behind, and our relationship resumed its on again/off again, dance. But our sense of closeness was not the same. I'd moved back into my dad's home in Petaluma and did my best to turn it into a Catholic Church. Icons went up and stared outward from the walls, holy water fonts graced the doorways, incense traveled down the hallways, and the sound of EWTN eclipsed my dad's favorite Mexican telenovelas. With a little weight on my bones and fashion in my closet, I looked more put together than he'd seen in a while, and my sense of humor was on its way back. Dad seemed relieved that the "old me" had returned, and I saw pride return to his eyes as he watched me decide to become a medical assistant, then go on to win student awards and receive the highest grades in my class, and ultimately work hard and responsibly in that field. When he could afford it and time allowed, Dad arranged for my brother and me to travel with him to Mexico, where we all enjoyed our time together. More than ever before, my father and I were the best of friends.

I also enjoyed a closer relationship with my brother, who began keeping a Bible by his bed and saying morning and night prayers, now that a Holy Roller was in his house. I resumed a tentative relationship with my sister and bonded tightly again with my niece and nephew. Yet despite the familial relationships I did have, I still longed for a loving, united family to call my own, and this intense desire drew me like a moth to a flame when the next boyfriend came around.

His name was Marcello. We had been good friends since we were twelve years old. His family and I adored one another, and I'd known him as a good friend since we were twelve years old. I took him to church, introduced him to the Lord, and cooked, cleaned, loved and prayed for him. If he found himself in trouble, which happened often, I was there to pick him up and straighten things out. Our good times together, filled with laughter and playfulness, endured for months. He told me I was "the one."

But Marcello was an insecure *machista.* Jealous to the point of madness, Marcello wouldn't let me go places alone, and even when I was with him, he would purposefully flirt with girls, leaving extravagant tips for waitresses and ogling female passers-by. I pretended to ignore him, all the while scanning his every move.

Even before we started dating, I knew he was a cheater. But I was so special in his eyes that I figured he'd never cheat on me. I was wrong. Sometimes he wouldn't come home for days, and when he finally showed up on my doorstep, he'd reel me back in with his charm and material gifts—even cars from his dealership, which soothed my fear of the constant want I'd experienced on the streets. If that didn't work, he'd lure me back through taking denigrating shots at me, which he freely shared in front of others, even his family: "You're never going to be anybody in life without me," he would say. I began to believe him.

Clinging to the illusion of a better future, I wasn't willing to give up relations with him, even though the moment we became intimate, my conscience started running on a treadmill of guilt. My prayers lost their peace and became a repetitive cycle of, "I love you, God . . . I'm sorry . . . Please forgive me again . . . I love you . . ." As it had been before, Dad pretended to believe that I was telling the truth when I stayed out on weekends at the home of a "friend," even when those weekends turned into entire weeks. Neither of us found a reason to tear down the good girl front that I wanted to show him and that he preferred to see.

When I needed to come home to get more clothes, Marcello would drop me off, usually on a Sunday morning. Slowing down to five miles per hour as we neared Dad's home, Marcello would hope—and I would pray— that my father wouldn't be outside and catch us doing what he already knew we were doing. But one morning as we turned the corner, there Dad was, washing his car at eight a.m. in the front driveway. "Damn!" cursed Marcello, slinking down below the wheel, as though that could fool my dad into thinking no one was driving the car. I wanted to disappear into a dark hole, but I got out of the vehicle in my pajamas and did the walk of shame.

During this time, hidden away in my father's home was the image of the Sacred Heart, the one with the piercing eyes from our early family days. Dad had stored the picture in his bedroom closet, where it sat forgotten and gathering dust. For years now, I hadn't thought of the image, nor was I thinking of it on the day I was cleaning my bedroom and received an interior message from Jesus: "Tell your father that I do not want to be in a closet. Tell him to take Me out and honor Me."

Without hesitating, I went to my dad and said, "You know that image you have of the Sacred Heart of Jesus that's in your bedroom closet? Well, Jesus wants you to take Him out and to honor Him."

"Oh, I will," he replied.

But he never did. Feeling convicted that Jesus' request wasn't being obeyed, I put the Lord's image in my room. But I wouldn't look at Him. The only reason I kept Him on my wall was because I knew what I had heard. Particularly painful was my reentry into my room after days with my boyfriend when I would feel the image "staring at me." Sometimes my soul was pierced with such disgrace from the flash of His gaze that I would turn the image toward the wall and tell Him with sadness, "I'm sorry, Jesus, but I can't look at You right now."

When Marcello proposed the idea of buying a house for the two of us, I jumped at the chance. I was forcing hope. Perhaps with the permanence of a home, he would be more stable and loving toward me. After all, our intention was to get married one day and to do things right. As a gift to me, he wanted the house put in my name. "Pick out whatever home you wish," he said with characteristic generosity. After eight months of searching, I chose a grand home, and we started the process of buying it in my name.

Not long after that, Marcello's casual cocktail hours devolved into bouts of angry drunkenness, and his jealousy turned a dark corner. He slapped my face hard in the presence of friends at a dinner party simply because I walked a young man down the hall to show him where the bathroom was. From that time on, his jealous outbursts turned increasingly violent. One day, he struck me with such force that I punched him back for the first time, giving him a bloody lip. That's when I said to myself, "If I don't leave soon, this is going to get worse." Only then could I get through my confused mind that I wasn't bringing my boyfriend any closer to God.

In the end, my heart stopped caring for him, and I wanted to get out of the relationship; but I couldn't bring myself to leave him because during holidays and whenever I was in need, I had a mom, a grandma, sisters, nephews, and nieces—a loving and complete tight-knit family to replace the one I had lost. I also found it hard to let go because my self-image had hit a new low. Marcello had twisted my mind against myself and succeeded in erasing all of the marks of self-esteem I had regained in the Lord. My mother's words to me, spoken with such power from on high—"You are a daughter of the King"—had been displaced by Marcello's jabs: "You are trash." "You are nothing. And you will never amount to anything."

A week before the real estate agent handed me the house keys, I learned that Marcello had gotten a girl pregnant. Devastated and distraught, I screamed, "How could he do this to me!?" At the same time, I was neither surprised, nor despairing, for a small voice within me whispered that Marcello had just given me the reason and the courage to finally leave him. There would be no joint home—no new life together.

> Do not give what is holy to dogs, or throw your pearls before swine, lest they trample them underfoot, and turn and tear you to pieces.
> –Matthew 7:6

To boost my shattered ego after our breakup, I made myself look special through new clothes, accessories, makeup, and beautiful possessions, which I purchased with the money I was making as a medical assistant. While catering to my shallow desires and pursuits, I tried my best to bury my past, which had sunk to a level of depravity I could not expose: having three abortions, falling into drug addiction, running away from home, and living with a cheater who abused me. "No good man would want a girl who has my history and is also too fat," I thought to myself (I was still thin as a rail). "I will have to lie." With my childhood desire to one day be someone special hanging over me like a curse, I figured I would do my best to fake it.

Faking it did get me my next boyfriend, Rodrigo, who treated me well and doted on me to the point of thinking I was some kind of goddess—and I let him. He lived far away in Chicago, and we loved each other, but on a superficial, materialistic level. I was charmed by his lavish declarations of love, romantic advances, and frequent visits, and he did want to commit himself to me—but not to the Lord. The more I revealed my faith, the more jittery he became. Eventually, when I saw that he wasn't budging in God's direction, I broke things off.

Meanwhile, the words of the priest at St. Hilary's were sounding an alarm in the depths of my conscience: "You do not play games with God." At twenty-six, my drug days were long gone. For three years, I hadn't experienced any cravings for methamphetamines or even so much as thought of getting high. With meth being so dangerous and a user recovery rate as low as 5 percent (only 12 percent with rehab), the absence of any physical damage or addictive feelings was nothing less than a miracle. The Christ Child of Atocha had truly healed me.

But now, with my periods of chastity never lasting long, I felt like I was "playing games." Instead of stopping sex, I had stopped going to Mass. What was the point of attending, I figured, if I couldn't receive the Eucharist? I didn't want to be a hypocrite. Only after running into the confessional following a break up (entering a different confessional each time so the priests wouldn't think I was doing exactly what I was doing) did I start going to Mass again. My barhopping days had long since ended, but my Confession-hopping days had begun.

I didn't understand the "why?" behind purity and chastity, and neither did my parents when I was growing up. I'd never gotten a chastity talk from them because they didn't have one to give, and my public elementary school had taught me that anything goes—just use a condom. My sex education took place in a classroom of embarrassed, giggling twelve-year-olds, where the teacher had us practice "safe sex" by unrolling condoms onto bananas. Chastity, for me, was a concept written onto the pages of Scripture and the Catechism rather than a commandment woven by God into the fabric of my soul.

One would think I would have gladly turned away from this sin since sexual relations stirred up my guilty conscience. But I just wanted those occasions to be as few as possible and over with quickly. My boyfriends always wanted to be more sexually active than I did, and my girlfriends gave glowing accounts of their hook-ups, which left me wondering if there was something wrong with me. But since I assumed that sexual relations were obligatory in a relationship, I gave in many times, blaming myself for making guys feel unhappy and frustrated. The foremost reason I consented to sex was because I worried that men would think less of me as a woman—and what people thought of me was everything. It was still my identity.

My plan, in the following order, was to give in to my boyfriend's desires, make him happy, cause him to fall in love with me, reveal my religion to him piecemeal, cause him to fall in love with God, marry him, and then go to Confession, clean up my soul, start a family, and be happy myself. But my beliefs and religious practices always seemed far-fetched and fanatical to my boyfriends, and I couldn't understand why my missionary efforts were proving ineffective.

God was speaking to me so plainly through these young men's resistance, but somehow I couldn't hear what He was saying: "You can't bring a person to me by bringing your soul and his into serious sin, which cuts you both off from Me." Time and again, circumstances were proving my method wrong, but the world had taught me it was right.

The Lord also tried to get my attention by sending me dreams. Sometimes, while asleep at night, I'd undergo a fatal tragedy. In the dream, I am falling off a cliff, or careening into a head-on collision, or running away from a man with a gun. In one dream, I get shot, and I am dying. I leave my body and find myself suspended in the air surrounded by midnight blue. I am in the very presence of God, and I feel His powerful wrath all around me. It is my moment of judgment. An angry Father is looking at me about to condemn me. At the second that I am about to enter into hell, I wake up.

It is two or three in the morning, and I am lying next to my current boyfriend, my heart pounding frantically in my chest. A tremendous fear of God overwhelms my spirit, and I start praying fervently. "I'm sorry, I'm so sorry, Father. I'm sorry, so very sorry . . ." But I wasn't sorry enough.

> Avoid immorality. Every other sin a person commits is outside the body, but the immoral person sins against his own body. Do you not know that your body is a temple of the holy Spirit within you, whom you have from God, and that you are not your own? For you have been purchased at a price. Therefore, glorify God in your body.
> –1 Corinthians 6:17–20

Fact: Former United States Surgeon General C. Everett Koop, warned: "When you have sex with someone, you are having sex with everyone they have had sex with for the last ten years, and everyone they and their partners have had sex with for the last ten years." For example, if you and your partner have each had sex with five former partners, both of you have been sexually exposed to thirty-one people. If each of you has had sex with ten people, you have both been exposed to 1,023 individuals. With twenty partners each, you have both been exposed to 1,048,575 people.

To see a visual chart of this fact, search for "Sexual Exposure Chart" on the World Wide Web. For example:
https://www.wvdhhr.org/appi/edresources/sexual_exposure_chart.pdf

Chapter Eleven

A Time to Heal

When I was twenty-seven, Dad began to court a woman from a small, extremely poor village next to his home town. Soon he was smitten, and I sensed that he would marry her. Within months, they eloped to Mexico, and Elvira came back to live with us. At first, she and I got along well. Over time, however, she began to show signs of distrust and anger toward me, which she never allowed my father to see. I tried my best to please her in everything, but even when she and my dad had a baby boy, I wasn't allowed to hold my new little brother for long because I never did it "right."

I told my dad that it seemed like Elvira didn't want me around, but he didn't want to hear it and accused me of making things up. My heart sank. He would take his wife's side, and that was that. It now seemed that Dad didn't need me anymore, and indeed he started to act that way.

Seeking comfort and place to belong, I drove to St. Hilary's Church, one day to pray. No one was inside when I arrived. As I walked forward down the center aisle, a tender peace touched my soul, like the soft caress of a loving hand. Drawn to my favorite statue, one of Our Lady of Fatima with stunning features and adorned with shining gems, I knelt before her. A nurturing presence swept through my most tender emotions, easing my sorrow. My soul wanted more. From a place deep within, my prayers erupted in words: "Oh Mother, I want to love you to the fullest. Show me how to love you. Guide me to know more about you and your heart."

Then I rose up from my kneeling position and sat down in a pew. A few seconds later, a woman came out of a side Adoration chapel holding a bag. I had never seen her before. Without saying a word, she put the bag next to me and walked out of the church. Curious, I reached into the bag and took out three paperback books on Our Lady's alleged appearances in Medjugorje. (1) Mary had responded to my prayer almost instantaneously. As I opened one of the books, a small paper fell out. I picked it up off the floor and turned it over: it was a pamphlet for a Rachel's Vineyard post-abortion healing retreat. "Must be a coincidence," I shrugged.

As soon as I got home, I plopped onto my bed with the books and started to read. I didn't know that Mary might be appearing on earth—and in my lifetime. She had allegedly started appearing to six children in 1981 in this small town of Medjugorje in the former Yugoslavia, now called Bosnia-Herzegovina, and she had already given thousands of messages to the world. Captivated, I read for hours, sometimes forgetting the need to eat and sleep as the Spirit carried me along. My soul devoured all three books in as many days. My love for the Blessed Mother was being set aflame.

Especially intriguing for me was Mary's response to a particular question the Medjugorje seers asked of her during an alleged apparition. In the words of the visionary, Mirjana:

> "When we were children, we asked her a childish question: 'How come you are so beautiful?'
>
> "She smiled at us and said, 'I'm beautiful because I love. My dear children, if you want to be beautiful, start to love.'"

Our Lady's words cut to the ugly core of my obsession with appearance. My thoughts were forever torturing me with worry over how I looked, what I wore, what people thought of me. Always desiring to be beautiful but never satisfied, I lived in fear and frustration over reaching an ever-impossible, aesthetic ideal. But Mary was talking about the source of real beauty. Anyone could dress themselves up; but only a person filled with love could be radiant. Love was what made Mary glow. Her heart was what made her so beautiful. This epiphany softened my crippling preoccupation, and I tried to show more and more love—more true beauty.

Three days later, I returned to St. Hilary's to join an evening prayer group, and there I met a woman from Kentucky about my age. She was new in town, and we struck up a friendly conversation, hitting it off immediately. I invited her out to dinner, but she declined, saying that she was preparing to go to Medjugorje with her parents, so we postponed our get together. When she returned, she couldn't wait to tell me about her experience, and I couldn't wait to listen. Over dinner, she shared excitedly how their pilgrimage had saved her parents' marriage. Before they left, her folks were on the brink of divorce, but in Medjugorje, they fell in love all over again; and toward the end of the trip, her mom and dad were holding hands and kissing, like two giddy teenagers. They even insisted on renewing their vows in the local Medjugorje church, St. James.

The minute Sarah came home, she said she wanted to go back. "Why?" I asked.

"I believe there's no place like it on earth. Once you feel the heavenly peace of Medjugorje, you never want to leave."

Sarah and I quickly discovered that we had more and more in common as we opened up our lives to one another and shared in confidence things we hadn't told anyone—ever. Leaning forward across the table, Sarah revealed to me in a whisper her most private and painful secret, that she had undergone an abortion in her past. She also mentioned that she had recently received tremendous healing from it.

"How?" I asked.

"From a Rachel's Vineyard retreat." My breath stopped. "Not again." Although I hadn't planned to reveal my checkered past to anyone, I told her that night that I, too, had had—one.

Sarah and I met again on Good Friday. As we were kneeling side by side in a pew before the Blessed Sacrament after praying the stations of the cross, I asked her, "What was the greatest turning point for you in your life of faith?

I waited for her to say, "Medjugorje."

She looked at me and answered, "Rachel's Vineyard."

"What?" I stammered. "Really?"

"That retreat completely changed my life. It transformed and healed me in so many ways I never thought possible. It is really, really beautiful." Looking me straight in the eye, she added, "Patricia, I want you to go."

For the first time in my life, my mind opened a mite to the idea. I trusted Sarah because she had already gone on the retreat, and I knew she was picky. Yet my heart kept me paralyzed with fear. "If she had the courage to go," I wondered, "then why don't I?"

> Be doers of the word and not hearers only, deluding yourselves. For if anyone is a hearer of the word and not a doer, he is like a man who looks at his own face in a mirror. He sees himself, then goes off and promptly forgets what he looked like. But the one who peers into the perfect law of

> freedom and perseveres, and is not a hearer who forgets but a doer who acts, such a one shall be blessed in what he does.
> –James 1:22–25

I went onto the Internet that same day and found that a Rachel's Vineyard retreat (2) was happening soon in my area. At Sarah's insistence, I reluctantly agreed to let her give the organizers my number, as long as everything would remain completely confidential. Soon I started to receive calls—ones I didn't dare pick up. But after playing back a few lovely voicemail messages, and some cajoling from Sarah, I finally decided to call back.

Unawares, I found myself in the midst of an intake interview. The organizer's voice sounded so soothing and welcoming that, much to my surprise, talking to her gave me peace. It was hard to wrap my mind around the fact that we were calmly discussing my abortions, and that this was somehow okay—though an arrow of anguish passed through me when I said the word "three." I hadn't told a soul in ten years. But I heard no judgment, purely understanding, in her voice. After asking me a few basic questions, this kind stranger named Valerie said, to my relief, "Patricia, I'm so sorry to tell you that the retreat has filled, and there is no more space."

"Good!" I thought. "It wasn't God's will that I go, after all. And it's not my fault. Oh well, I tried."

Valerie continued, "If it's God's will for you, someone will cancel and a spot will open up." I began to pray right away that nothing would open up. But God wasn't interested in my pleas. One day before the retreat was to start, she called me to say that a place for me had miraculously become available. "We're excited for you to come!"

"Oh great," I said facetiously. All that day, I planned on bailing. I simply wasn't going to show up. On the next day, Friday, I received a series of encouraging texts from Sarah. Each time one came in, my mind railed against it: "I don't really need this. I'm being forced into it . . . I can't believe people are going to know how many abortions I've had . . . I can't handle their judgment . . . I don't need any healing . . . There's always next year . . ." Finally, I forced myself to get in my car, almost against my will.

Fear pulsed through my veins, making me short of breath. To drum up courage, I thought to myself, "I'm going to go simply to make God happy and to get this over with. I'll get some healing, and that's it. I'm done. No one else will ever, ever know about my abortions, and I won't have to deal with this subject *ever again*."

When I drove up to the retreat center, my body was quivering. This would be my first overnight retreat, and memories of my being stuck at the Fr. Sudac retreat flooded in. "Once I'm in, I can't escape! What will I do? Maybe I should turn around." But when I saw two people waving at me—a sweet-faced religious brother wearing the brown Carmelite habit, and a beautiful young woman standing next to him, wearing a kind smile—my pulse slowed down. They helped me with my bags and received me with such love that I stopped trembling. When we walked in, my antennae were on the lookout for someone who might recognize me, even though I had been assured by Valerie that the chances were almost zero. "Whew! She was right." Then two arms extended toward me. Suddenly, I was hugging Valerie.

I walked into Rachel's Vineyard not knowing what I was carrying inside. The agony of my abortions had been repressed for so long and to such a degree, that I wasn't at all aware of my great need for healing. Through the exercises, prayers, and nurturing atmosphere of that weekend, I not only received healing for my abortions, but many long-held sorrows from past circumstances and resentments miraculously disappeared. In Rachel's Vineyard, there was no judgment, only forgiveness. We were all paddling in the same boat, fearful of being swept away by the currents that had buffeted our souls for so long, and we found safe shores in one another and in God.

Each exercise opened me up to a new dimension of healing, but one moment in particular affected me most profoundly. On Saturday night, the Lord gave me an enduring and life-changing gift. While deep in prayer with my eyes closed, I found myself on a grassy field. As I walked forward in the vision, I noticed three children, standing side by side in the distance, poised somewhat stiffly, like in the photographs of the three Fatima children who received apparitions of Our Lady in Portugal. Somehow, I knew in my spirit that this was a divine appointment, and that Our Lady herself had been preparing these children, even dressing them up for the occasion. I also knew, without question, that these children were mine.

My heart filled with a strange mixture of joy and grief. I could see the children clearly but without color, as the vision was in black and white.

The oldest and tallest stood on the left: a girl looking about age nine, wearing a long-sleeved blouse underneath a square-necked, straight dress that reached her knees. I noticed that she looked a lot like me when I was young—thin with big eyes and medium-length brown hair—but her personality seemed more reserved and serious than mine ever was. On her left (to my right), slightly shorter than she, was a strikingly handsome boy, about seven years old, whose features took after Saul's—his father's. Timid and shy, standing with his shoulders hunched slightly forward, he looked adorable in his checkered shorts with suspenders, socks up to his knees, and a beret. I'd always thought I would dress my boy in such a way. The third child, a little girl about six, possessed a round, doll-like face, and showed less resemblance to me or to Saul. The front part of her long brown hair was pulled back into a bow, and the rest ended in curly tips that reached down to her waist. She was wearing a short-sleeved, button-down shirt, a checkered skirt, and an exuberant smile.

All of them looked as though they didn't dare move, should their special outfits end up looking less than perfect for me. Then my field of vision zoomed in to my youngest girl's face—so close that I could see the dimple on her left cheek. Catching sight of me, she threw away all decorum and began to jump for joy. Turning her head to the side (which was how I noticed the bow in her hair) she grabbed her brother's shirt and began to scream, "Here she comes! Here she comes!" My spirit knew they had been praying for me and looking forward to this special encounter for a long time. And as I walked closer to them, I realized that I had, too. Smiles of great joy spread across all of our faces and, with a love deeper than words, we stared at one another adoringly. Then the vision vanished.

I was sad to lose sight of them, but I felt simultaneously overjoyed. I hadn't once thought of my abortions as children. To now know, without a shred of doubt, that they not only existed but were still alive—and not only alive, but basking in the joys of heaven—was an unparalleled gift. I wasn't a murderer anymore; I was a mom. And the fact that I would one day see my children again—not for a moment, not for a day, but for all eternity—was beyond my human concept of mercy.

I named my three children Mariana, in honor of the Virgin Mary; Emmanuel, in representation of Jesus; and Rosie, after the Holy Rosary. I rejoiced in the knowledge that they actually loved me and, being so pure and in the very presence of God, had forgiven me long ago. How could they not have? And the realization that they had been interceding for me, their mother, for the past ten years of my life, filled me to overflowing with gratitude. That weekend, my abortion procedures changed from unforgivable blights on my soul to human mistakes covered over by the Cross, which Jesus was now using to shower me with love. The Scriptures were true. *"We know that all things work for good for those who love God, who are called according to his purpose (Romans 8:28)."*

Late that night, I wrote my children this promise: "Since I didn't give you a chance to live and to walk the earth, I will do everything in my will to defend life. I will be the voice for those who have no voice."

> While he was still speaking, people from the synagogue official's house arrived and said, "Your daughter has died; why trouble the teacher any longer?" Disregarding the message that was reported, Jesus said to the synagogue official, "Do not be afraid; just have faith." He did not allow anyone to accompany him inside except Peter, James, and John, the brother of James. When they arrived at the house of the synagogue official, he caught sight of a commotion, people weeping and wailing loudly. So he went in and said to them, "Why this commotion and weeping? The child is not dead but asleep." And they ridiculed him. Then he put them all out. He took along the child's father and mother and those who were with him and entered the room where the child was. He took the child by the hand and said to her, "Talitha koum," which means, "Little girl, I say to you, arise!" The girl, a child of twelve, arose immediately and walked around. [At that] they were utterly astounded.
> –Mark 5:35–42

While driving home from the retreat, I received a text on my phone. It was from Saul. I was now twenty-seven and hadn't heard from him in seven years. I had long since changed my number. "Hi, how have you been?" read the text. "I really felt the need to say hello to you and to see how you were doing." An old, familiar feeling of repulsion came over me, but I recognized it as a symptom of post-abortion syndrome (3). I wondered what God was up to, but I already knew the answer. Had Saul not contacted me, I would have never looked for him to tell him the truth. The excuse I had long kept in my head was that since I no longer knew anything about him, not even his whereabouts, he would never know.

But my excuse was not part of God's plan. Too scared to speak to Saul, I texted him, asking for his address so that I could send him an important letter. That night, I sat down to write.

> Dear Saul,
>
> I am writing you to ask for your forgiveness, which I do not deserve. When you texted me, I was on my way home from a retreat called Rachel's Vineyard, for people who've been through abortion, where I found great healing and experienced the love and mercy of God. Now I must tell you the truth. I didn't abort one of our children, I aborted three. Our first pregnancy did not end in miscarriage, and I hid a second pregnancy from you, which I also terminated. It is hard for me to ask this of you, but I would like your forgiveness. I am so sorry for taking away your children and your right to be a father.
>
> Sincerely,
>
> Patricia

Three or four days later, I received a simple text back: "Thank you for telling me the truth. I hope one day I can find that healing that you have found. Take care of yourself." I felt the pain in Saul's words, and they were hard for me to read; but at the same time, I knew that because of my participation at the retreat, grace had also fallen onto him. The timing of his first text was far too uncanny. Perhaps our children in heaven had started pestering God to let them meet their father, too.

The following day, although dead tired in body, I still felt alive in spirit and decided it was time to reach out to my mom. Not only had she urged me to go to Rachel's Vineyard, but she had also invited me each year to go to the Walk for Life West Coast in San Francisco. where about fifty thousand people gather yearly to hear talks and testimonies and peacefully pray and walk for an end to abortion. She said that the experience was grace-filled, even amazing, but I'd never accepted her invitation because of my own hypocrisy. The retreat gave me the courage to tell her the "why," so I sat down with her and said, "Mom, I need to talk to you. I need to let you know that I didn't have a miscarriage the first time I was pregnant. The truth is I've had three abortions total, and this past weekend, I finally went to a Rachel's Vineyard retreat."

Looking at me without a trace of surprise, she responded, "I've been waiting for you to say that. The Lord told me about your abortions three years ago, and that's why I kept insisting that you go on the retreat." In truth, each of us already knew what the other would say. It was a conversation we'd had before in the awkwardness of silence, and when it was voiced, a tangible sense of peace descended on us both. What had seemed impossible only three days earlier had escaped our lips naturally, like the exhaling of a deep breath.

With the exception of my mother, I still planned to never reveal to another soul the fact of my abortions. As I descended from the mountaintop experience of the retreat, my vow to my children slowly retreated into a secretive, shadowy corner. I still wanted to defend life, but without ever revealing that I had taken life. The outside world was not like Rachel's Vineyard and, at the bottom of the mountain, the view looked different. What need could there possibly be to share my secret shame with a world that I felt would not embrace my story or me?

> If God is for us, who can be against us? He who did not spare his own Son but handed him over for us all, how will he not also give us everything else along with him? Who will bring a charge against God's chosen ones? It is God who acquits us. Who will condemn? It is Christ [Jesus] who died, rather, was raised, who also is at the right hand of God, who indeed intercedes for us. What will separate us from the love of Christ? Will anguish, or distress, or persecution, or famine, or nakedness, or peril, or the sword?
> –Romans 8:31b–35

Fact: Until the landmark case of Roe *v.* Wade in 1973, abortion was still a crime in America in most states. Because the facts surrounding abortion and abortion law in the first two hundred years of this nation's history are not common knowledge, many people are not aware that for nearly all of the country's existence, taking the life of a baby in the womb was prohibited.

In fact, to those who have grown up in the post-Roe era, who have been taught little history, and who listen to pro-abortion rhetoric, the opposite may seem true. To these young people, it may appear that the United States was founded upon and has always guaranteed "freedom of choice" in abortion.

Until 1973, however, the pre-born baby was protected by American law . . . In the mid-19th century, the newly formed American Medical Association undertook to organize physicians and medical societies in support of laws against abortion . . . By 1910, every state except Kentucky had passed an anti-abortion law (and Kentucky's courts had declared abortion at any stage of gestation to be illegal). By 1967, not much had changed. In forty-nine states, abortion was a felony; in New Jersey, it was a high misdemeanor. Furthermore, twenty-nine states banned abortion advertising, and many outlawed the manufacture or distribution of abortifacients.

In 1967, though, state abortion laws began to change, after years of organized campaigns by pro-abortion forces. And then in January, 1973, the Supreme Court handed down Roe vs. Wade. With one judicial stroke, over 200 years of legal protection for the unborn was rendered null and void. For the first time in American history, abortion was the "law of the land." Excerpts above are taken from Brian Young's article, "Life Before Roe: A Brief Survey of U.S. Abortion Law Before the 1973 Decision." (4)

CHAPTER TWELVE

Serenaded

Rachel's Vineyard not only healed me in a myriad of ways, it renewed and bolstered my Catholic faith. One of the fruits planted in my soul was the desire to finally, at age twenty-seven, receive the Sacrament of Confirmation. Instead of going through a lengthy preparation process in the United States, I figured I could travel to my dad's small home town in Jalisco, Mexico, where the parish priest knew everyone in my family and would confirm me in no time. During a ten-day festival every January honoring the town's patron, Santa María, confirmations happened in droves. Already, I felt a strong desire to one day get married in the Church, and with Confirmation, it could be fulfilled. My brother wanted to get confirmed as well, so the priest sent us books on Confirmation and on the seven gifts of the Holy Spirit, which we would receive through the Sacrament. The more I read, the more my soul brimmed with excitement. I would soon be anointed with many of the same gifts of the Messiah, which Isaiah mentioned when he prophesied:

> But a shoot shall sprout from the stump of Jesse, and from his roots a bud shall blossom. The spirit of the Lord shall rest upon him: a spirit of wisdom and of understanding, a spirit of counsel and of strength, a spirit of knowledge and of fear of the Lord, and his delight shall be the fear of the Lord.
> –Isaiah 11:1–3a

When it came time for the Sacrament, my uncle and his wife—my kindly godparents–stood behind us proudly in the small town church of Santa María del Oro. As the priest said the prayer from the Rite of Confirmation, empowering me and my brother with the gifts of the Holy

Spirit, I stood transfixed, staring at the wooden crucifix behind the altar. A tear of thanksgiving caressed my cheek.

That very night, the town carnival was in full force. My brother and I had arrived in the middle of the yearly fiesta. Almost no one worked during this ten-day romp of non-stop music, drinking, and wild, raucous celebrating until seven or eight in the morning, juxtaposed with prayer and special activities in the church.

By seven p.m., a large, too-many-decibels band was playing for the hundreds of people tightly packed into the town square. Four men lifted up a statue of Our Lady of Guadalupe at the church and carried her on a decorated platform, parading her majestically through the crowds. As she passed by, the townspeople threw rose petals and confetti her way to show honor to their Mother in heaven. While standing in the midst of the crowd, I noticed a young man a few feet to my right, one of several *muchachos* clutching tequila in their hands. "That guy is gorgeous," I thought to myself. My drooling girlfriends concurred. Tall and statuesque, with a quiet, cool demeanor and slicked-back hair, he reminded me of James Dean. Without seeking attention, he proved hard to ignore. He wasn't trying, and he didn't have to. As I was admiring his soft brown eyes with big black lashes, his head suddenly turned my way, and I could sense him looking at me. But I made myself look away, hoping he hadn't noticed my stare.

When the procession ended, all the girls walked around the plaza in the tradition of the town while the guys stood around its edge, admiring the girls and throwing roses and confetti their way. As I paraded arm in arm with my girlfriends, that same young man began to throw confetti and roses in my direction. I pretended not to see him. Terribly shy and nervous around the opposite sex, I couldn't even look him in the eye or smile. Undeterred, he yelled out, *"Bonita!" "Linda!" "Hermosa!" "Guapísima!"*—whatever variations of "beautiful" he could come up with. His friends egged him on in good fun, but his humorous tone couldn't cover up his obvious sincerity.

As is customary when the girls finished parading in a circle around the plaza, everyone, including the incessantly loud band, proceeded to a huge dinner-dance party, thrown by my cousin who owned the hall. Adjacent to the band and a platform for dancing were tables for ten, decorated with party favors and tequila and served by joyful locals. As my friends and I walked in, I could feel the young gentleman's stare, almost as if heat were warming the area of my body in contact with his gaze; but I continued to act as though I didn't notice. He sat down with his tequila-toting companions, and I sat down at a coed table, three tables away. My friends kept elbowing me to acknowledge him, but I refused to give him any eye contact, although I wanted to. He bought my table a round of drinks . . . and then another. . . and another. We drank them all. Out of the corner of my eye, I saw him lift up his glass at one point to say, *"Salud!"* Finally, his charm won me over. I looked over and lifted up my glass to him, motioning *"Salud!"* in return. Down went my fourth shot of tequila, and out flew the seven gifts of the Holy Spirit.

I wanted to dance with him, but my intuition was telling me that he was a bit prideful and wouldn't want to risk asking me unless he knew I'd say yes. Assuming he might think I was conceited based on my cool demeanor, I decided to agree to dance with another guy whose shirt fell halfway open, exposing several gold chains that matched his teeth. We started dancing with some difficulty, since he came up to my chest, and my strategy worked immediately. The moment I sat back down, my admirer walked over to my table, and with the gesture of a fine gentleman, extended his hand to guide me onto the floor. As we moved together to the mariachi rhythms of our home country, our interest in each other ignited. I learned that his name was Julian, and that he came from a nearby town called Valle de Juárez. Before the evening ended, he would ask me to dance again and again and fill my arms continually with roses.

At three in the morning, the celebration in the hall ended, only for more festivities to begin. While people spilled into the town plaza, Julian walked up to the band and said, "I'm going to pay you guys to play for this girl for an hour or two." Within seconds, I found myself standing near the steps of the church where I had just been confirmed, in front of the most handsome man of the entire fiesta, who was serenading me in an angelic voice under the moonlight with an entire mariachi band behind him.

My friends went crazy, and my brother looked baffled. He leaned into my ear to say, "*Ay Dios*, this guy is whooped!" I soon realized that everyone in the town who was still awake was watching this. Never had I felt so swept off my feet. When the singing subsided, Julian and I talked until sunrise. When we could stay awake no longer, he walked me to my grandmother's home and asked if he could meet me for lunch the next day since I was leaving for the United States that afternoon to return to work. He then drove to his hometown, only to turn around and drive back at midday.

In the sober daylight, Julian was a bundle of nerves. His hands were shaking so much over lunch that he couldn't eat properly. But his fumbling showed off his good heart and humility, endearing him to me. Politely, he asked for my number, and we started a relationship over the phone. My desire to be with him was fueled, more than anything, by my visit to meet his family during our three months of courtship. The moment he introduced me to his ten brothers and sisters, who were running around the house, laughing and playing jokes on one another, I yearned to be part of a family I could call my own.

Taking a dramatic leap, I moved to the tiny Mexican town of Valle de Juárez in the state of Jalisco to live with Julian in the large home he'd inherited from his father. I knew that I would be committing a mortal sin, but I figured I would quickly convert Julian, polish him up, flip him to my way of thinking, then marry him in the Church.

Julian proved to be a real gentleman, a true *caballero*, with a playful sense of humor tinged with a touch of seriousness, which intrigued me. He opened every door I walked through, helped me to don every coat. If he saw me struggling to open a bottle, he'd walk across the room to open it. If I was sitting with a group of girls, he'd walk over to ask if we needed anything. If I had a headache and wanted a glass of water in the middle of the night, he thought nothing of getting up out of a deep sleep to walk down the long hallway to the kitchen and back.

Once, when we went to a large lakeside barbeque with friends and family, many of the couples took turns going out on a Jet Ski with the man at the helm. When the couples jumped off the Jet Ski to come to shore, they had to wade up to their knees in swamplike muck with unknown things scurrying around in it. When Julian and I boarded the Jet Ski, I was the only woman crazy enough to want the front seat, and I drove like a maniac, almost knocking Julian off a couple of times as he struggled for his life. When we got to shore, I was about to get off of the Jet Ski when Julian interjected, "No, no, no. Let me carry you, so you won't get dirty." He swept me up into his arms, carried me safely above the water, and set me down gently on a rock. In the fashion of a true cavalier, he proceeded to take his handkerchief out of his pocket, dry and clean my feet, then slip my sandals on and buckle them. All the women looked over at their boyfriends and husbands and started nudging them hard with their elbows.

In Julian's eyes, I was his princess. One day, he looked over at me and started crying. "Don't leave me, ever," he pleaded. "Please don't ever leave me."

"What are you talking about?" I asked, for I had no intention of ending the relationship. I felt I truly loved him and wanted to marry him. But there was only one problem. Julian didn't know who I was, nor did he want to. The subjects of my former relationships or my drug addiction were taboo, as were my weaknesses, my faults, my failures—anything in my past that could rock the boat. I couldn't share with him all that I wanted to. But I was complicit when it came to my abortions. Julian would never know about those—no one in my future would. In North American culture, abortion is sometimes mentioned casually as a simple procedure, but in Mexico, never. There, abortion is still considered an anathema. People will openly refer to you as an assassin and place a virtual scarlet letter on your chest: "Oh, my God! That woman killed her child!"

My soul longed for the peace and freedom of my room in my dad's home, my little haven in this world where I could gaze at my Sacred Heart picture and spend time alone with Jesus. I missed Him so much. Traveling frequently to North America, I would escape from the spiritual emptiness that was hollowing my heart.

Whenever I came back to Mexico and stepped foot into Julian's house, I felt like a fish yanked out of a vast sea and plopped into a fish tank. One particular moment brought that feeling to the fore. In the small towns of Mexico, most people wash their clothes by hand. I was doing the same, standing on the roof and hanging up Julian's underwear and socks on a clothesline, to the sound of cows mooing and chickens clucking. All of a sudden, my arms fell to my sides. "Where are you, Patricia?" I asked myself, as my eyes surveyed the landscape. "And what are you doing?" I was in the middle of nowhere. I remembered that God had a mission for me and whatever it was, I knew I was not living it.

To make matters worse, dreams of offending God were coming more frequently, to the point that I was living in torment over having sexual relations. Julian got sex from me only three or four times a year, yet I started to cry every time. "Am I a beast?" he once asked me. Here before me was a gorgeous, sweet-hearted guy who loved me, and I didn't want to touch him. That's when Julian started to fear I was becoming an undercover nun. When I sat down to watch EWTN, he'd yell, "Change the channel! Change the channel!"

A month later, during one of my jaunts to California, I attended a healing Mass in San Francisco with Sarah and her new friend Jordan. When everyone stood up to receive Communion, I was the only one left in the pews, unable to take in the Lord's Body and precious Blood. My lips were dry and my soul felt starved as I prayed, "Lord, forgive me that I betray You and am not worthy to receive You. But please know that I love You, and I'm sorry."

A few seconds later, Jordan knelt by my side in the aisle after taking Communion. Knowing nothing of my relationship with Julian, he said to me softly, "Jesus just spoke to me, and He has a message for you. He says thank you for not taking the Eucharist for that would be a sacrilege. You are correct not to take it because that would be another mortal sin; but what would please Him more and show Him you truly love Him is if you didn't live in sexual sin and could then receive his Body and his Blood." No human being had told Jordan that I was living in mortal sin. It was one thing for me to know it, and quite another for me to realize that Jesus, the judge of my soul, knew it, too. I started to cry. The fear of God came over me, and my conscience stung horribly. I had thought I loved Jesus with all my heart, and here I was being told that if I truly loved Him, I would be fighting for my soul.

After that, more than ever, I felt a tormenting urgency to get married in the Catholic Church. When I returned to Valle de Juárez, I pushed Julian to enter into a sacramental union with me. He agreed passively without the slightest understanding of why it was important. He had committed his heart and his life to me and, for him, that was enough. Meanwhile, he was becoming more worldly and irresponsible, staying up late with his buddies and spending time with poker chips, tequila, and cigarettes, while I sat in my room alone with Gregorian chants and incense.

Seeking consolation and enlightenment, I grabbed the *Diary of Saint Maria Faustina Kowalska* and began reading. Intrigued, I learned that Jesus had begun to appear and speak to this poor Polish nun in 1931, calling her to be His apostle of His greatest attribute: mercy.

Nestling into the pages of Faustina's *Diary*, I became oblivious to the world around me, including Julian. I even began to dream of traveling to Poland, where I could trace the saint's footsteps. I wanted to see the cities where she had lived, be everywhere she had been. My heart felt such a strong yearning that I ran to the computer and looked up Kraków, Poland, to see how far it was, where it was. "I have no idea how, but I'm going to get there one day," I told myself. I felt both convicted and inspired by Jesus' words to the saint:

> Jesus told me that the most perfect and holy soul is the one who does the will of the Father . . . "Oh, if souls

> would only want to listen to my voice when I am speaking in the depths of their hearts, they would reach the peak of holiness in a short time." (*Diary*, 584)

I did desire holiness, and I wanted to bring Julian with me. When I learned that Jesus had asked for the institution of Divine Mercy Sunday one week after Easter, I found my hope. Ecstatic, I read on. Jesus had told St. Faustina:

> "I desire that the Feast of Mercy be a refuge and a shelter for all souls, especially poor sinners. On that day, the very depths of My tender mercy will be opened. I will pour out an entire ocean of graces upon those souls who approach the fount of My Mercy. The soul that goes to Confession and receives Holy Communion will obtain complete forgiveness of sins and a remission of all punishment. On that day all the divine floodgates through which grace flow are opened. Let no soul fear to draw near to Me, even though its sins be as scarlet. My mercy is so great that no mind, be it of man or of angel, will be able to fathom it throughout all eternity." (*Diary*, 699)

When Divine Mercy Sunday came around, I begged Julian to go to church with me. I wanted so much for the extraordinary graces of that special day to touch his soul. I dreamed of both of us confessing and receiving Communion together. If we did this, the sins of our entire lives would be forgiven, and all punishment—any time in purgatory—would be erased in a moment! What greater gift could we receive? But when Julian showed up one to two minutes before the Mass ended, I began to bawl. "He doesn't care . . . He just doesn't care," I lamented. A few days later, he retaliated, dragging me to the parish priest to say, "Help me! My girl thinks she's St. Faustina. Can you tell her to not be so extreme?"

Throughout the country of Mexico, church bells would ring in the towns to announce thirty minutes, fifteen minutes, and then one minute before Mass was to begin. One morning a few days later, when the first church bells rang at five a.m., a violent thunderstorm hit Valle de Juárez. As I lay in bed, the sounds of thunder and church bells entered into my last warning dream:

Three days of darkness had come upon Valle de Juárez, and Jesus' Second Coming was imminent. As thunder rolled louder and louder and the church bells pealed more and more insistently, I saw a cross of light with Jesus' silhouette behind it, coming down from the sky as the voice of God the Father spoke to me with great power: "There will be three days of darkness; then My Son, Jesus, will come again. And when he comes to this town, My wrath will be upon the unrepentant sinners here, and the church bells will ring in their ears, reminding them of all the many times they heard my call for Mass but chose to ignore it and instead went about their days as if I were of no importance."

I awoke. "Oh my, I am one of them. I am not receiving Jesus Christ in the Eucharist." And I trembled in great fear of God.

> Do you not know that the unrighteous will not inherit the kingdom of God? Do not be deceived. Neither fornicators, nor idolaters, nor adulterers, nor homosexuals, nor sodomites, nor thieves, nor covetous, nor drunkards, nor revilers, nor extortioners will inherit the kingdom of God.
> –1 Corinthians 6:9–10, NKJV

CHAPTER VIDEO
Patricia Sandoval Speaks to Those Who Have Lost Their Purity
See https://youtu.be/RGiECEQPgkg
Or go to YouTube.com and find the video by searching
Queen of Peace Media

In the days that followed, I kept wondering, "How am I going to get out of this? I need to cut ties before I'm pulled in any deeper." But I lacked the strength to leave. The courage I needed would finally come in an unexpected way from an unforeseen source . . . my Grandma Consuelo.

When I moved to Mexico to live with Julian, I made it a point to visit Grandma once a week in Guadalajara out of a sense of obligation, since she was eighty-three by then. This was the same grandma who had sent my mom running across the Mexican-American border. Growing up as a sensitive kid, I'd found her skin too thick, her heart too hard, her ways too ruthless, her words too rude. She was no Aunt Jemima, and we had never been close. But my sense of duty soon softened into endearment and fascination, for Grandma Consuelo had *Cristero* stories to tell.

Curled up in a love seat across from her while she crocheted in her favorite living room recliner, I'd listen attentively as she recounted the most intricate of details of her experience of the Cristero War. Grandma was only two years old when the war began on January 1, 1927 and the Mexican government launched a direct attack on the Catholic Church, forcing the closure of all churches throughout Mexico. Thousands of the faithful began to defend their religious freedom at the cost of their lives. Grandma's recall of stories and events was extraordinary, and she wanted nothing to be forgotten.

In Grandma's town of Tahul in the state of Zacatecas, a man by the name of Pedro Sandoval started a Cristero faction, and his soon-to-be right-hand man was her father and my great-grandfather, Medardo Lamas Correa. One day, he mounted his horse and said, "I'm a Cristero," and rode off.

At first, Consuelo's dad came home often to visit his wife and eight children. All of the Cristeros in the town would gather to drink in the back patio area of my great-grandmother Maria del Refugio's, home. At two years old, Consuelo wasn't allowed to go back there, but curiosity got the best of her, and several nights would find her peeking out a small window to watch the men and women drink. The spectacle that brought her little feet scurrying back to the window to spy each time, was Pedro Sandoval's mistress, Laura, who loved to show off in front of the men. Over and over, Laura would grab an empty bottle of tequila, mount Pedro's horse, pull out her gun, throw the bottle spinning high in the air, and shoot it to pieces while screaming the Mexican yodel, *"Ayayayayay!"* Consuelo admired her terribly for this.

Little Consuelo was kept close to home and wasn't allowed to play in Tahul, where bright and dark-red blood stained the streets and dead bodies lay in the dirt. So Consuelo's playground was the countryside where she spent much of her time skipping on top of rocks, sheltered from the chaos and carnage nearby.

In time, Consuelo saw her father less and less because he feared coming home, should government officials fighting the Cristeros follow him and kill his family. One day, when Consuelo, now age three, was standing on a small stool that made her tall enough to be able to reach into her soup bowl on the table and grab bits of food with her hands, her dad snuck into the home for a visit. Government officials had followed him and started shooting into the house. Everyone in the family ran into the hills, but Consuelo was forgotten—left standing on her tiny stool with her bowl of soup. My great-grandmother, Maria, darted back to the house amidst the gunfire, grabbed her little girl, and ran through the hills, carrying Consuelo on her hip. Grandma recalled hearing what seemed like endless rounds of bullets shooting past them and watching her father get on his horse and gallop away.

Amidst all the bloodshed, my great-grandfather, Medardo, was a just and peaceful man, known for his righteousness and his mercy. The song of his heart was the cry of the Cristeros, *"Viva Cristo Rey!"*—"Long Live Christ the King!"—which came from their lips, especially while they were being tortured and right before their executions. Christ was Medardo's Lord, and he would defend Him with his life and follow Him to his death. My aunt, Sister Olga, once met an old man from Tahul who said to her, "I knew Medardo Lamas Correa. That man was a saint to me. I'll never forget one day when the Cristeros were holding a government official captive, and they all pointed their guns at him to kill him. But Medardo was there, and being second in command, he told all the Cristeros to put down their guns and not kill the man. From then on, the Cristeros respected him. Medardo talked about righteousness. All he wanted was justice for the Church. Even government officials respected him because there was no hate in his heart."

One day, when Grandma was four, Medardo tried again to sneak home and visit his wife and kids. While his wife was cooking in the kitchen, she heard a noise on her doorstep. She walked to the front of the house, opened her door, and saw her husband on the front porch, beheaded.

Furious with grief that her husband's horse was also gone, Maria got a hold of a gun and walked over to the government official who had stolen the animal, pointed the gun at the man and said, "Not only did you kill my husband, but you also stole our horse. *Esto es una burla!*—This is a cruel mockery!" The man didn't say a word as she untied the rope that fastened the horse to a tree, mounted the animal, and rode home.

All of her sons had been courageous in their own way, like their father. Now they were high-priority targets for the government. They tried to save their lives by hiding out in their alcoholic uncle's home, since he was the doctor of the town and the government officials would never kill their doctor or search his home. Eventually, one after another, six of Maria's seven sons were hunted down and killed. The last one to die was my grand-uncle, Ruben, who went looking one day for the doctor and found him drunk in a bar. As Ruben was trying to drag him home, an official spotted him and said, "Hey, you're Medardo Lamas's son." He pummeled him with bullets right there in the bar. The boy was eighteen years old and about to get married.

There was another area of the family home that my grandma Consuelo was never allowed to enter. It was a small room that Maria alone went into. But one day, in search of something, little Consuelo walked in and saw hung up around the room her father's clothes, covered in blood, alongside her siblings' blood-stained outfits. Now she knew why her mother went there alone and cried for hours. When Maria buried her last son to be killed, she was numb. There were no more tears to be shed.

As Grandma Consuelo sat across from me on my last visit with her, I noticed that something was stirring in her memory. She took a breath and paused. Then she looked up, glanced out the kitchen window, and said, "I don't understand why my brother and I lived." Then her expression changed, and a sense of power and pride began to sparkle her eyes. Turning her head to look directly at me, she said with great conviction, "Patricia, martyrdom is in your bloodline."

The moment I heard those words, I felt an internal tsunami stir my blood. Courage pumped through my veins, electrical impulses burst like fireworks in my head, and my heart pounded with vigor. My sense of self instantly changed from a girl slouching forward in shame to a woman of great worth, standing erect with her head held high and her shoulders thrust back. To be the descendant of someone who gave up his life for Christ was a gift that meant everything to me. With a lineage of such committed belief, a powerful awakening came over me to be bold in my faith, and I imagined my great-grandfather and all of my grand-uncles praying for me from heaven.

The calling upon me was not small. I had come from the seed of a martyr! And all of these relatives were with me—all of them. My heart swelled. For the first time in a long time, I felt like someone special.

> No one has greater love than this, to lay down one's life for one's friend.
> –John 15:13

Fact: The religious persecution that launched the Cristero War in Mexico began on June 14, 1926, when President Plutarco Calles, a fervently anti-Catholic atheist and practicing Freemason (1) enacted anticlerical legislation. By the time the war ended in 1929, about ninety thousand people on both sides had died.

A major motion picture of the Cristero War titled *For Greater Glory* was released in 2012. Until then, many Mexicans did not know of this war in Mexico's past because it had been erased from their history books. (2)

Chapter Thirteen

Going Home

I came to understand that the Lord remembers the blood of the martyrs down a family line. It was no coincidence that Medardo Lamas's granddaughter, my mom, had returned to the Catholic faith and another of his granddaughters, my Aunt Olga, had become the leader of the congregation of the Sisters of the Sacred Heart of Jesus. Sister Olga had even been summoned to Rome to represent the twenty-five Cristero martyrs who were declared saints by Saint Pope John Paul II on May 21, 2000. At their canonization Mass, she handed the bread and the wine for consecration into the Pope's hands.

Grace had also touched my life from the very beginning. The Lord visited me in my room when I was a baby. He spoke to me as a child through shooting stars. He made sure I was clothed and fed when my mother banished me from the home and my father permitted it; and He was with me when I banished myself and did drugs on the streets. The Lord prevented bullets from entering my body and my body from going to prison. He rescued me through a Christian named Bonnie. He visited me as the Christ Child of Atocha. He saved my mother who, in turn, helped save me. He gave me visions and revelations to guide my steps. He sheltered me from fear whenever the evil one attacked me. He drew me to His mother and poured healing balm onto my darkest sins and secrets. He removed my addiction to drugs and protected me from meth's devastating effects without my ever having to go to a psychologist or psychiatrist, or taken medication—He knew well I couldn't afford them. Instead, He gave me the best and most inexpensive therapies I could get: The Eucharist and Confession. By my own actions, I should have been long gone from this world, but by His grace, I was preserved for a purpose.

Yet after all God had done for me, I was continuing to walk along my own selfish path, choosing my will over His. Instead of honoring my ancestors' legacy of heroic virtue, I was leaving my own twisted legacy of bad decisions. The wound in my heart from my fractured family had propelled me to practically force God's hand to give me a family of my own. But all I had achieved was an isolated life on a ranch with a bunch of Mexican chickens. Deeply troubled, I thought, "If my great-grandfather had the courage to risk everything—his marriage, his children, his life—in defending his faith unto death, then what am I doing? I'm not defending anything. I'm not even defending the Lord's Real Presence in the Eucharist because I'm not worthy to receive Him.

I escaped to the United States to delay a coming storm of change, and there my desire to serve the Lord ran headlong into a challenge. God was so eager that His call was on the cusp of bursting within me when I received a call from Valerie, the organizer of my Rachel's Vineyard retreat: "Would you be willing to help lead a new Spanish Rachel's Vineyard retreat, Patricia?" Before I could answer, she added, "And to help promote it, would you give your post-abortion healing testimony at the Cathedral of Christ the Light in Oakland to a group of Spanish-speaking lay ministers, priests, and the bishop?"

"Hell, no!" I thought to myself. To minister at a private retreat was one thing, but to publicly share the details of my sin in Spanish—to priests and a bishop, no less—would be a full-blown nightmare come to life. "I feel like my calling might be to minister to youth on drugs," I told Valerie, who then suggested we meet in person. Hanging up the phone, I wondered how I had missed the opportunity to decline on the spot.

Over lunch, Valerie explained to me that she wouldn't be able to get the Spanish retreat off the ground without a public testimony and how I was the perfect person to do it. I looked at her like the proverbial deer caught in the headlights—and one that had lost its appetite completely. "I don't want to," I told her honestly. My mind raced back to years earlier when I'd heard a pro-life speaker talk about abortion and the importance of defending life. "Thank God there are people willing to speak about this," I'd thought, "because I'm not. It isn't my calling."

"Not only will I pray for you," Valerie nudged, "but I'll get everyone in the ministry to pray for you."

"Ugh, she's not giving me an out." Feeling unnerved and cornered, I thought of women and men in the Spanish community who were trapped in their secret shame. "Okay, okay," I relented, "but this is the first and last time that I'll do it."

To prepare, I called Julian and lied to him. I told him that I was going to give a talk in California about drug addiction. But even this made him very angry. By giving my testimony, he said, I was involving him, too—by shaming him.

In the days following our meeting, Valerie and I got together for dinner several times and worked at writing out my testimony. One evening, as we were going over my story, I blurted out, "I used to work at Planned Parenthood. Would that help my testimony?"

She looked at me, dumbfounded. "Well, yeah! Of course!" As soon as she said that, every memory, every detail of my time there, started flooding back in. Even during the Rachel's Vineyard retreat, the dead babies that passed through my hands had never once crossed my mind. In over ten years, not a single memory had surfaced. Now I wondered how I could have ever forgotten.

I went home and wrote down my whole story. To have lived my life moment by moment proved a far different view from seeing it as a whole on paper. "Oh, my goodness!" I gasped. "This poor girl went to hell and back." My life painted an ugly picture, and I couldn't imagine sharing this mother lode of sin all in one package. Not only had I killed my own children, but others' children as well. A heavy brick of mortification came crashing down on me.

Walking into a room at the Cathedral of Christ the Light and seeing a group of people waiting to hear my testimony was a terrorizing, out-of-body experience. I didn't know if I had the mental strength to speak and not faint. The Bishop of Oakland stood up to introduce the event and then left. "Thank you, God, for small favors," I murmured. But as I stood up to speak, the power of people's prayers of intercession settled over me like a protective blanket. Inside my heart, I sensed the Holy Spirit giving me strength and grace that were not my own in order to say the next word . . . and the next. "Don't break down," I told myself. "One word at a time. You are doing this for your Lord in reparation for all your transgressions."

Looking out at the crowd, I saw that everyone, especially the priests, was crying. When the event ended, every single person in that room wanted me to speak for their parish or their prayer group. I found it hard to say no. Soon after that, my story came out in a newsletter and was splashed across the Internet.

Wait a minute. Wasn't this all supposed to be over?

> When they had finished breakfast, Jesus said to Simon Peter, "Simon, son of John, do you love me more than these?" He said

> to him, "Yes, Lord, you know that I love you." He said to him, "Feed my lambs."
> –John 21:15

I extended my stay in California to give my testimony a few more times before returning to Mexico. When I finally went back, I said to Julian, "I'm going home."

Intuiting something more in my words, Julian asked me, "Are you coming back?"

I hesitated to tell him the truth, so I feigned an unconvincing "I don't know."

I could tell he was deeply hurt. Although he'd always been kind and sweet to me, he knew he'd let me down and looked embarrassed about it. Then his pride asserted itself, burying the soft emotions that threatened to take over. Abruptly stoic and machista, he said with feigned confidence, "All right, that's fine."

My heart sank as I pondered the crushing blow I was inflicting on him. He loved me and, in return, I was hurting him terribly and shaming him not only in front of his family and friends but the entire town and beyond as well. Women in Mexico rarely leave their men, and small-town Mexican gossip travels at the speed of light.

Yet as I began to pack, a sense of relief lifted my spirits. I would have the chance to start all over, and I'd be home with Dad in my old room with my Jesus! But far more important to me, I was coming back to monthly Confession, to daily Mass, to the freedom to be me! Julian was a good man, and I would miss him. But what I really had been missing was myself.

The night before I was to leave Mexico, the phone rang. It was my sister calling from the States to give me a friendly warning. "Patricia," she said, "I wouldn't go back to Dad's if I were you."

"What?" I cried. "Why not?"

It turned out that my dad's wife, Elvira, had told my sister, "I don't want her back here, and if she does return, her father and I are going to have problems."

My chest caved with grief, and I found it hard to breath. "Why is this happening?" I asked myself—and God. "I have always been so nice to her." Yet in a way, I understood. Elvira had repeatedly encouraged my relationship with Julian and had assumed I was gone for good. Knowing that I was, in many ways, still my dad's little princess, she wouldn't have suggested directly to him that I not come home to be with them. Undoubtedly, she had shared her grievance with my sister, hoping that my sister would pass it on to me. Her wish had come true, and it hurt. I had felt safe with my father in the sanctuary of my room, and although Elvira had never hidden her dislike of me—except from my dad—I'd at least had a place to live. But now home was gone. My mother was living far away in Guadalajara, my brother with his girlfriend, my sister with her family, and no one had room for me. I had no money, no job, no security, and no clear path for the future.

In a panic, I called a friend who said I could stay with her for a month. After that, providentially, one of my cousins moved out of the house that Marcello and I had purchased, and I was able to live there. As soon as I moved in, I received a call from Julian, who ventured to ask again, "Are you coming back?" This time, I told him the painful truth.

I wouldn't hear from Julian for another two years. Even though I had caused the breakup, I felt discarded in my brokenness and wanted him to call. And so the theme of abandonment and rejection remained my constant, unwelcome companion. Over the next couple years, although my father lived around the corner from me, I never heard from him either. Soon after my plane had landed, he knew that I had returned from Mexico, but he never reached out to find out why I hadn't come to live with him; and I, fearing rejection, never had the courage to tell him.

In my thirty years of living, I hadn't once confronted my father about anything. The deflection, denial, and passive-aggressive silence that I suspected would follow were more than my psyche could bear. I didn't dare complain when I came to learn that Elvira had put all my things in garbage bags and thrown them away. I kept quiet when rumors traveled the grapevine that Elvira was smearing my name across town. But after many long days of wondering why my father did nothing about her behavior, I finally broke.

Caught up in a crescendo of resentment and anger, I picked up the phone and spoke my mind to Elvira. She hung up on me. Raging mad, I called my dad right after that and told him that he should tell his wife to shut her mouth concerning me. My father defended his wife, telling me that whoever had shared Elvira's supposed words should not be listened to, and that I should stop spreading lies. *Click.* Dial tone. He had hung up on me too.

In the weeks that followed, I sulked in a steaming-hot bath of self-pity. I couldn't fathom that this man who was shunning me was my very own dad. "How can he do this to me—again—especially after we've been the best of friends?" Further estrangement from my father sent me into depression, and my pain compounded into self-disgust as I turned his rejection back onto myself. Dad drove by my house on his way to work each morning, and passed by me on the way home each evening. As the months passed, my anger simmered in bitter resentment, with no outlet or resolution.

Two Father's Days and two birthdays in a row, I called him to wish him well, asking if my brother and I could take him out to dinner. But he said he didn't have the time. My brother, who was working in my father's construction business, couldn't understand why he was refusing our invitations. And I couldn't accept how completely Dad had shut me out of his life. In one last attempt at reconciliation, my brother and I planned a family get-together at a fancy restaurant in Tiburon, overlooking the sparkling lights of San Francisco Bay. It was to be an outing reminiscent of a time when my father and I were inseparable, when one of our favorite pastimes was to sample the foods of different restaurants and cultures. I had made a little money by then doing freelance makeovers, and I couldn't think of a better way to spend it. Planning for weeks in advance, my brother and I invited his godparents and their children and prepared to celebrate in style. An hour before our dinner reservation, my dad called to say, "I already ate." That night, we celebrated Father's Day without our father.

A few months later, I would see my dad for the first time in two years. While on my way to the bank on foot, I was about to jaywalk but thought, "No, I'll do it properly. I'll use the crosswalk." I waited at the curb for the light to turn green and, just as it changed, my father's car stopped directly in front of me. As I started to cross the street, neither of us did more than lift up a hand. It felt like I was waving hello to a distant acquaintance—and waving a painful goodbye to my dear dad.

> Be angry but do not sin; do not let the sun set on your anger,
> and do not leave room for the devil.
> – Ephesians 4:26–27

Trying in vain to fill the void in my heart, I stopped watching what I was eating or how much wine I drank. In my neglect, I gained a lot of weight, which only served to fuel my morbid self-perception. My worst fears became reality: I was fat, rejected, broken—and broke.

I needed to earn a living, and with my distorted physical image intensified, I allowed my obsession to choose my next job: a medical assistant at a plastic surgeon's office. Perhaps I could get free liposuction on my thighs. The mirror had become my nemesis, and I clung to the warped belief that if I fixed the outside of me, the inside would be happier.

After I'd been on the job for only one month, a married woman with three children came into the office for a consultation on getting breast implants, liposuction, and a tummy tuck. After meeting with the doctor, she walked up to the receptionist, scheduled her surgery date, and paid about seventeen thousand dollars cash for the procedures. Her enthusiasm was palpable. But a week before her scheduled date, she called the office to tell the receptionist that she was delighted to have unexpectedly discovered she was pregnant and asked if she could postpone the surgery.

After telling the patient she'd call her back, the receptionist yelled out the news to the whole office. I smiled out of joy for the woman, but the receptionist made a sarcastic comment about her pregnancy, and the rest of the staff laughed. The doctor grew furious and barked, "There's nothing funny about this. I have her scheduled for the whole day and that's big money I'm losing!"

The receptionist called her back to say that the doctor would not only lose time and money but was also extremely upset. The woman panicked. "Tell the doctor that everything is going to be okay. Tell him that I'm really excited about my breast implants, and I don't want anything to get in the way. I really want to respect his time, so I'll end the pregnancy before the surgery date he already scheduled."

The receptionist hung up the phone and called out, "Nothing to worry about, Doctor! She's getting an abortion." The staff tittered, and the doctor calmed down. My mental state raced between horror and helplessness. My job was to prepare the packets of the fifteen-to-twenty surgical instruments to be used in her procedures. Then and there, I knew I couldn't do it. So I quit.

I had no idea of the high cost I would pay for my action in support of life. Normally, jobs came my way fairly quickly, but after sending out résumé after résumé after résumé without a single call back, I began to spiral into hopelessness. And then came the scorching flames of divine purification.

No job meant no money to buy jewelry, accessories, makeup, or fashionable clothes that could hide my ever-expanding body. I wouldn't dare let anyone see me. I couldn't bear to have a family member ask, "So what are you doing with yourself these days?" In my cloister of a home, the mirror reflected back to me a sordid picture of social leprosy. The few times I did go outside for Mass, I prayed to disappear from view. Back when I had means, my money flew into department stores. Back when I could afford designer clothes, I strived to look like models and pretty actresses. Back when I was stylishly svelte, men's glances flashed my way. But now, as I turned thirty-one, no one seemed to notice me. All the compliments fell silent.

I had no idea how sick I really was. There is a name for it: body dysmorphic disorder. It causes its sufferers to have a distorted view of how they look and to spend far too much time worrying about their appearance. For decades, the bombardment of images on the Internet, on television, and in fashion magazines had fed my morbid preoccupation with appearance. When poverty came suddenly and took that all away, I was forced to stop the comparison game. I had to look at myself differently . . . but my eyes needed a long time to readjust. There were days when I could barely stand myself. To get the mail, I'd quickly dart outside and back, lest a neighbor catch a glimpse of me.

My façade was crumbling. Nothing was left to prop up the superficial wall I had erected over the years to hold up my self-esteem—a wall so thick that even God couldn't reach through it to touch my deepest wound: worthlessness. With all artifice gone, I was now face-to-face with the real me. And in my estimation, I had nothing to show for myself but ugliness and failure. Yet of all my sufferings, the most painful was the fact that my dad lived just two blocks away; but not once did he call, not once did he visit. At night, he would often show up in my dreams, fueling my forlornness. Although I was never suicidal, there were times when I simply wanted to die.

I'm lying on my parents' bed watching television. My dad is calling me from the hallway. I can tell by the sound of his voice that he is inviting me to go somewhere fun with him. I start to bounce up and down excitedly on his bed, which I know is a no-no. Turning around in a mid-air swirl, I see Jesus in the Sacred Heart picture on the wall. He is staring right back at me. All of a sudden, the image grows bigger and bigger . . .

In time, I felt so tired of being alone and rejected that I wanted a live human being to take care of me, to love me. "I'm ready to give up," I told Jesus one night before going to bed. I'm going to look for Julian and take him back. If You don't want me to do this, I need You to answer me."

Early the next morning, I had a dream in full color:

One of my aunts is sitting down, watching television. She tends to criticize me, making my life difficult in her rudeness. I am standing behind her right shoulder, and we stare at the screen to see a wide shot of myself in a wedding dress, walking down the aisle away from the camera, while my husband-to-be, who is someone well-known, waits for me to approach him. My aunt's jaw drops, and the first thing to enter her mind is, "Why is my niece marrying him*? And how is he marrying* her*?" He is beautiful, a true man of God, and she can't believe her eyes. Then God's voice echoes, "You see how I prepare a banquet for you in front of your enemies."*

Then the television disappears, and a huge ball of light explodes above my aunt. She looks up at the ceiling and sees a great, luminous sphere surrounding two transparent silhouettes. Gleaming white, my groom and I are facing each other, holding hands and looking into each other's eyes as the Holy Spirit flies in a circular motion from my heart to his, unifying our spirits as one. Through the light of God's glory, I can see that he is tall and becoming.

I was given my answer. The Lord was making a point to remind me of the prophesied husband in the blue suit, and I was not to go back to Julian. As my eyes adjusted to the dawn and my mind pondered the picture I'd seen of exquisite love and holy fire, my mood transformed into elation. But then, as I looked about my small bedroom, the reality of my present situation threw a dirty, wet rag on my dream. The thrill of it left my heart, like air escaping a punctured balloon. My looks, my poverty, and my past were no match for such a beautiful man, and I began to doubt that God had communicated with me at all. But a seed had been planted, one that grounded me and gave me hope, and prevented me from running into the arms of the next unsuitable suitor to come along.

After four months of reclusive misery, my meager savings had been spent on the home, food and gas; all my money was gone. I was thirty-two, and I could no longer pay the mortgage. First one foreclosure notice came, then another, and another. When I received a notice that my electricity would be turned off, I started to despair, wondering if I might lose my mind.

"I need you, Jesus," I called out. "I need you close! Why is this happening to me! Is this the thanks I get for following Your will?" One morning as I lay in my tears, unable to get up and face another empty day, I began to pine for the Sacred Heart picture, which still hung on the wall of my former room in my father's house. Not only was the image sacred in the Lord's eyes—He had told me so Himself—but it was the only thing I owned from happier times past.

I sat bold upright in bed, giddy with guilty excitement: "I know what I'll do. I'll steal it back!" I waited in stealth-mode for exactly the right moment when my dad's and Elvira's cars would be gone. Then I pulled my car up into their driveway, jumped out, punched in the garage door code by memory, bounded up the stairs into my old room, grabbed my precious loot, sprinted into my getaway car, gave my Lord a kiss, put Him in the back seat, and peeled out of the driveway with a racing heart.

"I just kidnapped Jesus!" Swinging open the front door, I smiled for the first time in months. After creating a small altar for Him, I picked up His picture, gave Him a tight hug, and began to dance with Him around the room. "I need You more than ever now, Jesus," I told Him in between sobs of relief. "You're my everything. I have nothing else but You."

After that, somehow, the electricity was never shut off, and not long after I'd open the latest foreclosure mailing, a notice of extension would come. This dance of threatening paperwork lasted for an entire year. Miraculously, I stayed in my home for free while friends and extended family kept me alive. A dear friend, Norma, would appear on my doorstep with a bag of food when my stomach was growling with hunger. I'd never had a friend like her; she was there for me in every way and loved me at my worst. My cousin Graciela would speak God's Word to my heart to help lift me out of my abyss. Flipping open the Scriptures, she'd practically yell encouraging verses into the phone. And my loveable godparents—my aunt and uncle—continued to treat me like their daughter. Their mere presence would calm my jittery nerves, and the Mexican aromas from my aunt's homemade cheese and tortillas, combined with food from their garden, would soothe my senses. "This is your house," my uncle would say with every visit. "You can eat here whenever you like." He would kiss my cheeks and tell me he loved me. Everything I dreamed about my father doing and saying, my uncle did it all. But my self-pity and the dread of running into my father, who lived around the corner and popped in to see them often, prevented me from responding to many of their invitations and affections.

During that year and a half when I was out of a job, I received invitations to give my personal testimony at churches and conferences. Only by the grace of God was I able to say yes to every one; and in some miraculous way, I was able to preach in my crippled state. No matter how crushed my spirit felt, I was not going to let my Jesus and my three children down. A vow was a vow. After each of my talks, painful as they were to give, both women and men, and girls and boys, would shower me with compliments—not about my appearance, but about *me*. "You're so courageous!" "Thank you so much for sharing your life." "Your talk is the best I've heard." "You've touched me so deeply." "I will never forget you." "What a beautiful person you are." "Can I give you a hug?"

New life began to sprout through my soul's broken cracks. It was the love and appreciation of these strangers, my cousin, my friend Norma, and my dear aunt and uncle that showed me that Patricia Sandoval, stripped of everything she thought gave her value, was actually worth something.

> Therefore I tell you, do not worry about your life, what you will eat [or drink], or about your body, what you will wear. Is not life more than food and the body more than clothing? Look at the birds in the sky; they do not sow or reap, they gather nothing into barns, yet your heavenly Father feeds them. Are not you more important than they? Can any of you by worrying add a single moment to your life-span? Why are you anxious about clothes? Learn from the way the wild flowers grow. They do not work or spin. But I tell you that not even Solomon in all his splendor was clothed like one of them. If God so clothes the grass of the field, which grows today and is thrown into the oven tomorrow, will he not much more provide for you, O you of little faith? So do not worry and say, 'What are we to eat?' or 'What are we to drink?' or 'What are we to wear?' All these things the pagans seek. Your heavenly Father knows that you need them all. But seek first the kingdom (of God) and his righteousness, and all these things will be given you

besides. Do not worry about tomorrow; tomorrow will take care of itself. Sufficient for a day is its own evil.
–Matthew 6:25–34

Fact: Historically, the ideal female body in the United States was strong and full-figured. In the 1900s, the American public became increasingly consumed with thinness to the point where in modern times, a "slender at all costs" movement has come to define Western culture. (1) Currently, 80 percent of women in the United States are dissatisfied with their appearance, and more than ten million suffer from eating disorders. From a young age, women aspire to Barbie-like measurements that are physiologically impossible without surgery and/or starvation. The more a female is exposed to the media, the more she adopts role models disconnected from real life. Her goals are physically impossible and thus a setup for failure. (2)

Chapter Fourteen

The Utter Blindness

My self-esteem continued to improve as time passed and, on days when I felt confident, I believed in God's promise of the husband I'd seen in the dream. On days when I felt pitiable, I distrusted it. Yet even in my spells of doubt and fear, I still believed enough to offer up every Eucharist from that time forward on behalf of this tall, well-known, attractive Hispanic, Catholic husband in a blue suit. And when I learned that Mother Teresa of Calcutta urged single people to pray three Hail Mary's daily for their own chastity and that of their future spouse, I did that and more: since the Angelus prayer contains three Hail Mary's, I made it a point to pray it every single day for this man's chasteness and my own.

Finally, after spinning my wheels in the job search, my trial of unemployment ended when I was hired as a medical assistant in a high-end dermatology clinic. It felt so good for my feet to hit traction and to have a purpose for my day other than seeking employment and ways to survive.

Three months into the job, my employer, a dermatologist and former Catholic, called a mandatory meeting for his entire staff. We gathered in a circle in the lobby, my fellow workers and I. I had yet to see my new boss so full of enthusiasm—quite out of character for him. This special noon meeting would introduce us to a particular skincare line of anti-aging creams so intriguing that one of my coworkers, who had that day off, drove into the office just to hear about this new product she'd tried. I even got excited about the prospect myself.

We listened attentively as a company representative for NeoCutis gave us a slick presentation on a new, cutting-edge technology for top-of-the-line skincare products. To start, he took testers of each of the eye creams: day cream, night cream, SPF 10 cream—variations of the superhero of creams that did it all—and rubbed some of each product on our hands so we could feel its smooth, soft, elegant texture.

The rep explained that the products were made out of PSP human factors, a natural substance that we already carry in our own bodies. Then he pulled out a large cardboard poster, a visual guide of the stages of product development, and began to explain what the human factors were. At the top of the poster chart was a human being in the early stages of gestation. "These fetuses," said the rep, "have been within women whose doctors told them their child would have Down syndrome or some other complication in life. So the doctor recommended abortion. The women decided for it, and they donated their fetuses."

The rep continued, "They boil the fetuses in water, making a broth—just like chicken soup! It's like when you boil a chicken and the protein ends up in the water." I blanched in disbelief. An arrow pointed from the picture of a fetus to the bubbly broth. "Then they use the proteins and cells from the boiled tissue to make a cell bank, which they freeze in liquid nitrogen; that's what they then use to make the anti-aging cream. This cream contains youthful cells with skin-repairing properties." My eyes followed the arrows from the dead fetus to the bubbly broth to a small 120-dollar jar of cream.

The group of employees looked starry-eyed. The rep, the doctor, and my coworkers couldn't help but echo that this was the cleanest, purest, most natural organic product out there on the market. Two of my fellow employees had already taken some of the creams home and rubbed them onto their husbands' faces. This inspired a discussion of how this product was going to be a big launch for men as well because it was light and not oily. Not only did their husbands want the product on their faces, but on their hands as well. The rep nodded, clearly pleased that their enthusiasm was making his job so easy. "When you introduce this product, it shouldn't only be put onto your patients' faces, but onto their necks, and hands, and chests, too."

I looked around in horror as my intrigued coworkers took notes without a trace of disgust. My dermatologist employer shared that he had been doing marketing research for months, and he thought this was going to be the "cream" of the crop of all of the products he sold. In a chorus, the doctor and rep declared, "If you try it and love it, and you believe in it with all your heart, like your boss and I do, then it will be easier for you to sell it."

I couldn't speak. I felt like I had the blood of martyrs rubbed into my hands. One of my coworkers asked, "How should we respond when the patients ask us what human factors mean and what this product is made out of?"

The doctor responded, "We cannot use the term 'fetal tissue' because then the people in this county would say, 'You're killing humans for an anti-aging cream.'" After that, the conversation turned into a staff brainstorming session with the rep's help over how to conceal the word "fetal."

I flashed back to my training at Planned Parenthood, where they had taught us to lie and deceive patients. Then I thought of all the people already using this product who were deceived and unknowingly have the tissue of aborted children rubbed on their faces. More shocking to me than the presentation was the fact that I had never seen my coworkers more on fire. Overjoyed by the free samples, they were jumping at the opportunity to sell it and lie.

Trembling, I went up to the doctor after the presentation and said, "Today I'm quitting. I'm Catholic, and I defend life and human dignity. Thank you very much for the opportunity that you have given me in your practice." He looked down at the floor, with shame covering his face. "I know, Patricia, and I'm sorry."

My promise that I would do everything in my will to defend life would cost me dearly—again. Another seven months ensued of a daily online search for work with no results. My money ran out again, and I returned to relying on Providence for my daily bread. Then one day, while I was sitting at the computer, searching listlessly on the Internet for employment, God spoke to my heart in a strong voice: *"Stop looking for a job today. I have a job for you. Today you will rest at home in prayer."*

"Okay," I thought, "but this is crazy." In obedience, I turned my computer off and remained in prayer all day. That afternoon, I got a call. The woman on the line had received my résumé a few months before. She was the manager of a dermatology practice and wanted me to come in that very day for an interview. The next morning, I was hired.

I couldn't understand why God wanted me to work in this particular office. It didn't make sense, and I didn't fit in. Just two weeks into the job, while I was eating with four female coworkers in the lunch room, one of them, a nursing student on my right, said excitedly, "Oh you guys, yesterday in class it was so cool. We got to cut open and dissect a four-week-old fetus." Then she formed with her hands its shape and size.

"Oh, Lord, not again," I complained silently. "Please let me stay out of this and keep my job."

A girl on my right piped up, "I got the opportunity to dissect a fetus too. I got to scrape the skin and cells. It was awesome!" Her voice bubbled with fascination and pride.

A third girl offered, "Oh, in my class, we got to dissect a cat."

Agony and alarm gripped the table. "That's animal cruelty. How is that possible? That is so mean!"

I put down my fork and could no longer eat. "What's wrong with this picture?" I thought. "With our culture?" Nobody is even flinching at the mention of a murdered fetus getting scraped. It isn't dawning on these girls that this was a human being. But to them, to dissect a cat is 'inhuman.'"

"I get it, God. I understand," I said in the sad silence of my heart. "I don't know why you have me here, but you are letting me see how cold and distorted our human hearts have become. This mindset is pervasive. It is everywhere. We have compassion for animals but not for human life." An intense need to be quiet and alone drew me outside to a bench, where I sat down to pray.

As soon as my eyes closed, the Lord spoke to me interiorly. His tone was emphatic: *"You will speak. Others will not. So I am calling you, my daughter, because you have the courage to tell the truth. You will be My voice."*

That night, while looking into the eyes of Jesus on my bedroom wall, I garnered the courage to say to Him, "No matter the humiliations that come, I promise I will speak for You. I will help You expose the darkness that has blinded us to the sacredness of human life. But, Lord, I feel very small, scared, and weak, so please don't let me fail You."

Then I tucked myself into bed, wondering what exactly I'd just agreed to. That night, Satan let me know of his great displeasure with my yes. As I lay on my back, shadows of different shapes and sizes appeared in my room. Some advanced slowly from my left, others from my right, and some from directly in front of me, like cougars surveying their prey. Despite the pitch black of night, I could see them through the "eyes of the soul." As I waited for their assault, a sickening feeling came over me, and the hair on my arms stood straight up. Then it came—the sound of steps racing toward me on my carpet as several demons swarmed my bed in a rage, charging on top of me. I cried out, but to no avail. They lunged at me, pulled at my hair, tried to scratch and strangle me. I could feel the pain of their sharp nails, but when I looked down, I couldn't see any scratch marks on my body. One demon grabbed me by the tongue, which caused me to drool and prevented me from swallowing. He wouldn't let go. In vain I tried to utter the name "Jesus!" Finally, after what felt like a half hour of struggle and strenuous prayer, they disappeared into the night.

A week later, shortly after I had given my testimony in a parish, a woman stopped directly in front of me, reached out to gently hold the sides of my upper arms, and said, "Don't be scared when he comes into your room at night, because he cannot touch you. He cannot touch you."

"Wait," I stopped her. "Who are you talking about?"

"You know who I'm talking about," she responded. "Satan."

"So, I'm not crazy. The Lord gave you this word for me."

"That's right."

It reassured me to know that God had revealed my painful nights to this woman, because ever since my recent promise to be God's voice for life, Satan was making his upset known to me in constant and "creative ways. When he didn't pay me a visit himself or send his "friends" to harass me, he tried to stop me by throwing arrows through the weaknesses of people.

He incited my first public attack when I received an invitation to give my testimony before a Spanish-speaking prayer group of about one hundred seniors. I asked my friend Sarah to be by my side for support. Staring at the crowd, I noticed that they all looked similar to my grandparents—just off the boat from small towns and ranches in Mexico where modesty is still a virtue.

By the time we arrived, the seniors had been set on fire by Hispanic praise and worship music, extolling God's love and mercy. They were in the jolliest of moods, dancing and waving their arms high. Their favorite song seemed to be one called, *"Písale la Cabeza al Diablo"*—in English, "Stomp on the Devil's Head." Twisting their hips and stomping their feet, they were moving rock 'n' roll-style, putting swagger and flavor into it. I was even getting into the groove myself, crushing the devil with my high heels.

Then the music ended, and it came time for my testimony. "We are fortunate to have with us today Patricia Sandoval," said the host, "a young woman who will share her story of abortion." As I walked up to the microphone, my soul sensed the heaviness of judgment in the rigid postures of the room, and my heart began to race. Scanning my audience, I saw closed-mindedness in their eyes.

Staring out at them like a caged animal, I began to speak. When I got to the first abortion, a tall Mexican cowboy in his late seventies—one of my people—sporting ostrich-skin boots and a belt buckle with a rooster on it, flung his big sombrero in the air and huffed, *"Hija de su madre!"*—the Mexican equivalent of "Son of a b----!"

My first spiritual tomato had just been hurled at me. I proceeded in a daze. When I got to the second abortion, the man's fist flew angrily through the air. With his cowboy boots stomping loudly on the floor and his sombrero shaking violently back and forth, almost flying right off his head, he hollered it again: *"Hija de su madre!"*

I could feel the crowd eating me with their eyes. I was terrified to continue. "What am I doing up here?" "Why am I doing this to myself?" My voice began to quiver, but I managed to say: "And then I had a third abortion . . ." Gesticulating wildly, the old cowboy looked at his neighbor, nudged him hard, and squawked, *"Hija de* toda *su madre!"* loosely translated, "Daughter of a mucho bitch!"

After that, my mind went blank and I lost my train of thought. My speech turned into stuttering, and I don't remember what I said or how I finished. Feeling cheap and degraded, I walked off the stage and sunk low in my seat. There was no applause. One could have heard a bug crawl.

Glancing over at Sarah, I searched for an assuaging look or comment. I would have settled for "Don't worry. You did a pretty good job." But her big blue eyes shot me a startled look of pity, and she tapped me on my left shoulder and whispered, "It's okay, Patricia. It's okay. It's a very hard crowd," which made me feel even worse.

After the loudest silence I'd ever heard, a woman began to walk forward from the back of the church with a Bible in her hand. *Click, click, click* went the sound of her heels. Passing through invisible waves of tension, she reached the podium and took the microphone. "The Lord gave me a word for everyone here: Matthew, chapter seven, verses one and two: 'Stop judging, that you may not be judged. For as you judge, so will you be judged, and the measure with which you measure will be measured out to you.'" A small drop of consolation reached my battered ego, but I was sorely tempted to call it quits that day and never accept a speaking engagement again.

As Divine Mercy Sunday approached, Satan's helpers came back to visit me more than once. During my presentations and in my conversations with people, I couldn't help but encourage men and women who had been part of an abortion to receive the graces of Divine Mercy Sunday. With the force of love and persuasive conviction, I brought many people to the Sacrament of Reconciliation and Mass on that special day, including families who hadn't confessed in years, and friends who'd never known what Confession truly is.

Satan's most vicious assault occurred the following Monday. That night, my room suddenly grew cold. As I was lying on my back about to fall asleep, a familiar, eerie presence of fear entered the room. But the fear didn't enter me. In the corner appeared an ominous, six-foot-tall being. My spirit knew who the shadowy figure was. Satan had sent himself this time, so frustrated was he that the little demons he'd been dispatching hadn't bothered me as much as he would have liked.

In a split second, Satan leapt on top of me and shoved his fingers down my throat. I felt my body press into the mattress, and at that moment was given the knowledge that he was infuriated because I had taught so many people about the Divine Mercy promises. Too many people had been forgiven all their sins. Completely contrary to the Holy Spirit, Who is forever self-controlled, the devil was moved and compelled by uncontrollable bursts of rage.

I couldn't breathe and truly thought that I would not survive. In my mind, I called out, "God why are you permitting this!" But, I reassured myself, at least I would make it to heaven, even if I had to go to purgatory, for I knew I was in a state of grace and had just accomplished something very good. Unafraid of losing my life, I reached for my crucifix in order to have Jesus close as I prepared to die.

At that moment, St. Michael the Archangel appeared next to Satan with the force and power of a mighty wind. He was tall and majestic, his wings hitting the ceiling. I could see his vest, skirt, and sandals, and the sword in his scabbard. Overpowering the devil in size and sheer presence, he grabbed Satan's hands with great strength, took them off of my neck, and told him in a stern and thunderous voice, "You will not touch her any further."

I heaved and gasped for breath, trying to calm the adrenaline shooting through my system. Still panting, I reached for the phone and called Sarah's friend Jordan in San Francisco, who had since become my friend as well. "Please pray for me, Jordan! I'm getting strong attacks from the devil at night—one after another, and I don't understand why this keeps happening to me."

"Hallelujah—praise the Lord!" he said. "I would be more concerned if you *weren't* getting attacked."

I didn't expect that response at all. "But why?"

"Because this means that your speaking and your actions are doing something very effective for God's Kingdom. You are in the company of the saints, many of whom were attacked in the very same way—like St. Faustina." (7)

I realized he was right. Until then, I had never thought of the spiritual attacks as being in any way good, and his words completely changed my way of coping with them. Instead of praying that they would cease, I accepted them as part of God's inscrutable plan, even as a backhanded compliment.

> The word of the LORD came to me thus:
> Before I formed you in the womb I knew you,
> before you were born I dedicated you,
> a prophet to the nations I appointed you.
> "Ah, Lord GOD!" I said,
> "I know not how to speak; I am too young."
> But the LORD answered me,
> Say not, "I am too young."
> To whomever I send you, you shall go;
> whatever I command you, you shall speak.
> Have no fear before them,
> because I am with you to deliver you, says the LORD.
> Then the LORD extended his hand and touched my mouth,
> saying,
> See, I place my words in your mouth!
> This day I set you over nations and over kingdoms,
> To root up and to tear down, to destroy and to demolish,
> to build and to plant.
> –Jeremiah 1:4–10

Fact: A fictitious biomedical research company, called The Center for Medical Progress (CMP), was created by David Daleiden and other anti-abortion activists in order to expose to the masses a horror that some already knew to be true: Planned Parenthood has been illegally harvesting the body parts of babies in order to sell them for profit—sometimes going as far as to remove a baby's brain through its face when its heart was still beating. (1) On July 14, 2015, CMP

released to the public the first of many undercover videos in which workers at Planned Parenthood and from organizations buying the human parts were caught on tape, indicting themselves. The videos can be viewed on the following website:
http://www.centerformedicalprogress.org/cmp/investigative-footage/

One of the fastest growing markets for the sale of fetal tissues, parts, and organs is cosmeceuticals—the unholy marriage between pharmaceuticals and cosmetics. Seeking to profit, some biotech companies, mostly in the United States, have turned to developing and making miracle claims for these beauty products, none of which have been evaluated by the FDA or have any proven efficacy. (2)

Cannibalism is also occurring in connection with abortion. In May of 2012, it was reported in newspapers and on television stations across the world, that officials in South Korea were intercepting thousands of capsules filled with finely ground human baby flesh. In parts of Asia, the powder is touted as a stamina enhancer and medical cure-all. This grim trade is being run from China, where thirteen million abortions are performed each year. Medical staff are selling tiny human corpses, which are ground into capsules along with herbs to disguise the true ingredients from health investigators and customs officers. Tests carried out on the pills, intercepted by officials in South Korea, confirmed that they were made up of 99.7 percent human remains. The tests also successfully established the genders of the babies used. (3)

CHAPTER FIFTEEN

Across the Airwaves

BEFORE LONG, I was flying across the country at Valerie's invitation to a Rachel's Vineyard leadership conference in Pennsylvania. I was there to learn how to help lead a new Rachel's Vineyard retreat in Spanish. At least, that's why I thought I was there.

During one of the breaks between presentations, I turned around and recognized Fr. Victor Salomon, a jolly, round Hispanic priest, with a smile that could warm a thousand hearts. "Oh, wow! That's the priest on EWTN in Mexico!" I had often watched his show *Defendiendo La Vida* (Defending Life). *"Es verdaderamente una bolita de amor"* ("He truly is a little ball of love") I remarked to myself. Without hesitating, I ran up to him and said, "You are Fr. Victor!"

His smile broadened even farther, if that were possible.

"Yes," he said. *"Tú hablas Español."*

"Sí." I gave him a big hug. We started talking and became instant friends. Over the course of the four-day conference, I learned that, in addition to having a television and radio show, he was the spiritual director of the international Latino branch of Rachel's Vineyard. Inspired, I asked if he would be my spiritual mentor. In spite of his busy schedule, he said yes. I also struck up an acquaintanceship with Fr. Frank Pavone, the national director of Priests for Life and pastoral director of Rachel's Vineyard. I had been wandering around lost, looking for one of the seminars, and he walked forward to help me. For the remainder of the conference, these two formidable priests and I ended up chatting at meals, and their friendly manner put me completely at ease.

During a break on the second day of the conference while sitting next to Fr. Victor, I ended up sharing my story with him. When I finally finished, he looked at me as if in shock. "We have to get you on my show," he stated emphatically. "After dinner, we're putting you on TV."

"What? After dinner tonight?" I gulped.

"Sí."

"Oh, no, I'm not ready," I protested. And I wasn't. My body dysmorphia kicked in immediately, and I got extremely nervous. I wanted to back out—but God's will would have it otherwise. Not only did I end up telling my story extemporaneously in Spanish for *Defendiendo La Vida*, but the news of the impact of my testimony spread, and Janet Morana, assistant to Fr. Pavone, got word of it. As part of my dying-to-self marathon, I ended up sharing my story again in English for the *Silent No More* show.

The filming went well enough, but I was shell-shocked throughout, telling my story without fully embodying it and unconsciously leaving out some of the more embarrassing details. I knew in my heart that the Lord wanted me to *preach* my testimony, not merely speak it. He wanted me to be confident, to be bold, to lay myself bare without fear.

To be able to do this, God knew I would have to die to a sin that I didn't even know was one—the sin of people-pleasing. *"Am I now currying favor with human beings or God? Or am I seeking to please people? If I were still trying to please people, I would not be a slave of Christ." (Galatians 1:10)* Caring what others thought of me and seeking to earn their approval was a serious sin that God would no longer tolerate in me, and He planned to use the job He had given me to strike a mighty blow.

His tool in hand was my supervisor's assistant at my job, who singled me out as her favorite torture toy. Every day, she made her dislike of me known. If I asked her to hand me an object, it came flying my way. When I asked a question, disdain curled her upper lip. Whenever I made a mistake, she waited for others to come around so she could scold me publicly.

Every day, I wanted to cry. Every day, I wanted to quit. Crumbling into apologies for my mistakes, I'd then slip into the nearest closet or side room to hide my tears. At times I would come home from work, stand directly in front of my image of the Sacred Heart, and exclaim, "Why did You give me this stupid job? Don't You know how depressed I am? Look at me!" I hoped that Jesus would feel guilty and get the point. But I fought the temptation to leave because I knew God had some unknown reason for me being there.

When people had mistreated me in the past, I'd brushed the dirt off my feet and declared, "I don't need this, and I won't put up with it. I'm outa here!" But my heart was beginning to understand the sin behind my cut-and-run, need-to-be-liked-and-praised-wherever-I-went approach. There was no humility in it. Waiting on God for discernment, I said, "Lord, I'll stick it out for six months, and then I'm gonna leave . . ." "Okay, Lord, another month, and then I'm gonna leave . . ." But I never heard back from Him.

Time passed and I survived. Help came from my friends the saints. I was inspired by St. Therese of Lisieux, a Carmelite nun and Doctor of the Church, when I read in her *Diary of a Soul* how she offered up her pain to God when mistreated by her Sisters. St. Josemaría Escrivá de Balaguer, founder of Opus Dei, taught me through his book *The Way* how sanctification could be nurtured in the day-to-day struggles and tasks of work. I also studied the life and words of St. Mother Teresa of Calcutta, who said, "If you are humble, nothing will touch you, neither praise nor disgrace, because you know what you are."

With this newfound awareness, I no longer instantly assumed that my supervisor's assistant's abuse meant that there was something wrong with me. I also made good use of my suffering and began to offer up every mistake, every embarrassment, every excoriation—especially her displays of bombastic yelling—for the souls in purgatory, for an end to abortion, and for the salvation of her soul. Her cruelty and my work duties became a chisel in God's hands to strengthen and sanctify me.

Over time, my timidity turned into boldness, and I even complained to the head manager about the assistant's rude manner. But I knew that the real solution lay in my own attitude. I couldn't change this woman, and there was nothing I could do to please her. "Let her be miserable," I thought. "Let her get mad!" Her emotions were out of my control. "And who cares what she thinks or feels about me!" Finally, I was loosed from the chains of people-pleasing, which had shackled me for a lifetime. A sinful bondage to the opinions of others, like an iron lock, broke within me, and its chains fell away.

I literally felt a cracking followed by a release in my soul. And an old memory surfaced of the young African American woman who was driving the dilapidated car and singing a love song to Jesus at the top of her lungs. I realized that I was experiencing now what she must have felt! For the very first time, I was riding an exhilarating wave of true freedom in Christ in which the opinions of others mean little to nothing, because the opinion of Christ is everything.

> But as we were judged worthy by God to be entrusted with the gospel, that is how we speak, not as trying to please human beings, but rather God, who judges our hearts.

—1 Thessalonians 2:4

Toward the end of my thirty-second year, I was invited to speak on a show called *Cara a Cara* (Face to Face), a highly rated Spanish program aired in several nations by EWTN. By then, my hesitant public speaking had flowered into passionate preaching. God had orchestrated my trial-by-fire in the crucible of work. Since I had learned not to care much what someone who knew me thought of me, it had become all the easier to shrug off the opinions of mere strangers. Now at age thirty-three, I was bold, focused, and unafraid to share my testimony, even in all its gruesome details.

EWTN flew me out to their headquarters in Irondale, Alabama, where Mother Angelica had started the station in a garage in 1981. EWTN was now available in over 150 million homes in more than 140 countries. Good thing I didn't know those numbers when I arrived. My spirit felt at peace, and as I began walking the grounds, I remembered that my soul knew long ago that I would not only be on EWTN but also filmed at the EWTN headquarters. God's dream, not mine, was coming true. A dream of my own, though, was to pray in the chapel where daily Mass was filmed; and come the morning of my interview, I found myself participating in Mass on the other side of the cameras. The reality of sitting physically on a wooden pew in the beautiful chapel decorated with angels and brilliant lights, tickled my spirit. All my silly questions were answered: Was the chapel really as small as it looked? Yes. Where were the cameras? Nestled in the side walls. Who were the people attending? The EWTN crew, visitors, and people from the surrounding neighborhood.

Then it came time for the filming. Alejandro Bermúdez, the host who would interview me, was a brilliant man: a well-known journalist; director of ACI-Prensa, the largest Catholic news agency in Spanish; executive director for Catholic News Agency; host of several Spanish shows on EWTN; guest commentator on religious issues for the New York Times; translator for Cardinal Jorge Bergoglio's (Pope Francis's) book *On Heaven and Earth*; and more. His show, *Cara a Cara*, was known for its intellectual excellence and theologically astute guests—bishops, cardinals, and the like. I was its first nobody—some chick from Petaluma.

Before filming, Mr. Bermúdez and the show's producer said to me, "This is the first time we're not going to insert a commercial. There will be no breaks. Your story is so powerful that we don't want to stop the camera from rolling."

My nerves kicked in. "No breaks for an hour? God help me." Even though I'd become much more confident as a speaker, doing this program meant a whole other level of exposure, and worries about how I would look and sound spun around in my head: "A ton of Spanish speakers watch this show, and my Spanish isn't 100 percent . . . I'm going to look ten pounds heavier on TV . . . Worst of all, my dad is going to see this one day." But another part of me said, "No, you're doing this for the unborn. You're doing this to save lives. You're doing this for those who have no voice, for your children in heaven, for those men and women who have suffered through abortion." That voice was winning. To press forward, I literally had to push my emotions of fear into numbness, using the mantra, "I just need to get through this interview. I just need to get through this interview . . ."

Before the camera rolled, I started joking to ease my nerves, "You'd better not ask me any hard questions."

Mr. Bermúdez smiled. I found him to be the one of the sweetest men I had met. "Oh, don't worry," he responded gently. "If you mess up, I'll help you. I'll redirect you. You'll be just fine." He made me feel so comfortable that when the show started, I acted like I was having a conversation between only the two of us. At first, I stuttered a couple of times, but the interview got better and better as Mr. Bermudez encouraged me to keep going. I spoke from the heart. I spoke with passion. I talked about the gruesome details of my testimony: the drug addiction, the abortions, the body parts at Planned Parenthood—everything.

When I heard the word "Cut!" the producer ran out from the back and hugged me, saying, "That was wonderful!" Mr. Bermúdez reached over to hug me as well.

"You'd better edit that!" I half-joked.

"No! This is the first show where we're not going to edit anything. It's real. It's original. You were just great."

"Don't you see?" said the producer. "Usually we interview people who have statistics or opinions. But you're saying something that is truth. Nobody can change what happened. Your past isn't simply your opinion.

It is something real, and nobody can take that away. Nobody can change what happened. Don't you see that you have a gem? Do you understand how valuable this is? This is a strong weapon you have in your hands." Feeling consoled and fortified, I heaved a sigh of relief.

Later that day, while eating in the EWTN dining area, I saw Johnnette Benkovic walk in. Her program *Women of Grace* was, in my estimation, one of the best on EWTN—my favorite of the shows I'd watched with my mom. "Oh, you're Patricia," Ms. Benkovic said to me. "You're going to be on my show tomorrow."

Star struck and honored, I somehow managed to respond graciously, all the while thinking, "Holy cow! You're working overtime, God." I would be interviewed alongside Fr. Ben Cameron, who founded the Confraternity of Our Lady of Mercy (1), a prayer ministry for the sanctification of post-abortive men and women.

Before the filming, Ms. Benkovic leaned over to say, "Be careful with your words, and do your best not to mess up. This is a live show, and there will be over one hundred million people watching it." Hearing that didn't help my jitters; but the program, while more subdued than *Cara a Cara* and with much less speaking time, went well, and Ms. Benkovic's eyes often filled with tears.

A couple of months after the filming at EWTN, as I was walking into a restaurant with a girlfriend, I stopped in my tracks and said, "I think the *Cara a Cara* interview is launching sometime this week." As soon as those words flew out of my mouth, my phone rang, and I picked up. It was Julian.

"Hello?"

"*Mentirosa!* (Liar!) I saw you on *Cara a Cara* last night!"

That man never watched EWTN, and that was the first show he saw when he did. He bristled and then exploded. "I cannot believe you. You liar! You piece of shit! I can't believe you never told me any of that. Thank God you left me."

I retorted, "You know, you don't need to speak to me that way. You would have never accepted who I am. That's why I never told you. You would have reacted in just this way. I forgive you for insulting me. God bless you." And I hung up in tears.

Most everyone in Valle de Juárez had probably seen the *Cara a Cara* interview—towns and cities across the globe had seen it. "Now the whole world knows," I thought. "I will always be labeled as the woman who killed her three children." I had always wanted to be known as someone special, and now I was the poster girl for abortion.

Later that day, I remembered my great-grandfather who shed his blood. He gave up everything, even his own life, for the sake of religious freedom, for truth. The people-pleaser in me, the girl who always wanted to be loved, admired, desired, and accepted, was gasping for her last breath. She would have to die once and for all. "Well, maybe no man will ever want to be with someone like me," I lamented, curling up on the couch in tears. "I'm dying for the sake of the unborn. I'm even giving up being merely acceptable in the eyes of men. This is my martyrdom."

That night, my friend Daniel, a Hispanic speaker and singer who is endowed with the gifts of healing and evangelization, called me from his home in Guatemala. "Patricia," he said, "I never watch EWTN. You know I'm always preaching at night. But I happened to turn on the television, and there you were."

"Oh, great," I responded, thinking to myself, "here goes another one—round two."

"Why didn't you ever tell me this about you?"

"Because it's hard for me. It's hard to tell people I care about, and it's so embarrassing."

"I want to tell you," he said, "that you are even more esteemed in my eyes now. I think you're the most courageous woman I have ever met. I support everything you do. You are God's beloved, and now I admire you more than ever."

Daniel is a holy man. When he sings, people are slain in the Spirit at the sound of his voice. These words from him, from a well-respected, humble servant of the Lord, were healing something in me. I put him on mute and began to sob profusely. His compliments didn't stop, and neither did my tears. Finally unmuting for a moment, I managed to say, "Thank you so much. That means a lot."

A couple of months later, Julian called me to say he was really sorry. I appreciated his apology, but by then I had realized the difference between the eyes of a man of the world and the eyes of a man of God.

> Amen, amen, I say to you, unless a grain of wheat falls to the ground and dies, it remains just a grain of wheat; but if it dies, it produces much fruit.
> –John 12:24

Fact: Uncovering the past of Planned Parenthood reveals an unsavory history. Margaret Sanger, the founder of the abortion provider, was a known racist and eugenicist. In 1921, she stated, "We do not want word to go out that we want to exterminate the Negro population, if it ever occurs to any of their more rebellious members." (*Woman's Body, Woman's Right: A Social History of Birth Control in America*, by Linda Gordon). Referring to African Americans, immigrants, and poor people, in her book *Pivot of Civilization,* she spoke of "human weeds," "reckless breeders," "spawning . . . human beings who never should have been born." "The most merciful thing that a family does to one of its infant members is to kill it." (1)

Today, Planned Parenthood carried forward Mrs. Sanger's sordid legacy by strategically placing the majority of its surgical abortion facilities in locations that target black and Hispanic Americans for abortion. (2) Before Roe *v.* Wade, which legalized abortion and allowed the proliferation of abortion clinics in minority neighborhoods, whites were five times more likely than African Americans to seek out an abortion. (3) Nowadays, according to the Alan Guttmacher Institute, African Americans are five times as likely to obtain an abortion than whites are.

CHAPTER SIXTEEN

The Heart of Mercy

WORD WENT AROUND IN MY home parish that a pilgrimage was being organized to the Divine Mercy Shrine in Poland where St. Faustina Kowalska had received her visions of Jesus. My interest was piqued. When I learned that the pilgrims would be there on Divine Mercy Sunday, the day that the sins of one's entire life and the punishment due for them could be washed away in God's mercy, I simply had to go. For an entire year, I didn't buy a single unnecessary item for myself, sacrificed comforts, even to the point of skipping meals. My joy-filled reward came when I boarded a plane headed for Kraków with my friend, Norma. God had shown me such an abundance of mercy in my life, and now He was taking me to the place where His twentieth-century message of mercy began. I felt giddy.

The man leading our group was an adorable Polish priest in his late twenties who spoke Spanish perfectly, was deeply spiritual, and couldn't help but giggle at his own jokes. Our destination city was near Fr. Kotas's farm-town home. During an orientation meeting a couple of days before we flew off, he told all the pilgrims that he knew the area well: "Take thin sweaters and light jackets. We're going to have great weather. The temperature will be around sixty to seventy degrees." When we landed in Kraków, it was snowing. Fr. Kotas found this hilarious.

I could scarcely believe I was across the world in that faraway place I had longed to see, wandering through a wintry landscape on point B of my Google map. Each morning, I felt like I was waking up to a beautiful dream. Our third day in Kraków was Divine Mercy Sunday, one of the best days of my life. We visited the Shrine of the Divine Mercy, a small brick chapel where Jesus had appeared and spoken to St. Faustina, initiating his worldwide message of mercy. This was also where the saint had been laid to rest in a tomb, and where the miraculous image of the Merciful Jesus still hangs—by request of Jesus Himself: "I desire that this image be venerated, first in your chapel, and [then] throughout the world"

(*Diary* #47). "By means of this image, I shall grant many graces to souls." (*Diary* # 742). (1)

That day, only sixty thousand people wanted to pay the same visit. A line had formed from here to eternity in order to enter the shrine. Happily, I took my place with Norma and Fr. Kotas, feeling like I'd won the lottery. Through flakes of falling snow, I noticed a small nun standing outside the shrine's doors. She was holding a microphone in one hand and *The Diary of St. Faustina* in the other, and speaking in a gentle voice in Polish. "Father," I nudged him, "is she reading the *Diary*? What is she saying?"

"No, she's not reading. She's talking about what her congregation, the Sisters of Our Lady of Mercy, used to do—and still do. They go out into the night to find and pick up troubled women and girls living on the streets—prostitutes, drug addicts, drunkards, the homeless, the abused—and bring them back to the convent to help them. St. Faustina was specifically called and assigned to do this work." The fact that these nuns risked their safety to walk out into the night to roam the slums impressed me profoundly.

Finally, we arrived at the chapel entrance. Because of the large crowd of pilgrims, we would have only seconds to kneel before the inspired painting. When my turn came, as soon as I dropped to my knees and looked up I felt as though I were kneeling before the Lord Himself. I couldn't believe I was in front of *the* image. To see the very picture that St. Faustina's eyes saw, to pray in the very chapel where Jesus spoke to her, to know that I was passing through a place of profound sanctity that shook the foundations of the world—I could not absorb it all.

I backed away from the image, not wanting to keep it out of my sight. Then one of the nuns extended toward me an exposed relic of St. Faustina, which I venerated with a kiss. Filled with graces that the Lord had promised would be given through the veneration of His image, I walked away from the crowds and leaned against one of the chapel's four walls. All of a sudden, I heard a woman's voice speak to me from within. Without knowing how, I knew exactly who it was. The voice said in English: "When you were troubled and on the streets, when Bonnie came and hugged you, I was there. I went out to get you."

St. Faustina! She had gone out into the streets, as she did when she was alive, and rescued me, a troubled girl! She had known me years before I ever knew her, and she had prayed to God for that moment of divine mercy to come true for me. I could hardly believe that a saint in heaven had just spoken to me. No wonder I had been so attracted to her, to Divine Mercy, and to this place. God had brought us together long ago.

> Merciful and gracious is the LORD,
> slow to anger, abounding in mercy.
> He will not always accuse,
> and nurses no lasting anger;
> He has not dealt with us as our sins merit,
> nor requited us as our wrongs deserve.
> For as the heavens tower over the earth,
> so his mercy towers over those who fear him.
> As far as the east is from the west,
> so far has he removed our sins from us.
> As a father has compassion on his children,
> so the LORD has compassion on those who fear him.
> –Psalm 103:8–13

The next day, our tour group piled into a bus—a loud, rowdy entourage of bad singers with a priest leader who couldn't help but grab the microphone to tell jokes.

"Knock, knock."

"Who's there?" we answered back.

"Polish burglar." Fr. Kotas chuckled at his own joke, and we gave him two giggles and a groan. Undeterred, he forged on: "A Polish man goes to the eye doctor. The bottom line of the eye chart has the letters: C Z Y N Q S T A S Z. The optometrist asks, 'Can you read this?'"

"'Read it?' the man replies, 'I know the guy.'"

That one had us rolling in the bus aisles. Between jokes, Fr. Kotas shared stories of faith and history from his beloved home country. As we approached the city of Częstochowa in central Poland, his playful demeanor changed to a tone of joyful reverence and Polish pride. "Tomorrow," he said, "we are going to visit Jasna Góra monastery, which holds Poland's prized possession, an image of Our Lady holding the Christ

Child. Legend has it that St. Luke, the Evangelist, painted this portrait of the Virgin on the cedar wood table where the holy family ate their meals. This icon of Our Lady of Częstochowa is associated with many miracles, usually big ones." Fr. Kotas clearly loved Our Lady and her image and shared some of its history with us:

"Our Lady of Częstochowa is one of very few Black Madonnas in the world. She is likely black from the smoke of candles that lit her over the centuries. St. Helena, when she was searching for the True Cross in Jerusalem, supposedly discovered the icon in 326 AD and gave it to her son, the emperor Constantine, who had a shrine built for it in Constantinople, where it stayed for five hundred years. The image was displayed during a battle, and it is claimed to have saved the city from attacking Saracens.

"After that, the picture is said to have ended up in Russia for nearly six hundred years in an area that became part of Poland. In 1382, it was hanging in the castle of the Polish prince, St. Ladislaus, when an arrow from an invading Tartar struck Our Lady's image, leaving a scar on her neck. Then, for the next six hundred years, it rested peacefully in the monastery of the Polish Pauline Fathers in Jasna Góra near Częstochowa, where our very bus is headed.

"But our Black Madonna ended up in trouble again there too. In 1430, Hussites sacked the Jasna Góra monastery. When a raider slashed the image with his sword, trying to get Our Lady's jewels and gold, he put two deep gashes into her right cheek. While preparing to strike the image a third time, the invader fell to the ground and twisted in terrible agony until he died. Then the other raiders fled, thinking that God might strike them dead, too. Now get this—the two slashes on Our Lady's cheek, along with the gash on her throat, have always reappeared, even after several attempts at restoration. Over time, people have come to understand that this was a supernatural occurrence. In Poland, we now believe that it is God's will that her scars remain.

Intrigued by the history of this sacred image, I couldn't wait to see "her" and began daydreaming of what she would look like "in person."

We arrived at our destination that evening and carried our bags into a convent across the street from the Basilica National Shrine of Our Lady of Częstochowa, where we would be staying. After we settled into our rooms, the Sisters of the Holy Family, six gracious nuns who lived there and served pilgrims, had a dinner prepared for us. I seated myself at the dinner table next to Fr. Kotas, whose female counterpart stood on the other side of him—an elderly giggling nun, as deep, wise, and silly as he was. The two of them had clearly met before. As I was marveling at the perpetual good cheer on her extraordinarily cute face, she looked over at me, wide-eyed, and pointed in my direction. Taking two steps back, she began to speak with serious authority, and her tone of voice changed. The room fell silent. Everyone was aware that she was saying something important, although none of us pilgrims could understand her.

When she finished speaking, Fr. Kotas turned to me and said, "Sister Maria said that she feels God's presence upon you very powerfully—that you are very special to God. God has a strong hold on you and will take you very far, all in God's time. But sacrifices are required of you. If you accept these sacrifices for God, you will go far. She also said that she will be praying for you in front of the image of Our Lady of Częstochowa. She will entrust you to her." At these words, the nun put her hand over her heart in a gesture of prayer. Our eyes met, and the moment seemed to drop outside of time and through any barriers of culture or language.

Breaking the holy tension in the room, Fr. Kotas stood up and said, "Tomorrow, we will wake up early and go to "the Unveiling." He then shared with us how this Polish religious custom, which pulsates as the spiritual heart of the nation, occurs in the early hour of five a.m., when the silver screen that covers the image of Our Lady of Częstochowa behind its frame is slowly and ceremoniously lifted.

Norma and I woke up before dawn the next day. We entered the Jasna Góra monastery and, filled with awe, we walked below the stunningly ornate, high-vaulted ceilings toward the gothic chapel of the Black Madonna. Approaching the floor-to-ceiling, arched iron gate that separates the inner sanctuary from the rest of the chapel, we sat down in a pew closest to the Madonna. I remembered how I once read that St. Faustina, when she visited Częstochowa, would sit for six hours in front of the sacred image and say, "This is truly my Mother."

Precisely at five o'clock, a loud drum roll began, and everyone present fell to their knees. As the drums continued to boom and the majestic fanfare of live trumpets sounded a royal melody of hope and promise, proper to a queen's crowning, the silver veil over the sacred image of Our Lady of Częstochowa slowly lifted. For a moment, I felt like a true visionary about to witness her Queen Mother in heaven, stunning and radiant. When the image of Our Lady holding the Christ Child was finally exposed, the face that gazed intently back at me was a visage of Mary unlike one I'd ever seen. Her expression was one of suffering. She looked wounded and tired, as if from a fierce battle. The scars on her cheek and neck revealed that something terrible must have happened to her, and yet she didn't seem to be thinking of herself. The way she held her Son in her left arm and gestured toward Him with her right hand showed me that, even though she was wounded, she was thinking of and protecting her Son. Staring intently at her, I felt that she was doing the same for me.

Looking up at Mary, so sad and scarred, I felt the center of my chest starting to ache, and I spontaneously gave to her my family, my brokenness, my wounds. I gave her everything. This painful ache within me began to stir—a sensation akin to water in a dark, hidden well far beneath the earth, churned into chaotic waves by falling rocks. She was calling out to me. The waves in my heart were growing larger and larger, overflowing into my eyes, which were filling rapidly with tears.

Then the gates of pain within me flung open. I began to weep uncontrollably. A profound sorrow, hidden for years underneath drugs, behind boyfriends, within my desire to be noticed and pretty and loved, gushed forth in deep sobs. Although the agony being released from my spirit caught me by surprise, I knew the meaning of every tear. Each drop splashing on the stone floor was a broken piece of my shattered family.

I cried for almost an hour. Never before had I grieved over my family in this way. The process was wrenching, and to help me through it, Mary came. I felt her holding and protecting me in the gentle curve of her arms, as she was doing for the Child Jesus.

For the remainder of our time in Częstochowa, I longed to be with the Black Madonna every moment I possibly could. Each time I approached her image, I felt as though I were discovering my Mother for the first time. Her gentle spirit reached out to soothe mine, like the touch of a doting mother wrapping her crying baby in a soft blanket. Norma had to literally pry me away from her. I never wanted to leave. All I wanted to do was sit and be with my Mom.

My mind couldn't comprehend why I was sensing such a deep connection with an icon from across the world. Only later did I find out why. Our Lady of Częstochowa is the patron saint of post-abortive women and of anyone with childhood wounds and scars.

> Standing by the cross of Jesus were his mother and his mother's sister, Mary the wife of Clopas, and Mary of Magdala. When Jesus saw his mother and the disciple there whom he loved, he said to his mother, "Woman, behold,

> your son." Then he said to the disciple, "Behold, your mother." And from that hour the disciple took her into his home.
> –John 19:25–27

With my heart still in Częstochowa, we boarded our tour bus again. It was headed for Auschwitz, the infamous Nazi concentration camp. This was the only bus ride on our tour led by a serious Fr. Kotas. With the specter of the Holocaust looming in our minds, the pilgrims scarcely spoke to one another on the three-hour trip. In one of the most brutal wars of the 20th century, millions of Jews, Catholics, and Protestants, among others, were exterminated. (2)

"Patricia," Fr. Kotas whispered to me in Spanish so others couldn't understand, "tell your story to the pilgrims."

"Father, I'm not gonna do that! It's way too embarrassing. No, thank you."

A half hour later, Fr. Kotas asked again, "*Pssst.* Patricia, I really think you should give your testimony. It is so powerful."

"Father, I really think I shouldn't. No way."

An hour passed.

"*Ola*, Patricia," he whispered, "guess who. Please, please, share your testimony."

"Father, think about what you're asking me. Think about how cheesy and awkward this is. You want me to speak into a microphone—on a tour bus—about my three abortions. Who on earth would want to do that? Who on earth would want someone to do that? And who on earth would want someone to want to do that?"

He chuckled. Then, changing back to a serious whisper, he said, "I know of a couple Catholics on this pilgrimage who are all for abortion. They don't think it's a big deal. I need you to talk about it so that they can hear the truth." Feeling uneasy and unwilling, I looked at him with skepticism and mistrust and mustered my most respectful sneer. Fr. Kotas begged me one last time: "Please, Patricia? There is a young man on this bus who has come on this pilgrimage as my guest because he is an alcoholic. He's gotten himself into a lot of trouble, and I wanted to take him away from his troubles for a while. I believe this young man needs to hear what you have to say. I want to help him so that he might have hope."

I knew immediately which young man it was. Fr. Kotas had found my weak spot. For the benefit of that young man, I walked forward, took a front seat next to the driver, and grabbed the microphone. Staring off into the windy road ahead, I began to speak—telling every good, bad, and ugly detail of my story to the "captive" audience behind me.

When I finished, the bus continued forward in a deafening silence. Not a word. When I got up to go back to my seat, I heard nothing . . . nothing but the young man's crying.

When we arrived, the pilgrims with whom I had prayed and laughed throughout the trip skirted by me in a file of awkward, silent tension—all except the young man. With eyes red from crying, he came directly up to me and said, "I was actually mad that I was forced to go to Auschwitz on this trip. I'm detoxing from alcohol, I'm away from my wife and kids, and I certainly didn't want to hear your story, so I put on my headphones to block you out. But through the music, I could still hear your voice, and I began to relate to everything you were saying. Out of curiosity, I took off my headphones, and then suddenly I couldn't stop crying, and I couldn't bring myself to put my headphones back on. I really want to thank you, because your story has given me hope." We hugged, and I said a prayer aloud for him. Then I uttered a silent prayer of thanksgiving for the opportunity to be God's instrument.

Turning around, I joined Norma who stood underneath a wrought-iron arched sign, which read in German, *"Arbeit Macht Frei"* ("Work Will Make You Free"). All those in this camp were told that everything taken away upon their arrival would be returned to them: their freedom, their possessions, their family—plus an easier life than the one they'd known, if they simply worked hard. The entrance to the place of their death began with a lie.

As we wandered, speechless, within the electrified barbed-wire fences, we visited a gas chamber, a crematory, barracks, the cells used for different kinds of torturous deaths, and the platform where prisoners were sorted after coming off the train and sent either directly to work or to the gas chambers. Among the sights of horror, three displays spoke to me most loudly. The first consisted of a giant pile of thin, tangled strands behind which hung a jacket and a blanket. Leaning forward to look closely, I noticed that the jacket and the blanket were woven out of human hair.

They were used to keep the German soldiers warm. With a turning stomach and watery eyes, I walked down a long hallway with walls covered in floor-to-ceiling glass cases of baby clothes. It struck me that each precious child who once wore these clothes had been brutally killed, perhaps shot, or starved, or picked up by a soldier and thrown into a gas chamber. "But how?" I wondered. "How could the SS men in the Nazi party have simply grabbed a child and killed him? How did they do that without any love or mercy or compassion in their hearts? None!"

Toward the end of the tour, we came to the cell where Maximilian Kolbe, "the saint of Auschwitz," was held and left to starve to death. Saint Kolbe was a Polish Franciscan priest who founded a worldwide Catholic evangelization movement in 1917 called *Militia Immaculatae* ("the Army of the Immaculate One"—Mary). He was posthumously declared by the Church a patron saint of the pro-life movement. When Maximilian was only twelve, the Virgin Mary came to him holding two crowns, one white, the other red. She asked if he were willing to accept either of them. The white one meant that he would persevere in purity, and the red meant that he would become a martyr. He told her that he would accept them both.

As I stared into the saint's small chamber, cell #18, in which a Paschal candle flickered on top of a small altar, our female tour guide shared stories of Father Kolbe's suffering and sacrifice. In the camp, when others had scrambled for their meager portion of daily bread or soup, Fr. Kolbe stood aside to let others eat first. Frequently, there was none left for him. After being severely beaten and left for dead, he made sure to hear Confessions in the infirmary, looking for ways to offer hope and healing. He gave his fatherly love to all. Auschwitz survivors who had met Fr. Kolbe said that he never seemed to think of himself and never tired of speaking about God's infinite goodness. He was once asked whether such self-abnegation made sense in a place of animalistic survival, and he answered, "Every man has an aim in life. For most men it is to return home to their wives and families, or to their mothers. For my part, I give my life for the good of all men."

Fr. Kolbe was the only person in any of the German concentration camps who offered to die in place of someone else. When one of the prisoners assigned to his barrack escaped, ten people from that section were randomly marked for death by starvation as punishment. Among the chosen was a young Polish man, a sergeant named Franciszek Gajowniczek, who cried out, "Oh, my poor wife, my poor children. I shall never see them again!" That is when Fr. Kolbe offered his life for this man he didn't know.

Transferred along with the other nine unfortunates into a small cell, Fr. Kolbe led the inmates in prayer and song, praising God for His goodness. One by one, they collapsed dead on the stone floor until none but him was left alive. Whenever the SS guards stopped by the cell, Fr. Kolbe would smile at them with the love of Christ. "Don't look at me," they would say to him in return. After more than two weeks without food and water, Fr. Kolbe was still alive, so to do away with him, they injected him with a poison that traveled directly to his heart. For this last insult, he freely offered his arm. (2)

Staring into the candle flame within cell #18, I began to cry. I felt more proud than ever to be Catholic. At the same time, my soul recoiled in sadness as I pondered the brutal and senseless ending of St. Kolbe's life. To the Nazis, he was nothing more than Number 16670. But then a thought came to me, as if from outside myself, asking me the question, "Can you see how important it was that St. Maximilian Kolbe lived for as long as he did?" Yes, I could. I could see how he must have helped save countless souls through his life's witness, service, and prayers—even through the holy example that he left behind, which still lives on.

Then another insight came His life had no price. What if St. Kolbe had been killed in the womb and not in Auschwitz? Which killing would be worse?

The voice of our female tour guide interrupted my internal dialogue: "As you can see, this camp was a human killing factory." I thought of how during the Holocaust, good people knew that the extermination camps were wrong, even if they chose to be silent. But nowadays, good people cannot even *perceive* that the modern human extermination camps all around them are wrong.

At that moment, I heard within my soul the chant of millions today: "We need to fight to keep abortion safe and legal!" And behind this smokescreen, evil's hidden chant of absurdity: "You must fight for the right to kill your own children!" Holding my stomach, unable to swallow the enormity of it all, I threw myself on God's endless mercy. "Oh, the blindness in the world . . . the dark and utter blindness."

"There were people aware of what was happening," continued the guide, "but they chose to be silent."

"I will not stand back and do nothing," my heart swore. "I will not be silent . . . I will not be one of those who turns a blind eye . . . I cannot be . . ."

> Did you fail in a day of adversity,
> did your strength fall short?
> Did you fail to rescue those who were being dragged off to death,
> those tottering, those near death,
> because you said, "We didn't know about it"?
> Surely, the Searcher of hearts knows
> and will repay all according to their deeds.
> –Proverbs 24:10–12

Fact: Dr. Martin Luther King Jr., renowned leader the modern American Civil Rights Movement, preached the following words on Christmas Day of 1967:

"The next thing we must be concerned about if we are to have peace on earth and good will toward men is the nonviolent affirmation of the sacredness of all human life. Every man is somebody because he is a child of God . . . Man is more than . . . whirling electrons or a wisp of smoke . . . Man is a child of God, made in His image, and therefore must be respected as such . . . And when we truly believe in the sacredness of human personality, we won't exploit people, we won't trample over people with the iron feet of oppression, we won't kill anybody." (3)

Half of all Catholics believe that abortion should be legal in all or most cases (4), and abortion is seen in many countries—in particular the United States—as a civil right. But civil rights activists, by and large, have decried violence and killing. Somewhere, in the case of abortion, there is a disconnect.

Chapter Seventeen

Let Me Live

MANY SURPRISES—SOME WELCOME, some not—greeted me when I returned home from Poland. In my mail was an eviction notice that finally meant what it said. In two weeks, I would have to be out. I pushed it aside, choosing to face the lesser evil of my backlog of unanswered e-mails.

Word of mouth, a new website bearing my name, and the *Cara a Cara* interview on YouTube had caused my story to spread like a firestorm. (1) My in-box was filled with requests for me to speak in the United States, Colombia, and Mexico. A woman from Tijuana had written, "I do marriage preparation talks, and I show your video to all the couples before they get married."

"How random," I thought.

Another e-mail read: "Thank you so much for your *Cara a Cara* video. I work at a pregnancy center in Veracruz, and here we show your video to women who are unwavering in their desire to have an abortion. I'm writing to tell you that today, a twenty-one-year-old woman came into the clinic for the third time, determined to have her late-term abortion. Since it would cost her approximately 28,000 pesos (approximately eighteen hundred dollars), she put her house on the market to pay for it and already had a buyer. I told her, 'I understand that you're going to have an abortion, but before you do, there's a YouTube video I'd like you to watch.' As your video played, she openly cried, and when it ended, she said, 'I can't abort. There's no way.' Thank you, Patricia, for being so courageous. Your video is our last hope and our greatest Christian weapon." (1)

"Wow, God! Thanks for doing all the work. Does this mean I can retire?" Feeling a tad overwhelmed because I knew his answer was no, I closed my laptop for another day. Looking in the mirror at my travel-worn self, I decided to put off the daunting tasks of moving and speaking across nations, and went to get my hair done, instead. When I arrived at my favorite local salon, the stylists descended upon to let me know that they had taken my advice and gone to their first retreat, given by missionary Sisters from Mexico. One of them chattered, "At the retreat, the nuns showed us a video that they show everyone . . . While it was playing, we couldn't breathe and we had to grab onto our chairs . . . Guess what! It was you!" I offered a fake smile as they picked up their smartphones and started texting furiously, their thumbs flying in the air. Ten minutes later, the nuns showed up in their habits.

"You've gotta be kidding," I murmured, as I sat with foils sticking out all over my head and a black plastic cape around my shoulders, wondering how I could melt to the floor and become a puddle of hair conditioner.

The next day, I was ready to embrace the task of finding a new home. Fortuitously, I found a very small one-bedroom apartment in Petaluma—which was all I could afford. On the day I was to move myself out of my house on a short sale, I woke up happy. "Thank God I'm moving," I reflected. "Not one more day of knowing that my dad lives two blocks away, drives by my house every day, and doesn't attempt to see me. At least, by moving out of town, I'll have the excuse in my head that I'll be too far away for him to visit, and I can remain safely in denial about how he doesn't care."

Before picking up my U-Haul that morning, I decided to get some coffee at a local café. As I finished paying for my latté, I glanced over my shoulder and saw my father standing two people behind me in line. He turned his head away quickly, and I could tell by my brief glimpse of the evasive look on his face that he was acting like he hadn't seen me. I grabbed my coffee and bolted out the door. The fear of being rejected once again was too much for me to bear. Crumpled over in my car, I wailed like a crazy woman it hurt so much. How could a father see his daughter, and a daughter see her father, and they act like complete strangers?

Struggling forward through buffeting waves of sadness, I settled into my new apartment and eventually decided to distract myself by answering the e-mail requests. Soon, I forgot my grief as I boarded a plane to Colombia for what turned out to be a grueling whirlwind mission—and by God's grace, an overwhelming success. Assuming that I would be the speaker for one pro-life event, I was alarmed to learn when I arrived that I was scheduled for a minimum of two events a day, with a music ministry to accompany me, in front of crowds of five hundred to a thousand people.

Wherever I went, the band followed, and whenever I reached the point in my story when I arrived at the abortion clinic for the first time, a four-year-old boy in a mariachi suit would sing the plaintive words of the song, "*Déjame Vivir*" ("Let Me Live"), by Vicente Uvalle Castillo. The song rarely left a dry eye. After all of the presentations, which lasted an hour or two, people quickly lined up to wait their turn to speak to me, and I listened to their stories—often staying another three or four hours. I didn't care how long it took. I would hug them. I would kiss them. I wanted to embody God's care, especially for the youth. Wherever I went, I made a point to love. As St. Paul said, *"If I speak in human and angelic tongues but do not have love, I am a resounding gong or a clashing cymbal." (1 Cor. 13:1)* It was love that could heal them. Love was more important than any words I could say.

The youth openly showed their hearts in return. Most were crying. Many physically clung to me, as if grabbing onto the safety of a buoy in high waters. Girls were screaming, "Thank you, thank you!" in between sobs. I later learned that many went home and freely confessed to their parents their disobedience and their sinfulness, saying that they wanted to change.

Many teens flung open their lives to me, revealing their secret pain, things they had never told a soul. A pack of ten female friends shared with me their addiction to cutting. If one wanted to stop, the others wouldn't let her. I met girls who had been raped by their stepdads or their professors and were forced to have abortions. I spoke with children who were prostituting themselves with forty-year-olds in order to get drugs. Twelve-year-old boys and girls told me about their orgies with one another. Eleven-year-old boys shared their desire to be free of their addictions to pornography. A rich young girl lamented having given herself over to older boys and men out of her yearning for her father's attention instead of his money and permissive freedom. A ten-year-old girl sobbed in my arms, telling me that her cousin had been tricked by her mom and aunt into getting an abortion at ten years old, and was now, a year later, in a psych ward after several suicide attempts. A thirteen-year-old looked at me with alarm and said, "I think I'm pregnant. I just had sex this morning with some guy."

Of all those I spoke with, the face I cannot get out of my mind is that of a fifteen-year-old girl, more beautiful than a precious flower, who said to me, "I'll do anything to hurt myself, I hate myself so much. I'll hit myself with a pan, and I'll scrape, bite, and stab myself." I looked at her body and saw that her face and her arms were bruised and cut. The girl looked like a fashion model, yet her worst fear was the mirror. When I asked where her pain came from, she said, "From my parents' rejection."

Grabbing her hand, I confessed, "I've struggled with similar problems, so let's ask the Holy Spirit to help both of us. You are not alone. I, too, suffered the abandonment of my parents, but God can do anything. Pray with me now . . ."

Of all the problems I encountered in the youth, the divorce or abandonment of their parents was the source of the deepest pain. I understood them all.

> Blessed be the God and Father of our Lord Jesus Christ, the Father of compassion and God of all encouragement, who encourages us in our every affliction, so that we may be able to encourage those who are in any affliction with the encouragement with which we ourselves are encouraged by God. For as Christ's sufferings overflow to us, so through Christ does our encouragement also overflow.
> –2 Corinthians 1:3–5

While on the road, I hardly had a moment to myself and was often viewed as a celebrity. People followed me and clung to me, asking for my prayers, my advice, my ear—while back home, Patricia was on her own in a small apartment, doing her best to make sure she had enough food in the fridge for another day. I found the contrast surreal. When travelling, I never felt lonely. But living at home by myself with little or no contact with my family left a void in my heart, so I did my best to remind myself that I was never truly alone. My constant companions were the saints. Coming home at the end of a hard day's work to an empty apartment, I'd fling open the front door and exclaim, "Hello, everybody! I'm home!"

The saints were my friends, but Jesus was my mainstay. I grew to depend on Him for everything, even the smallest of matters, and I engaged Him in conversation while working, driving, eating, doing the dishes. Before falling asleep, I'd tell Jesus I loved Him and sing songs of consolation to His picture. Staring blurry-eyed into my closet in the morning, I'd ask, "Lord, what are we going to wear?" Before speaking to people, I'd ask, "What do you want me to say, Jesus?"

In a short time, requests for me to give talks became so frequent that saying yes to them meant my job saying no to me. "We love you here," remarked the doctors at my clinic, "but we can't have you leaving for such long stretches of time." I understood their situation, and yet I also understood my position with God. I had no choice but to throw my temporal cares onto Providence yet again.

Clinging to the Lord, like a saddle-free rider grabbing a wild horse's mane, I began to travel extensively in the United States and to countries in Latin America. I never imagined being asked back even once, but many places asked me back again and again—sometimes even for a fourth visit. Youth who heard me in one location would collect clusters of friends and show up in the town where I was speaking next, leaving me wondering, "Who would want to hear the same lady talk again?" Everyone, it seemed—the young and the old—could relate to something in my story. Even from the smallest and simplest things I said, people were receiving insights, healings, and dramatic transformations of heart.

On all of my trips, I did my best to check in constantly with Jesus, for only He knew exactly what the people around me needed. During one mission in particular, a tour primarily focused on schoolchildren during my third visit to Ibague, Colombia, my habit of conversing with the Lord made the difference between life and death.

Before speaking at the first school on my tour, I asked Jesus what He wanted me to say, and within my spirit, I heard the word, "suicide." A few minutes into my talk, my pulse started to quicken, and I began to share thoughts about the value and meaning of life and how God has a plan for each of us. After I was finished, two pretty twelve-year-old girls came up to me, crying. "We're best friends," said one, "and we're cutters." Then they pulled back their sleeves to show me their arms. "Our cuts aren't superficial. We cut deeply into our wrists and our forearms because we don't get along with our mothers. I can't cry in front of my mom because it makes her mad, so I slice myself with a knife instead to relieve the pain."

I took them aside and started to pray for them, telling them that God loved them and had a purpose for their lives. A friend of theirs, sitting nearby, overheard our prayers and crumpled forward, crying hysterically. Motioning the members of our prayer group to surround and pray over the two girls, I slipped out of the circle to sit with the young girl. "You don't understand," she sobbed. "If you hadn't come to my school this morning, my two friends would be dead. Right now they have pills and knives in their backpacks, and they made a pact this morning to commit suicide. I tried to talk them out of it, but they were really determined. Their plans were stopped when the teachers started rounding us up to hear your talk. They've cut themselves so frequently that they're not afraid of it. They were going to take the pills and then cut themselves right here at the school in order to bleed to death. If you hadn't come, it would have been too late."

This occurred in the first few hours of my mission trip. The next day, some young boys and girls came up to me after my testimony, saying they wondered if they were homosexual because of certain feelings and experiences they'd had. I hadn't spoken in my talks about the Lord's view on this issue because I didn't want to offend anyone; but I checked in with Jesus Who told me I had to tell them the truth, so I did, and I tried my best to speak it with love. To my surprise, the kids weren't the least bit offended and hugged me out of gratitude for freeing them from their confusion.

Unusual transformations were commonplace. After one of my testimonies, a boy covered in black leather and tattoos, with long hair and black fingernails, wept in my arms, feeling God's mercy wash over him. When I left, he followed me on his motorcycle to where I was staying in order to pray the Rosary. After another presentation, two of the biggest troublemakers in their school—avowed atheists—went straight to the office of their school disciplinarian, a Legionary priest. Crying, they declared to him that my talk had changed their lives: "We didn't know before how much God loves us. Now we want to be good."

Following each testimony in front of the youth, I answered questions that they had written down anonymously. Unnerved to find out how many of these kids were having sex, I responded in the light of Church teachings to questions about condoms, diseases, and how not to get pregnant. "There's only one way that God is asking you to live," I told them, "and right now, it doesn't involve sexual relationships. You've been told that you're having safe sex if you use contraception. But using any kind of contraception means adding one sin on top of another. And certain forms of birth control can kill a newly formed human being—not to mention that the Pill causes cancer and ruins the environment. There is no such thing as "safe sex" simply because you use contraception. Think about this: What will keep your soul safe, your passage to eternal life safe? Only abstinence can give you that." How blindly the youth were copying what they'd seen in the movies or on TV, with little to no understanding of the consequences to their bodies, their lives, their future children's lives—and their very own souls.

In Ibague, most of the ten- and eleven-year-olds with whom I spoke were sexually active; most of the girls having sex were getting pregnant (no one thinks of using condoms at that age); and most of those girls were getting abortions. Since the law allowed abortion in the case of rape, the youngest and poorest ones I spoke with told me they would lie to the doctors, say they were raped, and get a free abortion at the government's expense. If they had money, they'd run to get the RU 486 pill illegally from certain local pharmacies. No questions asked. No parents notified. Sadly, Ibague was not an isolated case. Of all the kids I've spoken with personally in Latin America—and this amounts to thousands—the majority of those who were sexually active started having sex at age ten or eleven. They either revealed this to me in our conversations or frankly and openly gave me this answer when I asked them. By age thirteen, these kids were fully initiated into a sexual lifestyle.

With so much moral decay continually unveiled before me, I was left stunned and overwhelmed. I didn't know, as I ploughed through each day, if I was supposed to cry or grow numb. Kids were coming up to me with such awful, ugly truths. Children were killing their own children, and this was going to mark them for the rest of their lives. They were far from God, and there were so many things I wanted to do for them but couldn't. "What's going on with this world?" I wondered. "Where are all the people who should be speaking up?" *"These are your children,"* I wanted to shout.

With each child, only ten minutes was given to me to make a difference. Ten minutes. "Help me, God," I would cry inside. "How can I help these little souls heal from sexual sin and abortion when they're only eleven years old? They don't even know what being a woman or a man is!" With arms outstretched, I would pull the children toward me and hug them. I let them cry on my shoulder. I told them how much Jesus and Mary loved them and wanted goodness for them.

On that tour, I spoke at another school where a fifteen-year-old boy happened to take one of my cards. Two days later, he called the house where I was staying and said in anguish, "I need to talk to Patricia. I need to talk to her now!" I picked up the line. "I heard you speak, and today my older sister found out she's pregnant. She's about to leave for a pharmacy to get the abortion pill."

"I'll come over right now, and we'll pick up you and your sister." My host family and I hopped in a car and brought them back to the house. I shut myself in a room with the girl for two hours. I told her my story. I told her that the life inside of her was a real baby. I told her that God had a plan for that child. But my words fell flat. She couldn't hear me. Her stare was blank, almost catatonic. "My parents are going to kill me," she repeated. "I want to go get an abortion. I'm only nineteen. I've got to have one."

I felt so desperate. Nothing was in my control, and I was wrestling for two people's lives. Still wondering what might make her see what her choice would result in, I walked her into the living room and motioned for her to sit in a comfortable rocking chair. Looking around in a panic, I prayed, "What do I do, Jesus? What do I do!" My peripheral vision caught sight of a statue of the Virgin Mary, which happened to be "pregnant." "Hold onto this," I said, placing "Mary" in her hands. "Hold her belly and ask her to help you gain strength and to take your fears away." As the girl sat in the chair, rocking and crying, with her fingers around the statue, I scurried out of the room, calling back to her, "Hang on! I'm going to get you something!"

Frantically searching through my suitcase, I grabbed one of my tiny plastic fetuses, which traveled with me, and ran back to place it in the palm of her hand. "This is the size of your baby." As she stared at it, mesmerized, a weak smile began to lift the corners of her mouth.

The host family, the girl's brother, and I joined together in a circle around the rocking chair and started to pray aloud. Tears formed in her eyes and began to stream down her cheeks. She and her brother were not churchgoers and never prayed, but as I looked over at the boy with his eyes pressed shut in fervent supplication for the life of his niece or nephew, I saw something very holy in his face and thought to myself, "He looks as though he could be a priest."

When our prayers died down into a still and quiet peace, the girl looked up with a faraway gaze of gratitude. "We're here for you," the family said to her. "You're not alone. We will help you. Don't be scared." She nodded her head and smiled. Through the brother, we later learned that she kept the baby—and not only that. The boy started attending the host family's prayer group and going to Mass, and realized he wanted to enter the seminary to study for the priesthood.

Given all the pieces that had to serendipitously come together for this meeting that changed three lives and more, radically and forever—and with events like this happening on a regular basis, I stopped believing in mere coincidences.

Toward the end of that trip, for the first time, I was ready to come home to my tiny, lonely apartment. The Lord was squeezing out the last drop of juice left in me. At a certain point, I wasn't sure I could even talk anymore. "I'm done, Lord," I mumbled several times. *"Done."* Each time I was about to collapse, people who wanted my attention would come out of the rocks. Someone would corner me in the hotel lobby, or the elevator, or the parking lot, or even at the bank, to reveal their secret abortion. Strangers even started floating toward me in the hotel Jacuzzi.

My facial expressions and body movements were becoming more zombie-like, my eyes were blinking constantly, my legs were swelling from hours of standing during my presentations, my hair was headed in diverse directions, and my mind was discombobulating my speech. One lady, noticing my exhaustion, exclaimed, "You need a massage! I'm going to go up with you to your hotel room and give you one."

I thought, "This lady really gets it! She can clearly see how tired I am!" As I lay down on the bed, I could feel my whole body collapse from fatigue. "Ah, thank you, God, that I get to tune out the world and simply relax and receive."

After a squirt of the massage cream, I heard a sniffle. "Patricia," she said in a whimper. "This was my only chance to get you alone. I had an abortion!"

Nooooooooo!

> Hear me, O coastlands, listen, O distant peoples. The LORD called me from birth, from my mother's womb he gave me my name.
>
> He made of me a sharp-edged sword and concealed me in the shadow of his arm. He made me a polished arrow, in his quiver he hid me.
>
> You are my servant, he said to me, Israel, through whom I show my glory.
>
> –Isaiah 49:1–3

Fact: Women are aborting their children and are unaware of it. Certain kinds of contraceptives, such as the Pill, are abortifacients, which means that they cause abortions. It is estimated that each year in the United States alone, approximately 1,894,620 newly conceived children are killed in the womb by the birth control pill—and these women never even knew they were pregnant. Intrauterine devices (IUDs) also allow for a life to be conceived and a baby to grow but make the uterus uninhabitable so the baby is discarded. Sometimes, when the baby is not discarded early, IUDs have been known to embed themselves in part of a baby's body, causing its death. (2–8)

Women are also harming their health and are unaware of it. In 2005, the World Health Organization classified the birth control pill as a "Group 1" carcinogen—highly carcinogenic, equally cancer-causing as asbestos and tobacco. (9) Among the Pill's many deadly side effects—in addition to breast, liver, and cervical cancers—are pulmonary embolism, cardiac arrest, hypertensive disease, heart failure, and stroke. (10) With synthetic hormones from the Pill being unleashed into wastewater by passing through women's urine, scientists have discovered around the globe that male frogs, river otters, and fish are mutating to have female characteristics. In 2002, the United Kingdom declared hormonal birth control a type of pollution. (11) One scientist, John Wooding of Denver, Colorado, sampled fish from just below a sewage plant outflow pipes in the South Platte River and Boulder Creek and discovered similar findings in each area. In Boulder Creek, many more female fish were living: 101 females were living, as opposed to only 12 males (which means that males likely mutated into females) and 10 intersex fish whose reproductive organs were so mixed that they could not be assigned a gender. Wooding declared of his findings: "This is the first thing that I've seen as a scientist that really scared me" . . . "It's one thing to kill a river. It's another thing to kill nature. If you're messing with the hormonal balance in your aquatic community, you're going deep down. You're twiddling with how life proceeds." (12) Dr. Jose Maria Simon Castellvi, president of the International Catholic Medical Association, reported in January 2009, "We have sufficient data to state that one of the causes of masculine infertility in the West is the environmental contamination caused by the products of the Pill." (13, 14)

Natural Family planning (NFP) is an alternative method to artificial birth control in which a woman learns to follow her fertility cycle. NFP does not harm a woman's body or the environment, is more effective in preventing pregnancy than the pill, and also helps couples who are struggling to get pregnant. (See: http://www.pfli.org/nfp_faq.pdf) In her 1979 Nobel Peace Prize acceptance speech, St. Mother Teresa of Calcutta described how the practice of Natural Family Planning was proven successful even when used in the slums of Calcutta, India. (15)

Chapter Eighteen

In God's Time

I AM SITTING AT A *round table together with my parents. A pile of photo albums lies in the center of the table. One by one, we open up the albums and begin flipping the pages. Together we look at photo after photo: my brother in his baby crib . . . my sister and I having a water fight in the yard . . . my parents in their 1970s clothes. We start to point and laugh at my dad's mustache. In unison, my mom and dad say, "Those were beautiful days."*

Waking from the dream, my spirits sank. I would never have such days again. God seemed so far away that morning, replaced by a fierce yearning for a husband and a family of my own. Tired and beat up from my trip, I longed to spend a few days at home being taken care of. "Okay, God, that's it," I decided. "You had better give me the man in the blue suit darn soon."

By this time, I had received as many as fifty confirmations from God that I would meet and marry a very specific, well-known, Godly, Hispanic man—confirmations that even an atheist couldn't ignore. A priest whom I'd never met had spontaneously prayed with me and described to a *T* this same future husband. Random women in my audiences had shouted out that I was to marry this certain gentleman. A stranger from Colombia, a man I didn't even know, called me to tell me how knowledge of my marrying this specific man came to him spontaneously in prayer. Acquaintances and friends who knew nothing of my prophecies of "Blue Suit" said that God had shown them in detail whom I would wed. Always the same man, every time.

Consistent prophecies were well and good, but I was growing impatient. Seeking my own will, I began to hound Jesus for this future husband and devoted much of my free time to pestering the Lord. After a couple weeks passed and that didn't work, I tried to manipulate Him through the saints by praying novena after novena.

Finally, I realized that I had to cut it out, so I sat myself down in front of the Blessed Sacrament and asked Jesus to forgive me for not respecting

His timing. Weary of asking for this man in my life, I let the tears fall, releasing to Jesus someone I'd never had in the first place. Gently, ever so gently, I felt the Lord wrestle "him" from my grip. "Show me," I begged the Lord, "how to trust You, and how to wait."

Shortly after that, feeling a little more life in my bones, I decided to go to the gym one Saturday morning. Still dry in spirit, I told Jesus, "I need to know that you're with me. I haven't heard from you in a while." Bending over a new squat machine, I put some steel plates onto it but then couldn't figure out how to maneuver my arms and legs at the same time. Awkward and embarrassed, I continued my attempts to look hardcore with my heavy weights while feeling like the gym's newest dumbbell. "Holy Spirit," I said in silent frustration, "help me. I don't want to have to deal with this booby trap."

Nearby was a woman about my age, running on a treadmill. Looking over at her, I asked, "Excuse me. Have you, by any chance, ever used this squat machine?"

"No, I haven't, but let me help you figure it out." She kindly assisted me with the set up, then hopped back on her treadmill and started jogging while I did my squats. After that, every time I looked over at her, she was staring at me intensely. I felt the need to help her with something, but not knowing what it was, I simply prayed for her. When she got off the treadmill, she smiled and waved, "Have a great weekend."

"Thank you so much," I responded. "I really appreciate you helping me." Then she left.

A minute later, she came back in, shaking with nervousness, and walked toward me with a determined gait. "I'm sorry," she blurted out. "You're going to think I'm crazy, but the Lord spoke to my heart about you." As soon as she said this, my eyes started to tear because her words reminded me of Bonnie. "He told me to tell you that, yes, maybe I helped you figure out the machine, but it was really Him helping you, not only me." Then she looked into my eyes and asked, "Do you know the Lord?"

"Yes, I know the Lord. I am His servant." She told me she was a Christian, and I told her I was a pro-life Catholic speaker.

"I wasn't going to say anything to you, and the reason I walked back in was because sometimes I hear the Lord but I'm disobedient, and I didn't want to disobey Him again by ignoring His voice. I've been praying to God to hear from Him—I've been missing His voice for a long time now—and today He spontaneously spoke to my heart loudly while we were working out. I've also been asking Him for patience because I have three kids and, as a mom, sometimes life is tough and I'm hard on them."

"I have been praying to hear His voice, too, because I haven't heard it for so long; and I've also been praying for patience!"

Our conversation got louder and more animated, and the guys lifting weights nearby began to look at us askance, as though we'd lost a good number of screws. I started to sniffle, moved by the fact that God would send someone to speak with me merely to let me know He cared about something as insignificant as my frustration with a squat machine. He had been so close to me all along. The woman began to tell me a bit more about her life, and I shared some of my story with her, which made her cry, too. Embracing, we decided to become friends and work out together.

"Excuse me," interrupted an irritated weight lifter next to us, "Are you guys gonna use this leg machine?" We looked up at him, dazed, and then moved over, oblivious that we were now blocking the squat machine.

"And you're confirming something else for me," she said. "Sometimes I'm really concerned about what others think about me, especially when I talk to them about the Bible and Our Lord. That's why I haven't wanted to go up to people and do that. And now you're telling me that you're an international speaker who openly shares about your abortions. I thought I was giving you a message, but the Lord is giving *me* a message too." Then she told more about her struggle with impatience and asked about mine.

"Well, sometimes I'm lonely. Years are going by, and I really would like a family. Family is very important to me."

The voice of my new friend began to rise over the huffing, puffing, and clanging around us, and her eyes looked slightly away from me. "I know this is from God because I feel Him speaking to my heart right now. You are going to meet a strong Christian man—not a weak, mediocre Christian—someone who is going to help you grow spiritually. He's going to be a man on your same wavelength who walks alongside you. Together, you will further God's plan for His kingdom and His glory."

Then she looked directly at me, as if shifting from God's voice to her own. "God is good! You're gonna meet a great man!"

"I accept that in Jesus' name!" I shouted, and we started hugging and jumping up and down.

"Can you move?" asked one of the guys pumping iron, who was trying to get to the squat machine.

At that moment, we couldn't have cared less who squatted or who didn't. Squealing with the joy of the Spirit, our tears mixed with our sweat as we encouraged each other to press on in great hope and trust. "Remember," she said emphatically, "everything in God's time. Release your future into God's hands. Live only in the present. It is very important that you accomplish what God needs you to do now and that you focus on that."

> Wait for the Lord; be strong, and let your heart take courage;
> wait for the Lord!
> –Psalm 27:14, ESV

God knew my Achilles' heel: the need to be seen as special in the eyes of another and the desire to be part of a closely knit family. Were it not for the Lord's reminder to wait for a man who was right for me, I might have already settled once again for Mr. Right Enough and slipped outside of God's will into arms He hadn't chosen for me. My missions had made me realize full well that I wasn't alone in my temptations, so I started to include the subject of purity and chastity in my talks—and every time, I felt like I was speaking to myself.

While surfing the Internet one day, God introduced me to a new friend in heaven, St. Philomena. From her story, I saw more clearly than ever how chastity was a fight. She was a Grecian princess, born in 291 AD. At the tender age of thirteen, she gave up her life to preserve her chastity. After being brutally tortured, she was decapitated by the Roman emperor Diocletian, who had wanted to have her for his own. Philomena endured Diocletian's thwarted attempts to kill her by flogging her, drowning her with an anchor around her neck, dragging her through the streets, and shooting her with fiery arrows. (1, 2) Suffice it to say, he didn't handle rejection very well. Philomena's loyalty to Christ and her willingness to go through hell to preserve her chastity deeply convicted me. St. Philomena was everything I wasn't, and all I wanted to be.

The first time I included chastity in my talks was at a church in Mexico, in front of a small crowd of eighty teenagers, ages fourteen through nineteen. Invoking the prayers of St. Philomena, I stood in front of a statue of Our Lady of Guadalupe and began to speak freely in the Spirit: "Our

Lady is our greatest example of purity, and she desires to help you. She is asking for your chastity, which is not purely a discipline, like abstinence, but a way of life. Chastity affects your whole being—the way you act, speak, think, and dress. It propels you to reach out to others to give them love, to never use them for your own pleasure. Whoever wishes to be courageous, whoever would like to give this gift to Our Lady, come up to her now and ask for her help."

Every single youth came forward. One by one, they got up out of the pews and dropped to their knees around Mary. In an atmosphere of profound solemnity and prayer, they committed their chastity to her. I didn't know it at the time, but one of the teens who walked forward was newly pregnant and about to abort. That day, her baby and perhaps her very soul were saved.

After my talk, I witnessed an explosion of joy. The teens were effusive with happiness. They surrounded me, hugged me, and pulled out their phones to take multiple pictures. Many went back up onto the altar to take selfies next to the statue of Our Lady of Guadalupe. One fifteen-year-old girl, who was from El Salvador and studying in Mexico, immediately got on the phone to pro-life organizations in her home country, and within three hours had me booked to speak at a conference there. Another girl walked over to her school principal's office after I spoke and said, "We would never have believed the moral truths about abortion and sexuality through textbooks or classes. Patricia's talk was the only way we could understand it. Thank you so much for bringing her here."

What moved my heart the most, though, were the teenage boys. They surrounded me, cuddling my plastic fetuses in their hands, asking me more questions about how to practice chastity in their daily lives. "Read the story of St. Philomena," I urged, because I wanted the youth to know the lengths she went through to preserve her purity, the purity they were throwing away in the click of their mouse or an overnight stay. One sixteen-year-old boy held both my hands, looked into my eyes, and said, "Thank you so much for changing my mindset." A tall youth, age eighteen, leaned over to hug me and sobbed on my shoulder. No words were spoken. This time, I couldn't hold back my tears and cried with him.

With gratitude, I watched the fruits of my internal fight for purity become God's multiplying gift to others who were choosing it because of my example. The need was great. "Please raise your hand," I called out to crowds across Mexico and Colombia, "if you know the definition of 'chastity.'" Among over thirty thousand, a total of *fifteen* raised their hands—and the best answer they could give was "abstinence."

At the same time, I learned that chastity is an unpopular subject in hell, because it causes Satan to reenergize his ugly stare toward me and redouble his attacks on me. At times, he expresses his wrath by picking me up at night, and I feel like my body is being elevated about three inches above the bed. In full force and fury, he tries to throw me toward the wall or up to the ceiling; once, he even tried to slam my body into the Sacred Heart image. When this happens, I enter into a dimension where I don't know if what is happening is spiritual or material. I feel everything in my physical body, which turns as solid and heavy as a rock, preventing Satan from moving me any farther. I see the silhouette of his arms and hands, his elbows and shoulders, and how he is trying with all his strength to throw me—but he can't. Instead, he starts slashing at me and choking me. All the while, I know why he's angry and what he's thinking. He's furious that I've helped people choose to be chaste. Without actually hearing the horrible sound of his voice, I see his livid expression roaring and screaming, like a wild beast going crazy with rage.

But it's no matter. I'm still not afraid. Whatever greatly delights God and makes His people happy and safe will always infuriate the enemy of humankind.

> So be imitators of God, as beloved children, and live in love, as Christ loved us and handed himself over for us as a sacrificial offering to God for a fragrant aroma. Immorality or any impurity or greed must not even be mentioned among you, as is fitting among holy ones, no obscenity or silly or suggestive talk, which is out of place, but instead, thanksgiving. Be sure of this, that no immoral or impure or greedy person, that is, an idolater, has any inheritance in the kingdom of Christ and of God.
> –Ephesians 5:1–5

Fact: Globally, the average age at which young people have sex for the first time is sixteen and one-third years old. (3) In the United States, the average is about seventeen (4), but they do not start marrying until their mid-twenties. (5) The most common reason that sexually inexperienced teens gave for not having had sex was that it was "against religion or morals" (38 percent among females and 31 percent among males). The second and third most common reasons for females were "don't want to get pregnant" and "haven't found the right person yet." (6) See the appendix for more factors that influence youth to either have sex or to wait until they are married.

CHAPTER NINETEEN

Flowers from Jesus

As I FOCUSED MORE on my mission and let Mr. Right disappear into an unknown future, I began to receive more plentiful and beautiful bouquets of graces—multicolored flowers of lives saved and souls healed, which God would gather up and present to me with love. Time and again, He breathed His Spirit into the world through the fruits of my sacrifice, fruits only He could orchestrate.

After I'd given a reflection at Mass to about five hundred people in a church in the town of Tierra Blanca in Veracruz, Mexico, the Holy Spirit was set loose. Chaotic in their search to speak with me, people standing in line were openly confessing their sins for everyone to hear. Women (who almost never share the news of their abortions—not even to spouses, friends, or family) were crying hysterically and shouting out, "I had three abortions!" "Four abortions!" Newspaper journalists were running my way to snap pictures. *"This is not normal,"* I thought.

"Your presentation is still the talk of the town," the organizers later phoned to tell me. They hadn't had any type of spiritual retreat in eight years. Inspired, they brought me back six months later to be their speaker for a sizeable Divine Mercy event. I asked my friend Daniel from Guatemala to join me and, standing next to relics of St. Faustina on a grand outdoor stage, he sang and I spoke to close to two thousand enthusiastic people, who collectively and spontaneously raised their hands high to praise God.

Even when the Good News remained hidden, God would throw a spiritual bouquet my way to reassure me. When I was invited to speak in front of high-level government officials in Chile where there has been a push to make abortion legal (56 percent of doctors are in favor of it), I gave two talks to political parties. Sitting at a round table with ten officials of the Renovación Nacional party, I began to pour out my life story while half of them were busy on their cellphones. Pushing my hurt feelings aside, I continued and, one by one, they put their phones down and stared at me with silent fear in their eyes. When I pulled out my lifelike fetuses, and they held them in their hands, their expressions turned into shock. I could almost hear their thoughts. My next talk, to forty young-looking politicians within the Unión Demócrata Independiente party, went quite differently. Infused with zeal, the officials were asking for my advice, ready to fight for life. They even posted my talk on YouTube for more people to see. (1)

In Veracruz, when I gave the scientifically verified information that some contraceptives cause abortions, a woman attacked me in public, torpedoing screams at me: "Who do you think you are? Where the hell are you getting your statistics?" In the United States, a woman stood up after I mentioned the evil of pornography and lashed: "How do I know that what you're saying is truth? Everything is a lie. It's all a lie." At a wealthy parish in Colombia where I spoke about certain forms of birth control and their abortive effects, a dozen women got up and walked out. All of the men stayed, however, and I noticed that many of them were sobbing openly. One of them walked up to the podium to say, "I can't leave my daughter alone. I have to be with her—to love her more. Patricia's presentation completely changed my heart. I promise from now on I'm going to be a better father." Of the women who remained to listen, one had been feeling useless, that she didn't have a mission in life; but when she heard my story and what was happening to the youth in Colombia, her spirit caught fire and she jumped into action. Together with twenty women, she initiated a pro-life movement, called *Proyecto Esperanza* (Project Hope), connected with Rachel's Vineyard, to heal the victims of abortion in Colombia.

God also threw flowers on my path by introducing me to some of the people who sought healing at Rachel's Vineyard retreats. One eighty-year-old woman was inspired to go on a retreat after hearing my testimony in person. Ever since her abortion at age thirty, she had felt depressed and suicidal. After the retreat, she called me to say, "I feel so happy, so very different. Never in the last fifty years did I think I would be liberated from the torment of my past." Another woman traveled from Mexico to Texas to attend a retreat, which ignited her calling to be a pro-life speaker. Men, too, were inspired to go on their own to a retreat; others went to support their wives, at least initially, but the Lord broke their defenses. They acknowledged their sin and their children; and through their confessions, their souls and their marriages were healed.

Healing, I've learned, is a choice. An individual whose abortion is self-justified or unconfessed is entirely unprepared to stand before God. *"You shall not offer any of your offspring to be immolated to Molech [a false God], thus profaning the name of your God. I am the LORD"—Leviticus 18:21*. But for the person who seeks reconciliation and healing, all is possible with God, even in one's last moments on earth. God handed me a most fragrant and colorful flower when, at the request of friends, I went to visit and pray for a woman dying of colon cancer. Teresa also happened to have a twelve-year-old son with leukemia. Doing my best to comfort her, I held onto her delicate skeleton-of-a-hand while reading the Bible to her and teaching her the Divine Mercy Chaplet prayer. I could see within her feeble, decaying frame that her soul was worried and restless. I was supposed to bring her hope and love and light—to give her Jesus—but I just wanted to cry. Yet no matter how sick and fatigued she felt, no matter how many visits she had already declined, when she heard the words, "Patricia's here," she'd muster the strength to say, "Please, please, bring her in. Don't let her leave."

Teresa died during one of my visits to Colombia, and I felt shattered. But I didn't know that Teresa's sister had heard me tell my story at my parish and had immediately gone home to repeat it to her. So comforted was Teresa by the fact that God had forgiven me and I was doing well that she finally revealed she had undergone two abortions. A priest came to hear her confession and gave her the Sacrament of the Anointing of the Sick. Then as Teresa was dying, God gave her a vision of her two children in heaven, which left her in awe. Freed from worry, she then passed away in deep peace.

When I heard that Teresa had died reconciled and finally at peace with God and her aborted children, I felt elated for her, but I also winced at the thought of the millions of women who have been told at abortion clinics around the world, "This will take five minutes. There may be some cramping and bleeding, so take some aspirin." And that's it. She wasn't warned of the emotional and physical damage she could endure. She wasn't told that she would carry within her soul, knowingly or unconsciously, the weight of her abortion until her dying breath. She doesn't know that scores of women and men suffer from a very real but underacknowledged condition called post-abortion syndrome (2). Therefore, she has no idea that her current psychological struggles may be a result of abortion in her past—not to mention all the men who suffer abortion's mark on the soul and know nothing about how to cope.

After giving a presentation at St. Cornelius Church in Richmond, California, I walked to my car to see a note on the windshield: "My name is Juan Carlos. Please help me. I was part of an abortion about a year ago, and I haven't been able to forgive myself for not defending the life of my child." When I met with him in person, he told me of how his girlfriend had taken a picture of their aborted child on her bathroom floor and sent it to him in a text. He decided to go on a retreat and was healed of his long suffering from post-abortion syndrome. Committed to leading Rachel's Vineyard retreats and post-abortion healing Bible studies in California, he gave his testimony, along with other men and women, including myself, in a short and mesmerizing video called "Dark Secrets" (3), which accompanies a powerful video of my life story (4). (These impactful videos, including the full-length version of my story, can be found in the "Transfigured" DVD, which was shown on EWTN. (www.QueenofPeaceMedia.com/product/transfigured-dvd) (5).

Many of the colorful flowers I've received from the Lord have come through men. During a live radio show in Chile, a DJ began to weep when I spoke of how the Lord had inspired Bonnie to come to me when I was on the street. When I spoke Bonnie's words: "Jesus loves you," he suddenly couldn't talk, so he motioned for me to wait and for his assistant to put on a song on the air. When my interview ended, he said, "In my thirty-two years of being a radio DJ, I have never, ever, been impacted by a guest to the point of crying."

Through another man in Colombia, God gifted me with a particularly resplendent, sweet-smelling bouquet. In front of hundreds of people in an outdoor, glass-ceiling stadium in Ibague, I had given a talk for a conference on the family. Invited back six months later to speak to students, I gave a second talk and, as I was being rushed out of the stadium in order to arrive in time for another event, a man in a janitor's uniform found me in the crowd and shouted, "I can't believe you're back so I can say thank you!"

"Thank you for what?" I asked and motioned for the organizers to allow me a moment to speak with him. We sat down side by side in the bleachers and with animated excitement, he told me that when he was working outside the stadium six months earlier, he'd heard "the echoes of my voice" over the loudspeaker as he was cleaning up the gardens. Captivated, he stood still, leaning on his shovel and my every word.

"A few weeks after that," he continued rapidly, "my daughter, who's in college, told me she was pregnant and planning on having an abortion because 'it wasn't the right time.' I told her, 'No, no, no,' and I drove three hours to Bogotá to tell her your story. I remembered every detail of it. We cried together, and I told her that if she had the baby, I would support her completely. I want to thank you because my grandson will be born in three months." He looked ecstatic. "I can't believe I'm having this opportunity to tell you."

To see a father's smile so full of joy and a heart so full of support, rather than upset, over his daughter's pregnancy, left me in awe of both him and God. "Oh my, Lord," I marveled. "You take advantage of every single opportunity to save a life and a soul, even touching a janitor outside a stadium, listening to the echoes of my story . . ."

Having the privilege of seeing the hand of God has inspired me to keep going. Sometimes, when I've been bombarded by sixteen talks in ten days, back-to-back television and radio interviews, or seen story-high posters plastered across shopping center plazas with the words, *"Patricia Sandoval: Yo aborté. Un testimonio real"* ("I aborted. A true testimony"), I've been tempted to retreat into the shadows. But then I'd receive a text, an e-mail, a phone call about another baby saved. Such messages have been the most beautiful blossoms that Jesus has given me. Since I began my mission, dozens and dozens of children's lives have been spared, so many that I've lost count . . . But nothing has compared to God's gift of letting me hold in my arms the babies who would not have lived at all if I hadn't spoken out. When I've cuddled God's precious creations, contemplating the joy I see that they bring to their families and the generations that may follow, the wonder of life overwhelms me, and I've had not a single doubt that it's worth it all.

> You formed my inmost being;
> you knit me in my mother's womb.
> I praise you, because I am wonderfully made;
> wonderful are your works!
> My very self you know.
>
> My bones are not hidden from you,
> When I was being made in secret,
> fashioned in the depths of the earth.
> Your eyes saw me unformed;
> in your book all are written down,
> my days were shaped, before one came to be.
> –Psalm 139:13–16

CHAPTER VIDEO

Patricia Sandoval Shakes the Crowd with Her Amazing Testimony
See https://youtu.be/_qJR-IAtAe8
Or go to YouTube.com and find the video by searching
Queen of Peace Media

My sister, brother, and I are playing ring-around-the-rosy on our backyard lawn next to the rose bushes. We're laughing because my brother just tripped and toppled over backward. He thinks it's funny too. We all decide to fall on top of each other on the grass. Giggling and squirming, I make my way out of the sibling pile and roll onto my back. The sun hits my face, and joy widens my smile.

My eyes started to blink, and I woke up to the bright morning rays streaming in from my bedroom window. The dream came not long before I received an unexpected invitation from my big sister to meet with her, my sixteen-year-old niece, and my brother on the prestigious Stanford University Campus where my sister was studying on a full scholarship. She must have known that if she included an Advent Mass in the invitation, I wouldn't miss the occasion.

When I arrived, she greeted me with an exuberant smile and a joyful laugh. She enveloped me with a warm embrace, as though nothing remotely negative had ever happened between us. My brother looked happy, too, undoubtedly relieved to be part of a reunion. He and I felt genuinely proud of our sister, who seemed to be able to accomplish the impossible. After a tour of the campus, we stepped inside Stanford's crown jewel, the Memorial Chapel, where my senses soared upward, as if communing with the presence of angels. The chapel, the size of a grand cathedral, was breathtakingly beautiful—adorned with stained glass and sacred art, and filled with the comforting scent of evergreens and the celestial sounds of Christmas carols.

It had been twenty years since my siblings and I had gone to Mass together. I was now thirty-three, my sister thirty-five, and my brother twenty-nine. As we sat down side by side in a pew, my heart swelled with thankfulness. Looking over at my brother, I thanked God for his sweet spirit, grateful for how I had always been able tell him everything about my faith, and how he valued and treasured it. He once told me, "The faith I have is because of what you've taught me. Without it, I'd be lost." I was caught by surprise and smiled when my sister pointed out her favorite Scripture quotes engraved in the stone walls, which she told me she would read when stopping in for a rest between class periods. Together, we listened attentively to the Mass readings, which spoke of the coming of the Son of Man.

During the homily, an impassioned priest asked, "What are we doing for Christ? What are we doing to change the world? Are we His hands, His eyes, His mouth? Are we living for Him every day?" I felt so happy, but a twinge of sadness came when my siblings and my niece, none of whom normally attended Mass, were not able to get up to receive Communion. They sat there, like I used to, while I walked forward and offered the Eucharist up for them in the hope that one day, the Body and Blood of the Lord would flow through our veins and spirits, together as one.

For many years, the holidays had been difficult for us, especially for my brother and me, who didn't have our own families. He and I would sometimes meet for Christmas Mass and exchange a gift or eat out at a restaurant. But our times together were never complete. Every year, we yearned for family unity, and every year, we didn't know what we were going to do. My mother had long been estranged from my sister, spoke with my brother infrequently, and after the last argument she and I had gotten into, she had completely distanced herself from me. Yet today, for the first time in a long while, I felt like I had a family. After receiving Communion, I sat back down next to my siblings, feeling awash in answered prayers—my mother's prayers, too. It wasn't Christmas that day, but it was the best Christmas I'd had in a long time.

About three months later, while I was driving home, I noticed that I'd received a phone message. It was from my sister, which gave me a twinge of joy. As I listened to her voice, I noticed that it sounded different than usual, softer and filled with compassion. At intervals, her voice would break, as though she'd been crying: "I just saw you on the *Cara a Cara* video at Stanford during school hours."

I gulped, afraid of what she'd say next. "I was going to do research on Planned Parenthood, and I was told by my professor that there was a conflict of interest with a family member of mine. They traced my address history and found that at one point in my life, I had the same address as someone in my family who had signed a letter to a congressman in support of his investigation of Planned Parenthood's negligence. (6) I told them it was a mistake, that no one in my family would have done that. Then I googled 'Sandoval and Planned Parenthood,' and your *Cara a Cara* video came on the screen. I was stunned. Now I understand so many things and why you do what you do with the youth. I want you to know that we may not always agree on things or have the same beliefs, but I am so proud of you for fighting for what you believe in. Watching the video was very emotional for me. I want you to know that I support you, and I love you."

My heart's black secret had been exposed, and I hadn't expected it to be met with kindness. As my sister's words filtered past my panic, my fears began to subside, and growing in their place was a delicate blossom of freedom. I had hidden so much from my family, trapping myself in lingering shame, and if it weren't for the Lord moving His hand to help me through artfully uncanny "coincidences," I would never have let my sister into my world.

No less than a month after that, she called again: "Hi Patricia, I went to Dad's house and showed him your video."

I exploded. "What!? How could you do that? Why would you do that!" My father was the one person in all the world whose disapproval I couldn't bear. He'd always taught me to have a good reputation and to walk in integrity, and never to be disgraced in the eyes of the world. My whole being recoiled in pain to hear that he knew everything.

"No, no, no. Dad was really interested. He didn't say anything negative or get upset. Instead, he said, 'Patricia did a good job. It would be very hard for somebody to say what she had to say.' And he said it with compassion, I assure you. Then he asked me how he could look for the video so he could watch it again himself."

I didn't want to know anything else. Disarmed and overwhelmed, I began to weep. All my life, my father had never openly expressed that I'd done a good job or that he was proud of me. He didn't share his own feelings. And finally, now, after hearing the disaster of my life—the most disappointing and degrading things he could possibly ever know of me—that is when he said, despite his own pain and hurt, "Patricia did a good job."

Again, I felt God's hand liberating me from a prison cell I'd kept myself locked inside of, and soon I let go of any upset toward my sister. Although I felt I should have been the one to tell my father the searing news of my three abortions and their public broadcast to the world, the truth was that I never would have done it.

That night, when I finally calmed myself enough to fall asleep, I had a dream:

I'm in the living room, sitting on the carpet floor and brushing my doll's hair. I'm about seven years old. I can smell Mom's cooking from the kitchen, and I look out the window to see that the sky is getting darker. I know what this means. Dad will soon be home. My heart quickens, and I start to bug my mom every few minutes with the question: "Is he coming?" Then I hear the familiar sound of the garage door opening. "Dad!" I exclaim, grabbing my doll and running to the back door . . .

When I woke up, I told myself, "I'm not going to hide from my father and let fear of his disapproval take over my heart. For years now I've lived with the mantra, 'I'm rejected by my father.' I don't want to play that recording anymore."

Picking up the phone, I decided to put to rest the warring factions in my mind—"You're not calling me, so I'm not calling you." What did it matter, I asked myself, if he never reached out to me or thought of me again? With a shaky hand, I punched the familiar but almost forgotten numbers of my old home.

"Hi, Dad, it's Patricia. How are you?"

"Ah . . . good. How are you?"

"Fine, how's the baby?" (My little brother was now four years old, and I hadn't laid eyes on him since he was an infant.)

"He's doing well," answered my father. A five-minute exchange of niceties ensued in a conversation reminiscent of ten years earlier. Without forethought and perhaps from an old, buried habit, I ended with the words, "I love you, Dad. Take care," and hung up the phone, exhaling years of accumulated mental poison.

Not long after that, I paid a visit to my godparents, seeking comfort in their hearth of familial love and, in particular, the warm hugs of my father's look-alike. As my uncle and I stood chatting in the kitchen, the doorbell rang. There at the door was my father; and a few steps behind him were his wife and my cute-as-a-button little brother. My father's eyes sprung open, and he was further surprised to learn that I was often there. Undoubtedly, he could also see my godfather's great affection for me.

Turning my attention toward my brother, who looked more like he could be my son, I asked him, "Do you know who I am?"

"Yes, of course," he said. "You're my sister!" I could tell by his response that Dad hadn't made me a stranger to him. A friendly little chatterbox, he acted as though he'd known me for more years than his age allowed.

Shrugging his shoulders and grabbing his head in confusion, he asked me several times, "Why don't you come over to my house? I don't get it." But I never answered.

My father ended up staying, and we both settled into a semi-comfortable visit. Sitting down together at the dining room table, we talked about family trivia, and I shared what I was doing in my mission work, now that the cat was not only out of the bag but flying around different countries: "Look, Dad. Here's a flyer for a big event on Saturday where I'll be speaking southeast of here in Modesto."

"This whole event revolves around you?"

"Yes, and I recently returned from Colombia, where three babies were saved. I have short video clips on my phone that I can show you . . ."

My father and I hadn't spoken to each other for years, and ten minutes into our time together, his wife, Elvira, began to nudge him, saying, "Let's go. Let's go!" But unlike in the past, my father chose to ignore her, and we chatted for another half hour.

After a week went by, my father called me for the first time in five years. Reaching out to others was always very difficult for him, I knew. It crossed the grain of his personality and took a great effort on his part. Happy to hear each other's voice, we exchanged initial courtesies: "How are you? How was your week? "Have you spoken to your sister? brother?"

Then without premeditation or spite, I began to speak spontaneously from a place of truth. I wasn't going to dress up my life and make things look better than they were, like I always had, simply because being okay in the world and doing your job well made my dad proud. "I've gone through some really rough years," I told him, "and there were times when I cried so much because I felt alone and didn't know what to do. For months, I didn't have work, and sometimes I wondered how I was going to survive. But I've never gone without food or a roof over my head, because God has always been there for me: He's been my provider, my shelter, and my protection."

Dad fell silent, and I continued, careful not to say too much more. He had forever told me, "Don't ever leave your job. Make sure you're working," I said, "When I did get a stable job, I ended up leaving it behind again because I felt a strong pull to do God's work. I didn't know how I would pay the bills and had to trust in the Lord completely. It was hard, but God was good. He came up with a better outcome than I could have imagined. The doctors at my job, who had said they had to let me go because I was taking so much time off to go on the mission trips, realized in my absence that they couldn't replace me. I had become very good at my work. So they rearranged their schedules around mine and have given me the freedom to come and go as I wish. I can't imagine such a thing happening without God. Many times, I've had to trust in the Lord beyond what I thought I could endure; but He's always come through, and I've learned to depend on Him for everything. He is truly my Father."

Dad remained quiet. He had never said a word when anything emotional was conveyed. Seconds crawled forward in an uncomfortable silence. Then, like a hand reaching out across a chasm, I told him I loved him, and we said our goodbyes.

The next week, my dad called again for a quick and cordial check-in. I believe it was his way of saying he was sorry. Mom's punishment had always been through words, but Dad's had been through withdrawing them—and now he was speaking. "Why don't you come on over to the house?" he asked. But my spirit recoiled at the thought.

"I'll go one day," I told him, unsure if I ever would. "It's just very painful for me." At the mere mention, even intimation, of stepping through his front door, a distressing sadness and anxious intimidation would churn within me. I no longer felt safe or welcome in a home that wasn't mine anymore, where all my things were gone or thrown away. Yet I knew that God would never want fear to control my heart. Something in me needed to break. This time it was my dad who was reaching out across time and tragedy to build a bridge between us. But I just couldn't cross it.

Not too long after my father's second phone call, I had another dream:

I am driving my car, and I looked in the rearview mirror and see my father smiling broadly. He is the happiest I've ever seen him, ecstatic that I've ended up with the man who is sitting next to him in the backseat, my husband. Together they joke and laugh, causing the crow's feet at the sides of my father's eyes to wrinkle in delight. All the while, my husband is showing him great respect. "Such a good man," my dad is thinking, "a wonderful man to take care of my daughter." The man in the backseat is wearing a blue suit.

> "Whoever loves father or mother more than me is not worthy of me, and whoever loves son or daughter more than me is not worthy of me; and whoever does not take up his cross and follow after me is not worthy of me. Whoever

> finds his life will lose it, and whoever loses his life for my sake will find it."
> –Matthew 10:37–39

Fact: Pope Francis gave the following address to his General Audience in St. Peter's Square, April 8, 2015:

Dear Brothers and Sisters, good morning!

We complete today, in the catechesis on the family, the reflection on children, who are the most beautiful fruit of the blessing that the Creator has given man and woman. We have already talked about the great gift that children are; today, unfortunately, we must talk about the "stories of passion" that many of them live. So many children are rejected from the beginning, abandoned, robbed of their childhood and their future. Some might dare to say, almost to justify themselves, that it was an error to make them come into the world. This is disgraceful! Please, let's not unload our faults on children! Children are never "an error."

In our time also, as in the past, the Church puts her maternity at the service of children and of their families. She brings to the parents and children of this our world God's blessing, maternal tenderness, firm rebuke and decisive condemnation. One doesn't joke with children!

Think what a society would be like that decided once and for all to establish this principle: "It's true that we aren't perfect and that we make many mistakes. However, when it is a question of children who come into the world, no sacrifice of the adults is deemed too costly or too great, in order to avoid a child thinking that he is a mistake, that he had no value and that he is abandoned to the wounds of life and to the arrogance of men." How beautiful such a society would be! I say that much would be forgiven such a society, its innumerable errors—much, truly.

The Lord judges our life by listening to what the angels tell him about the children, angels that "always behold the face of the Father who is in heaven" (cf. Matthew 18:10). We must ask ourselves always: What will the children's angels tell God about us? (7)

Chapter Twenty

Press On

EVERY YEAR, THE STATE of Querétaro, Mexico, hosts a televised pro-life event called *Vida Fest Nacional*, and I was invited to be one of their speakers. When I arrived in the early morning for the all-day program, I was ushered into the ninth dugout of a soccer (*futbol*) stadium, where presenters, priests, and coordinators were mingling and socializing. The twenty-or-so organizers looked overjoyed to see me and shared excitedly that they expected forty thousand people to come. The year prior, twenty thousand people had attended the event—in the rain. When the eight a.m. starting time rolled around, we looked out at empty seats, and I overheard their nervous whispers: "It's okay . . . It's still early . . . Things are just starting . . . People will show up later." At nine a.m., the team looked worried. When ten a.m. came around, I saw tears forming in their eyes. Only about five hundred people graced a small side section of the stadium. The team had spent months of hard work and sacrifice—organizing, raising funds, foregoing sleep—and their spirits were being crushed. They had scheduled the event on December 13, one day after December 12, the feast of Our Lady of Guadalupe, when the people of Mexico celebrate all day and throughout the night.

I was curious to meet a certain priest who had been invited to lead a Rosary at the event—Fr. Daniel Gagnon, a North American living in Mexico City, whose reputation for holiness and gifts of singing and healing preceded him. From pictures, I knew that he was in his late fifties—tall, slightly knock-kneed, gray haired, and blue eyed. Surveying the dugout, I didn't catch sight of the likes of him, so I sank down into a bleacher seat and started to rehearse my talk in my mind. Two minutes later, Fr. Daniel sat down beside me on my left. After saying hello to me and briefly greeting those around him, he reached down to pull his rosary out of his pocket and began to pray it silently and with great devotion.

Eager to speak with him, I kept glancing over anxiously at his beads, hoping he'd gotten to the fifth mystery. When he finally finished, I introduced myself to him and, since one of the team members to my right was crying, I mentioned, "Father, I think we should pray for the organizers. They're heartbroken over the thousands of empty seats."

"It doesn't matter," he answered. "We're doing this for Our Lady. This is all for her." And then he went back to praying.

"Darn," I thought. "More prayer." Eventually, he looked up, and I seized my chance to stir up a conversation, which ended up flowing naturally between us. *"Tu me caes super bien!"* (I get along really well with you!) he said with fatherly kindness. I noticed that he had a holy presence about him: his smile conveyed love, his every word was gentle, and he wasn't rushed; he moved with a steady grace, like I imagined Jesus did.

When he asked me why I was there, I told him I was going to give my testimony about my abortions and how I used to work at Planned Parenthood. Immediately, he said, "You know the enemy doesn't like what you're doing, so I'm going to pray over you." Remaining seated, he raised his hands, gently placed them on my head, and with tender fervency said, "First, I'm going to pray for your protection from attacks from the evil one." His words were soft prayers to the Baby Jesus. Suddenly, he stopped speaking. His body curled forward into a fetal position, and he started to weep.

"F-Father," I stammered, "are you okay?" He looked up at me, his left hand clutching his heart and his right hand motioning for me to wait until he could catch his breath. Eventually, he looked directly in my eyes and said with great earnestness, "Your children are so proud of you!"

"Did you just feel them? Did you see my children?"

He nodded a yes and repeated, "Patricia, your children are so proud of you."

Then he bent forward again, and kept wiping his tears with his hands. Joy and awe flooded my soul. I didn't think to ask any questions or try to get details. Heaven had touched us both with a gift from above—one that would remain with me forever.

It was now late morning, and my time to speak had come, so I walked up onto the gigantic, high platform and began my story. But moments into my talk, feeling far from the small crowd to one side, I got down from the stage and stood on the grass, closer to the people, so I could see their faces and they could see mine. Forty-five minutes into my story, at the point when Bonnie came to rescue me, something unexpected happened to my soul. I fell into contemplation of all the unmerited love that God had showered on my life, and I started to choke up. For the first time in my life, I didn't only know that I was loved by God—I drank in His love and mercy, and a barrier within my heart melted away. Tears began to flow in the bleachers, joining with my own, and I felt a connection with my listeners like I never had before—because until that moment, I could only watch my audiences cry.

When my talk ended, I sat down in the dugout, dried my tears, and pulled out my rosary as Fr. Daniel began to lead a procession with the Blessed Sacrament. He ascended the platform, placed the Host on the altar, knelt reverently before it, and proceeded to lead a profoundly Spirit-filled Rosary, accompanied by a sublime choir. Pausing in between decades, he prayed for healing of the various stages of life—from trauma in the womb, to infancy, and on through the pains of old age. In the middle of the third Joyful mystery, the Birth of Jesus, I looked out into the virtually empty stadium and was drawn deeply into prayer. At the sight of the empty bleachers, I was thinking of all the people who were missing this sacred opportunity, when the Lord, quite unexpectedly, spoke to me. In my heart, I heard the words: "These seats are not empty. They are filled with little saints. The unborn are here, interceding for the intentions of this event to spread across the globe."

As the Rosary was coming to a close, one of the organizers tapped me on the shoulder to say, "Patricia, we're going to get you on the radio now." I was jolted out of prayer and whisked into a makeshift tent, where headphones were snapped onto my head and I was told to stand alongside two radio announcers, one male and one female. As the woman interviewed me, my eyes began to water and so did hers, even though she'd heard my same story moments before. Both announcers appeared deeply touched. Snatching the microphone from her hand, the man blurted, "I need to say this before time is up. I want all you listeners to know that I'm looking at Patricia, and you would be surprised to see how beautiful and young she is. But that's nothing compared to what you can see in her eyes. You can see Jesus in them. And I want you to know that the eyes are the window to the soul." I was stunned. His words, bursting from his heart, were the best compliment I could have received because he saw beyond me. He saw the Lord. He saw God's love and mercy.

After the interview, I took advantage of a break in the schedule to retrieve a sweater I had left behind the stage. As I walked across the stadium field, I heard my name being screamed from the crowd. I looked up to my left to see hundreds of hands raised and beckoning me to walk their way. When the people saw me turn toward them, they broke into applause and wouldn't stop chanting, "Patricia! Patricia! Patricia!"

"What the heck?" I gulped. "All this for my abortions?" Approaching the security guards in the area, I asked to be let into the crowd, and hundreds of people rushed forward to hug me. Most of them appeared to be poor, and all looked so grateful. The next twenty minutes became a controlled mosh pit as I took selfies with kids, comforted crying ladies, said blessings for teenage boys and girls who were shouting out words of thanksgiving, and even responded to requests for my autograph. I thought *that* was crazy. "What are they going to do with my autograph? Why do they want it? I'm nobody famous." But I didn't have to understand. I felt happy and loved, and I believe they did too, because they were seeing God's mercy when they saw me.

Extricating myself from the crowd, I waved goodbye to my "fans" and joined a luncheon with the other speakers, a lineup of well-known, impressive figures: Bishop Faustino Armendariz of Querétaro; Bishop Rodrigo Aguilar Martínez of Tehuacán, who was chosen for the 2015 Synod of Bishops on the Family in Rome; Fr. Salvador Herrera, an exorcist; Fr. Daniel Gañon, my favorite; Bridget Hylak, whose mother tried to abort her four times; Marco Antonio Gracia Triñaque, a member of the Biotech Advisory Committee to the Conference of Mexican Bishops; and Alexander Acha, a Grammy-winning, Mexican singer-songwriter. And then there was me, some chick from Petaluma.

As I sat down in an empty seat across from Bishop Armedariz, I wondered how my thoughts could travel so quickly and precipitously from a mountaintop of self-worth to a cowering sense of inadequacy. During a break in a conversation of feigned confidence with the bishop, I turned to say hello to a priest sitting next to me. He introduced himself as Fr. James Hyde, and I discovered the he had been entrusted with the mission of bringing a famous traveling icon to different parts of the world for veneration. "The Lord uses the icon quite powerfully. We've taken it for processions around abortion clinics, and a lot of them have closed."

"Which icon?" I asked.

"A six-foot-high exact replica of Our Lady of Częstochowa."

"Oh, I love her!" I exclaimed.

"Well, she's right here. She's on display next to the Blessed Sacrament in a hall annexed to the stadium."

I barely believed it. "What are the odds of my Polish Mother coming to Mexico, here, now?" I excused myself from the table and rushed out of the stadium and into the makeshift chapel. God, it seemed, was giving me my own healing retreat. Thrilled to sit down before the Blessed Sacrament and my favorite image, I exhaled into a few precious minutes of holy restoration.

The Lord knew I would need it, for the minute I stepped out of the chapel, one of the organizers grabbed my arm—"Oh there you are. Follow me"—and ushered me into a room where a radio station, transmitting the event live, was holding interviews of all the presenters. I told my story again. After that interview, the event coordinators said, "Come, Patricia. It's time to be on the panel. Like all the talks, this is being televised."

"What panel?"

"You're going to sit on the stage with the other presenters and answer questions. Get ready. You go on in five minutes."

I felt wholly inadequate, intimidated, unworthy, and unequipped. Were it not for my time in Adoration, I might have run the other way; instead, I walked onto the platform with the other speakers. As we sat down in a row of chairs, my mind started playing its own game of ping-pong:

"Patricia, God is having you on this panel for a reason. You can do this."

"No, go back into the chapel and hide. You're not qualified. You're going to make a fool of yourself."

"Just speak from your heart, and speak the truth."

"That's not good enough. You don't know anything compared with these people. You don't follow politics. You don't watch the news. You don't even have a television."

"Don't worry. You have a lot of experience working with people who've had abortions and who are suffering. Speak to them about the things you've encountered."

"All you can say for yourself is you've had three abortions, which equals—unqualified."

Sitting in the middle of the astute and learned lineup, I was handed a microphone. A famous reporter named Chucho, *El Observador* introduced us along with our titles and credentials. I was introduced as *La Mexicana-Americana* who had three abortions, and that's how I saw myself. Then Chucho proceeded to ask two questions of each of us. The second question thrown at me was, "What is Mexico lacking? What does Mexico need in order to end the violence present here?"

As I opened my mouth to speak, I felt the Spirit come over me, blanketing me with an inward sense of calm and wisdom. "I can only speak from my experience," I answered. "Having spoken to thousands of youths across Mexico and in other countries, I've noticed that there's a lack of chastity. Children are aborting their children. It's very tragic. Children and teens know about pornography, masturbation, and having sex, but they've never heard of chastity. And I'm talking about children in Catholic schools primarily. Standing before assemblies of hundreds of students, in schools where nuns are their teachers, I would ask the youth to raise their hands if they knew what chastity was. Not one hand would be raised. The nuns were so ashamed. In the United States, 85 percent of children are aborted by mothers who are not married. If we would educate our children in Mexico about chastity, many babies could be saved. We need to get to the root of the problem."

The clergy on the panel began to clap, followed by the other panel members, and then the stadium erupted in applause. "Wow, Lord," I mused. "You really take those who don't have anything and take them far. All of this comes from you."

I assumed that I'd have a chance to relax after the panel, but they weren't done with me. Another television interview followed, and then another. The last one, for Gloria TV, was hosted by a beautiful North American woman living in Mexico City. "I was sent by your spiritual advisor, Fr. Victor Salomon," she said. "He told me to seek you out to interview you on my show. I want to tell you that he's so proud of you, the way a father would be." My tired senses came alive and my heart pounded as her words filled an empty well of longing inside of me. All my life, I had never heard such a message directly from my own father. I was forever trying to get my dad's approval, never knowing if I'd truly received it. Fr. Victor's expression of pride in me was a soothing remedy for my soul.

The next morning, I sat around a large breakfast table with the event coordinators. They looked terribly disheartened, and their conversation revolved around a collective sense of failure, as if the devil had won. They wanted to get my opinion about the event but felt embarrassed to even ask. In all sincerity, I expressed to them that it was one of the most awe-inspiring events I'd ever been to and shared the many ways I had received healing from it. As I was speaking, I felt the Lord prompting me to encourage them, so I told them, "You are still worrying about the empty seats, but during the healing Rosary, I heard the Lord's voice say to my heart: 'These seats are not empty. They are filled with little saints. The unborn are here, interceding for the intentions of this event to spread across the globe.'"

The woman who was the primary director of the event began to cry, and a radiant smile spread across her face. I looked around to see twenty expressions transfigure from sullen to satisfied. Joy had entered the room, and more tears began to fall. "It's not easy to do pro-life work," I reminded them. "It's not all glorious. But don't be discouraged. What you have done was so beautiful and was accepted in heaven. You are saving the lives of children—and people's very souls. Press on, press on, and continue to defend life."

> Cast all your worries upon him because he cares for you. Be sober and vigilant. Your opponent the devil is prowling around like a roaring lion looking for [someone] to devour. Resist him, steadfast in faith, knowing that your fellow believers throughout the world undergo the same sufferings. The God of all grace who called you to his eternal glory through Christ [Jesus] will himself restore, confirm, strengthen, and establish you after you have suffered a little. To him be dominion forever. Amen.
> –1 Peter 5:7–11

Fact: Captured on a YouTube video, Cardinal Francis Arinze said the following words at a conference held at Familyland USA in Bloomington, Ohio, in 2007. Born in Nigeria, Cardinal Arinze is the prefect emeritus of the Congregation for Divine Worship and the Discipline of the Sacraments. He was widely considered a leading contender to be elected pope at the 2013 conclave that elected Pope Francis.

"To the person who says, 'Personally I am against abortion, but if people want to do it, I leave them free,' you could say, 'You are a member of the Senate or the Congress. Personally, I am not in favor of shooting the whole lot of you. But, if somebody wants to shoot all of you in the Senate, or all of you in Congress, it's just pro-choice for that person. But personally, I'm not in favor.' That is what he's saying. He's saying that, personally, he's not in favor of killing these millions of children in the womb, but if others want to do it, it's pro-choice." (1)

Chapter Twenty-One

Jesus, I Trust in You!

LAST YEAR DURING LENT, as I was heading toward a church in Santa Rosa minutes before I was to give a talk there, I found myself standing on a street corner—next to my mom. She was so close that I could reach out and touch her. Our eyes met, and I opened my mouth to say hello. Before I could utter a word, she turned her back to me and walked off. As I watched her brisk footsteps carry her away, sorrow rose up in my chest. The painful sting of abandonment, however, was gone.

The Scripture passage from Isaiah that had first inspired my mom to read the Bible, the very same passage she had read to me as she nurtured me back to health, came immediately to mind—Isaiah 49:15: *"Can a mother forget her infant, be without tenderness for the child of her womb? Even should she forget, I will never forget you."*

Shaking my head and fighting back tears, I turned and walked into the church. Five minutes later, I was telling my story and speaking highly of my mom, giving thanks for all she had done for me.

Not long afterwards, I was boarding a plane for Colombia for a three-week, whirlwind speaking tour. At a small church in Ibague, the pastor wanted me to speak as part of his homily for a healing Mass. Word had spread that I would be at that parish, and late on a Friday night, the six-hundred-capacity church couldn't hold the overflowing crowd, which spilled out onto the front steps and back parking lot, where my words blared from an outdoor speaker.

In one of the parked cars sat a thirteen-year-old named Juanita, wearing headphones and listening to music. She and her mother had grown very close to me over the course of my many trips to Ibague, and Juanita had recently entered a stage of teen rebellion. On this particular day, her oppositional antics were in full form; despite her mother's urgings, she had refused to enter the church. But a few minutes into my testimony, Juanita heard an interior voice say "Go inside the church because Patricia is about to cry." Curious, Juanita obeyed. She took off her headphones, got out of the car, walked across the parking lot in the dark, and entered the front doors of the church. At that very moment, I was walking down the center isle toward the entrance, having felt prompted to come closer to the people.

Juanita looked in my direction and was immediately blinded by an immense bright light, only inches behind me. At first, she assumed it was coming from the church lights, but as it lessened in vibrancy, it morphed into the unmistakable form of Our Lady of Guadalupe. She was outlined in dazzling white, with luminescent stars sparkling on her mantle, like those that shimmer in the night sky. She was exquisitely beautiful. Juanita gasped and stood transfixed.

As I walked up and down the aisle, Juanita watched intently as Our Lady followed behind me. With her every step, the floor around her feet illuminated. As I began to speak about the breakup of my family, tears of grief and heartbreak overwhelmed me, and I had to pause to catch my words. Juanita looked over at Our Lady's face and saw that she was beginning to cry too, feeling my pain and suffering with me. When I said the words, "God is my Father and Mary is my Mother," Our Lady's tears became drops of joy. Juanita was shown in her spirit that this was the first time I had ever publicly acknowledged Our Lady as my Mother, and for this reason, Mary was crying from sheer happiness.

When I began to speak of God's mercy on my life, I couldn't help but cry again. This time, though, it was out of gratitude. The crowd burst into applause. Juanita later told me that all throughout my talk, Our Lady never left my side. Whenever I stood still, she was on her knees praying for me. When I started to talk about my promise to my three children that I would defend life, I crossed my hands over my heart, exemplifying my promise; simultaneously, Our Lady stood up behind me and put her arms around and over mine, covering me gently with her mantle. Then she reached her hands over mine and held my heart with me. As my story came to a close, Juanita then saw the hands of angels above Our Lady, reaching down to touch the top of her garments. Slowly, the angels drew her up off the floor. As she ascended upward, she looked down at me and smiled, showing her appreciation of all that I was doing for her Son.

After the healing Mass ended and before Juanita had the chance to share with me her vision, a woman approached me, weeping, telling me how strongly she had sensed the Virgin Mary's presence alongside me while I was speaking. "She was with you the whole time!" she exclaimed and then added with emphasis, "Patricia, God is going to heal you from everything you've gone through—everything."

When I got back to my hotel, I flung myself across the bed, exhausted but exceedingly grateful. Picking up my phone, I saw that a text message had come in at the time the Mass had ended. It was from Saul. I hadn't heard from him in seven years. The text read: "Hello Patricia, It's Saul. I had a great desire to say hello."

I responded, "Saul, thank you so much for writing. I'm in Colombia, and I must share with you what God has done in my and your life. I'm an international pro-life and chastity speaker. I've now shared with millions of people all the pain and suffering I put you through because of the abortions and the way that I treated you. God has had so much mercy on me that I've given my life to defend life. I should tell you that the Holy Spirit let me see our children, and I've named them Mariana, Emmanuel, and Rosie. They are so beautiful and precious. I pray for you all the time, and I know that they're praying for you, too. You will see them when you reach heaven. Here are some of the babies who have been saved through my testimony." I attached pictures of five of the children and ended with, "I hope everything is well in your life, and I send you blessings."

I held onto the phone and waited with bated breath for his response. It would only be fair if he shot back: "I still can't believe how you lied to me and how much you hurt me. . . You owe me an explanation . . ."

But instead I got a text back that read, "What an amazing and incredible woman you are. Thank you." That's all he said. He was so merciful. I wept in disbelief.

> But you are "a chosen race, a royal priesthood, a holy nation, a people of his own, so that you may announce the praises" of him who called you out of darkness into his wonderful light.
>
> Once you were "no people," but now you are God's people; you "had not received mercy," but now you have received mercy.
>
> –1 Peter 2:9–10

After the day-long marathon event in Querétaro and the healing Mass, my mind could no longer convince me that I was rejected or without worth. For the first time, I had drunk deeply from the well of God's mercy and Our Lady's love. How easy it now was for me to battle and reject any sour and self-deprecating thoughts or feelings. As my own mother had told me years ago, I was the daughter of a King. No matter what another voice might say, my identity was secure in my Lord and my Lady's love.

Come that Easter morning, as the rays of dawn streamed through my bedroom window, I woke up underneath a waterfall of grace, filling me repeatedly with such irresistible joy that for three hours, I couldn't stop crying. I was lifted into a higher elevation of love than I'd ever known. Gratitude for all God had done for me burst from my heart in such a torrent that I couldn't contain it. Overcome with what felt like every possible positive emotion, I looked at my image of the Sacred Heart and thanked Him aloud, again and again. I never imagined the human heart could feel such happiness.

Reflecting on my past, I marveled how high above my former misery and shame the Lord had lifted me, and my thoughts traveled to a long-forgotten moment. Transported back in time, I saw myself sitting in the Rosary prayer group with my mom, with blind Grandma Yolanda ministering to me while I had one foot out the door, ready to return to a life of drugs. Then I saw Grandma Yolanda reach out her hands to pray over me, and I heard her proclaim, "The Lord wants you for Himself. He is going to use you, and you will travel across nations."

"How could I have forgotten? Way back then, she was right!" My story had now spread far and wide through television interviews and newspaper articles in various countries. (1) I was being asked to speak in Peru, Argentina, Spain, El Salvador, Guatemala, and new territories in Mexico and the United States, and the invitations weren't slowing down. That prophecy was being fulfilled.

A week later on Divine Mercy Sunday, my thankfulness was still flowing unabated. Grabbing a microphone in the front pew of my church, I began to spontaneously lead the Divine Mercy Chaplet and added my own twist. I'd made up my own little tune and wanted everyone else to sing it too, so like a crazy woman in love, I belted out, *"Jesús, yo confío en ti!"* ("Jesus, I trust in You!") It sounded horrible, but I was determined to captivate His heart. For years, I had asked Jesus for a beautiful voice to adore Him with, but never received any talent in response, so I told Him, "Well then, I'm going to sing for you with this awful voice—a true sacrifice for You (and perhaps for many)." But to my surprise, people loved it and joined in wholeheartedly, *"Jesús, yo confío en ti!"*

Only days after that, I looked down at my phone and saw my mother's number light up the screen. My heart smiled. "Hi, Mom!"

"Hello, *mi hija.*"

"Mom, I'm so happy to hear your voice."

"I'm so happy to hear *your* voice."

I just want to say . . . please forgive me for everything I've ever done to hurt you in your entire life."

With those words, I felt multiple places in my soul, empty and cold, fill with warmth. I had heard "Forgive me" from my mother's lips many times before, but never had she asked for forgiveness for *everything.*

Desiring to give her the same gift, I responded, "And please forgive me for every way that I've ever hurt you." We spoke of how we loved each other and wanted to move forward and not rehash the past. Not a twinge of pain or resentment rose in our voices. She said that she was happy working as an English teacher and had been distant from me in order to have time and space to heal. With the passing of years, a strong desire had surfaced within her to see me, so she asked God to let her know when she should reach out to try. One day, a commercial came up on her TV screen, announcing my visit to her hometown of Guadalajara. That was her sign.

"I've been following you on television and in the media, and I'm so proud of what you're doing. I've been praying for you ever since I left, and I've fasted for you because I know that God has given you a very difficult mission."

"Thank you. That means a lot." Beyond our words, a palpable feeling of love passed between us. We said our goodbyes, assured that they were actually sweet hellos.

I hung up the phone and dissolved into tears. It was a short and simple apology. And it was one of the most spectacular miracles of my life.

One day, a couple of weeks later, I went into the bathroom and stared in the mirror. For the first time I could remember, I saw beyond my body and noticed a servant of God. Beauty for me was no longer skin deep. My true beauty lay within the questions, "Have I loved today? Have I pleased God today?" Feeling mysteriously happy with who I was, including my imperfections, I actually smiled into the mirror. Then the thought hit me: I'm going to call my father. I picked up my phone and, after we said our hellos, I plunged in. "Dad, I don't know my brother. Will you let me pick him up and take him out with me?" For the first time, his wife relented and said yes when my dad asked her. Perhaps the graces of Divine Mercy Sunday were more than her reluctance could handle.

The following Saturday, I went to my father's house for the first time in five years. Standing on the front lawn was my little brother, shifting his weight nervously from one foot to the other. Catching sight of me, he began to jump up and down and then ran to throw his soft arms around my waist. "Why are your cheeks so red?" I asked him.

"They started burning up because they couldn't wait to see you!" he chirped.

Taking his small hand, I walked with him toward the front door. For years, an iron wall in my heart had kept me from crossing the threshold of my father's home. Like a force field of unworthiness and self-rejection, his front door had repelled me backward; but today that barrier crumbled. Whatever my father and Elvira thought of me—and more importantly, whatever I thought of me—held no sway. I stepped through the door and walked in. I greeted my dad and his wife in peace, and we chatted with a friendly, heartfelt ease, as if life had never been otherwise.

A full day of five-year-old fun ensued. I traipsed around town with my sibling, who was sociable, inquisitive, funny, and obedient. While never at a loss for words, he refrained from asking me for anything and humbly waited for me to announce what would happen next. We stopped at the park, the bakery, for pizza and ice cream, and then took a train ride and ended up at the zoo. All the while, he sang my new song with me, *"Jesús, yo confio en ti,"* making sure we added happy clapping. Thus I discovered I had a brother who, through no merit of my own, had always loved me.

Not long after our day of indulgence, he called me early one morning while I was half-asleep in bed to announce, "My graduation is tonight, and I expect you to join me."

Propping myself up on my elbow and pulling myself awake out of a powerful dream, I asked, "Oh really? What are you graduating from?"

"Preschool."

"You're graduating from *what*?"

"Preschool!"

"Do they even have that?" I asked groggily.

"Yes!"

Tickled by his boldness, I told him I would be more than happy to accept his invitation; then I hung up the phone and collapsed back on my pillow. Closing my eyes, I recalled my dream. I was inside my childhood home again, retracing familiar steps. This time, however, things were different.

I am about to purchase the home I grew up in. As I walk through the living room, a real estate agent is at my side, and I notice a few pieces of familiar furniture and how clean and bright everything looks: the doors, the carpet, the kitchen tile. "Oh my," I declare to the real estate agent, "I get to have my home back!" And I cry profound tears of joy.

Opening my eyes, I thought to myself, "I've had dreams like this now for over twenty years, and they've been recurring more often than normal lately. Please Lord, help me to understand . . . I need closure. I need to go inside that house."

That evening, I attended my brother's "graduation," where I ran into my cousin Xochil, whose children my mom had taken care of at our home when I was young. Neither of us could help but smile broadly as we watched my brother hold up his head up high to receive his special "diploma." "He couldn't look more proud," said my cousin.

"Yes, and he should be proud of his mighty accomplishments of playing with building blocks, squishing Play-Doh®, and eating Goldfish® crackers."

She chuckled. "Please come over for dinner afterward," she said, and I accepted her invitation.

While we were eating, Xochil, who was now working as a real estate agent, said, "Guess what house is on the market for sale?"

I froze. "Don't tell me it's my childhood home."

"Yes. It's for sale."

"Xochil," I said in disbelief, "I dreamt of this house right before I woke up this morning. I was walking through the living room with a real estate agent. The home was staged with very little furniture, and everything in it was clean and bright. In the dream, my intention was to buy it, to take ownership of the place where my family had been happy and together. I felt so relieved, so grateful."

Xochil's was clearly moved. The house had been like a second home to her and her children. Reaching my hand across the dinner table to grab her wrist, I pleaded, "You have to take me there."

"It won't be a problem, Patricia. I can schedule a home viewing and get the key to the lockbox. You'll have to act like a buyer, even though you're not."

"That's fine. I'll get to pretend for a day that I can afford a house."

"How about meeting me there tomorrow? I'll let you know what time."

The next morning, while praying in the shower, I asked God to guide me through the day and show me what He was up to. I couldn't help but beg Him, yet again, for the healing of my family, so I poured out my desire to Him. Immediately, I sensed Jesus speaking to my heart through His Sacred Heart image: "Take me with you, and make Me the King of your family and home."

"This is it!" I thought. After twenty-some years of the same old dreams, I felt that God was finally going to bind up the wounds that were causing them. No matter what He was orchestrating, I knew it would be something beautiful. *"Jesús, yo confío en ti!"*

I figured that starting off that day with Mass would help the Lord's efforts along, so I placed "Jesus" in my passenger seat, right where "He" wanted to be, and we rode off together to church. After Mass, I hopped in the car next to "Him" and drove toward the home where my family had been united and happy. Standing at the front entrance was my cousin, waiting for me with a wistful look in her eyes. As I walked toward her through the front yard, with the Sacred Heart image held tightly under my arm, I couldn't help but notice that the scenery looked no different than I remembered it.

"Patricia," she said, her voice cracking with emotion, "I remember you playing hopscotch here. You'd get colored chalk and draw wobbly squares on the walkway."

"And I remember my sister skateboarding up and down the driveway while I went round and round here on my roller skates," I said, recalling how I loved the wind brushing against my cheeks and the feeling of freedom it gave me.

Turning to embrace me, Xochil bumped up against the frame of the Sacred Heart image and exclaimed, "That's the picture that used to hang over your parents' bed!"

"Yes," I said, "that's the one. Xochil, it's so strange . . . everything looks exactly as I remember it. Not a stone my father laid has been moved. Every plant is the same. Even all the flowers are exactly as my father planted them over twenty years ago."

"I know. It's uncanny, isn't it? It almost feels as though no time here has passed at all."

"It must be only the yard," I thought to myself, as my cousin inserted a key into the lockbox. I couldn't imagine the interior of the house looking or feeling like my old home. But when she opened the front door, I stepped into what seemed impossible. Nothing had changed. The house looked impeccable—bright, shiny, and clean, like in my dream—and except for the fact that it held very little furniture, I might as well have been eleven years old returning home from a stroll around the block. The original carpet was there and no different than before; the kitchen appliances hadn't changed or moved an inch; the woodwork, the windows, the curtains, the color of the walls, the tiles carefully selected by my mother—all the fruit of my dad's hard work, suited carefully to my mom's taste, was exactly as we had left it.

With a *real* real estate agent by my side, I walked across the living room floor, somewhat unnerved by the parallel to my dream. Then I perused the kitchen whose four walls echoed multifold memories of lively family meals. A lump of nostalgia rose up in my throat. My feet were standing in the spot next to the stove where Mom used to put her arm around me, call me her beautiful princess, and cook me pancakes with hot chocolate for breakfast. Taking a deep breath, I left the kitchen and walked toward the bedroom I had shared with my sister. Stepping through the doorway, I traveled even further back in time.

Rays from the noon sun streamed into the room through the same high window where Jesus had paid me a visit in my infancy. My mind pictured Him there in His stunning gold, green, and burgundy gown—with His adoring expression and His arms extending toward me. Then my eyes traced the path along the sunrays, where He had lifted me into the air to whisk me off to heaven. How was it that such a marvelous and unusual thing had happened to me? "Did You know, Lord," I silently asked Him, "that I would later squander the beautiful gift of Your visit? Of course You must have."

The last room to enter was the same one where I would crouch down and crawl to avoid Jesus' piercing gaze from above my parents' bed. With my cousin at my side, I felt my knees weaken, and I dropped to the floor in gratitude for the miracle of being there. Kissing the carpet underneath me, I finally let my tears fall. "How all-encompassing God is," I marveled, as I peered out the same window I always had, into the garden view I had enjoyed as a child. "There must be a reason why the owners of the home didn't alter or remodel a single thing," I thought. It seemed to me that Jesus wanted everything to look exactly as it was so I could have this occasion for healing more than twenty years later. That is how special and important He made me feel.

Aware of what I must do, I took my image of Jesus and hung "Him" up on the wall above where my parents' headboard used to be, and I prayed. The Lord was giving me the chance to complete what had never been done. I would consecrate my family to Him in the very place where we had once been united. Weeping with gratitude, I first thanked Jesus aloud for His goodness in bringing me there, and I asked Him to heal my cousin, who was kneeling beside me. Then I asked for mercy and forgiveness for all the New Age practices that had been welcomed into that house—and for the fact that Jesus Christ was never allowed to be the Lord of our home and of our hearts. Finally, still on my knees, I said a prayer of consecration to His Most Sacred Heart and declared Him aloud as the Lord and King of our family:

> Lord Jesus, King of all families and of all that is: In this moment, one that should have happened long ago, I consecrate my family to Your Sacred Heart. Your Heart always burned so brightly and with such tender compassion for all of us. You were in this home with us every second. You sat with us at meals, tucked us into bed every night, and stood by us in our sleep, but we didn't know You were there. Your picture graced our walls but not our hearts. We rejected Your presence and Your gifts and broke what You had so beautifully put together. But now, Jesus, I ask You to change all that. I believe that You can do the impossible, that You can reach through time and heal and restore everything. I thank You for bringing my mom back into my life, Lord, and I pray that You will fully restore our relationship. Place us side by side in Your Heart.
>
> Please, Lord, heal the rifts and broken ties with my dad. Draw us together again in close friendship, and in unity with my stepmother. Nothing is forever lost in You. I rejoice in the hope that the unity in our family will be gloriously restored. I know that no matter what may happen here on earth, we will again have the chance in

> heaven to embrace one another in holy love and true joy. May heaven open its doors to us, where we will all see my three children and the martyrs in our family who went before us, and where we will sing with great abandon of Your endless mercies for eternity. All glory be to the Heart of Jesus, our King and our Father!

When I finished, a warm stillness and peaceful air of reassurance came over me. With that act of consecration in my parents' old room, the Lord sutured the last bleeding wound within me from the trauma of suddenly losing my family as a child. This was the rupture in my soul that had triggered my hair-pulling and paved the way for a distorted self-image. This was the blow that had made me vulnerable to unhealthy partnerships and premature sexual intimacy—which opened me to the act of abortion, pulled me into drugs, and left me anxious for the man in the blue suit. This was the wound that propelled me to squander God's gifts over and over again in search of a replacement for the family I had lost.

I had assumed I would leave my childhood home feeling sad that day. But I walked out of there with a profound sense of liberation and joy. For the first time since age twelve, I felt whole. And from that moment on, my nostalgic dreams of times past have not returned, for the Lord is now set properly on His throne. He is King.

> I praise you, LORD, for you raised me up and did not let my enemies rejoice over me.
>
> O LORD, my God, I cried out to you and you healed me.
>
> LORD, you brought me up from Sheol; you kept me from going down to the pit.
>
> Sing praise to the LORD, you faithful; give thanks to God's holy name.
>
> For divine anger lasts but a moment; divine favor lasts a lifetime. At dusk weeping comes for the night; but at dawn there is rejoicing.
>
> Complacent, I once said, "I shall never be shaken."
>
> LORD, when you showed me favor I stood like the mighty mountains. But when you hid your face I was struck with terror.

To you, LORD, I cried out; with the Lord I pleaded for mercy:

"What gain is there from my lifeblood, from my going down to the grave? Does dust give you thanks or declare your faithfulness?

Hear, O LORD, have mercy on me; LORD, be my helper."

You changed my mourning into dancing; you took off my sackcloth and clothed me with gladness.

With my whole being I sing endless praise to you. O LORD, my God, forever will I give you thanks.
–Psalm 30:2-13

A NOTE TO THE READER

AMAZON REVIEWS

If you were graced by this story, would you kindly post a short review of *Transfigured* on Amazon.com? Your support will make a difference in the lives of souls and help spread the Good News.

To leave a short review, go to Amazon.com and type in *Transfigured.* Click on the book and scroll down the page. Next to customer reviews, click on "Write a customer review."

BOOK TRAILER & VIDEOS OF PATRICIA SANDOVAL

If you are curious to see the trailer for the book and videos of Patricia Sandoval speaking that are so impactful that they have "gone viral," go to YouTube.com and type in "Queen of Peace Media." Search for "One of the Best Pro-life Speakers in the World Today: Patricia Sandoval shakes the crowd," among other popular videos. Please share them with the world.

OTHER BOOKS

BY AUTHOR, CHRISTINE WATKINS

Available in Print, E-book & Audio Book Formats
at QueenofPeaceMedia.com and Amazon.com
Go to:
www.queenofpeacemedia.com/catholic-bookstore

OF MEN AND MARY

HOW SIX MEN WON THE GREATEST BATTLE OF THEIR LIVES

"*Of Men and Mary* is superb. The six life testimonies contained within it are miraculous, heroic, and truly inspiring."

—Fr. Gary Thomas
Pastor, exorcist, and subject of the book and movie, "The Rite."

(See www.queenofpeacemedia.com/of-men-and-mary For the book trailer and to order)

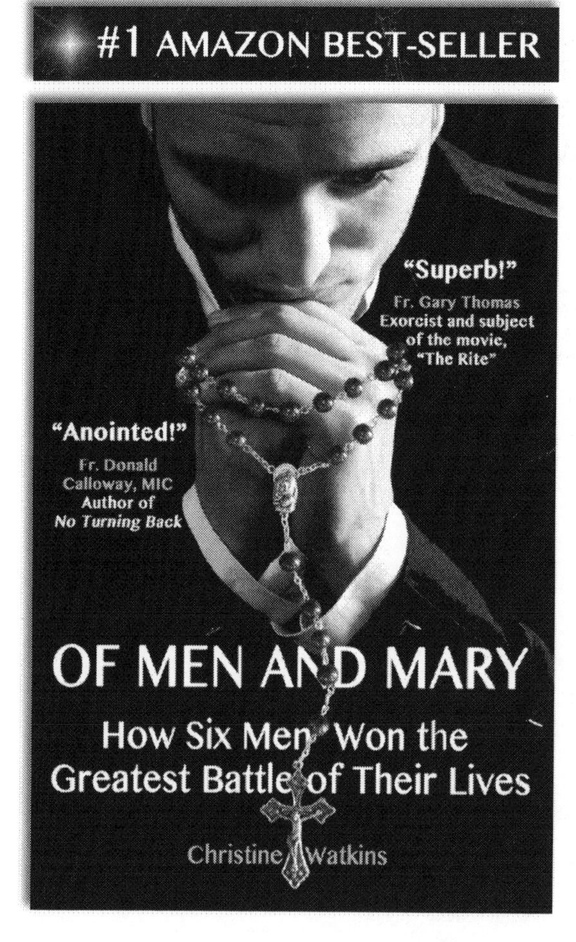

Turn these pages, and you will find yourself surprisingly inspired by a murderer locked up in prison, a drug-using football player who dreamed of the pros, and a selfish, womanizing dare-devil who died and met God. You will root for a husband and father whose marriage was a battleground, a man searching desperately to belong, pulled by lust and illicit attractions, and an innocent lamb who lost, in a single moment, everyone he cared about most. And you will rejoice that their sins and their pasts were no obstacle for heaven.

MARY'S MANTLE CONSECRATION

A SPIRITUAL RETREAT FOR HEAVEN'S HELP

Also available in Spanish—*El Manto de María: Una Consagración Mariana para Ayuda Celestial*

Endorsed by **Archbishop Salvatore Cordileone** and **Bishop Myron J. Cotta**

(See www.MarysMantleConsecration.com to see a video of amazing testimonies and to order)

"I am grateful to Christine Watkins for making this disarmingly simple practice, which first grew in the fertile soil of Mexican piety, available to the English-speaking world."

—Archbishiop Salvatore Cordileone

"Now more than ever, we need a miracle. Christine Watkins leads us through a 46-day self-guided retreat that focuses on daily praying of the Rosary, a Little fasting, and meditating on various virtues and the seven gifts of the Holy Spirit, leading to a transformation in our lives and in the people on the journey with us!"

—Fr. Sean O. Sheridan, TOR
President, Franciscan University of Steubenville

MARY'S MANTLE CONSECRATION

PRAYER JOURNAL

to accompany the consecration book

Also available in Spanish—
El Manto de Maria: Diario de Oración para la Consagración

PREPARE FOR AN OUTPOURING OF GRACE UPON YOUR LIFE

(See <u>www.MarysMantleConsecration.com</u> to see a video of amazing testimonies and to order)

St. Pope John Paul II said that his consecration to Mary was "a decisive turning point in my life." It can be the same for you.

This *Prayer Journal* with daily Scriptures, saint quotes, questions for reflection and space for journaling is a companion book to the popular *Mary's Mantle Consecration: A Spiritual Retreat for Heaven's Help:* a self-guided retreat that has resulted in miracles in the lives and hearts of those who have applied themselves to it.

These pages will take you even deeper into your soul and into God's transforming grace.

FULL OF GRACE

MIRACULOUS STORIES OF HEALING AND CONVERSION THROUGH MARY'S INTERCESSION

BEST-SELLER

"Christine Watkins's beautiful and touching collection of conversion stories are direct, honest, heart-rending, and miraculous."

—Wayne Weible
Author of *Medjugorje: The Message*

(See www.queenofpeacemedia.com/full-of-grace for the book trailer and to order)

In this riveting book, Christine Watkins tells her dramatic story of miraculous healing and conversion to Catholicism, along with the stories of five others: a homeless drug addict, an altar boy trapped by cocaine, a stripper, a lonely youth, and a modern-day hero.

Following each story is a message that Mary has given to the world. And for those eager to probe the deeper, reflective waters of discipleship—either alone or within a prayer group—a Scripture passage, prayerful reflection questions, and a spiritual exercise at the end of each chapter offer an opportunity to enliven our faith.

THE WARNING

TESTIMONIES AND PROPHECIES OF THE ILLUMINATION OF CONSCIENCE

Includes the riveting story of Marino Restrepo, hailed as a St. Paul for our century

(**See www.queenofpeacemedia.com/the-warning for the book trailer and to order**)

"Tremendous…invaluable…timely." **—Mark Mallet**

"Read this prophetic book and believe." **—Msgr. Ralph J. Chieffo**

Authentic accounts of saints and mystics of the Church who have spoken of a day when we will all see our souls in the light of truth, and fascinating stories of those who have already experienced it for themselves.

"With His divine love, He will open the doors of hearts and illuminate all consciences. Every person will see himself in the burning fire of divine truth. It will be like a judgment in miniature."
—Our Lady to Fr. Stefano Gobbi
Marian Movement of Priests

Appendix with Endnotes

CHAPTER 1:

Statistics for divorce in the United States consistently reveal that the children of divorced parents are more at risk for certain struggles in life, such as lower self-esteem, a tendency to trust others less, and lower grades at school. They are also more vulnerable to child abuse (this is more common in stepfamilies) and less able to make friends. Boys, in particular, are more prone to aggression. (1)

New research presented in the book, *The Good News About Marriage*, by Shaunti Feldhahn clarified that the actual divorce rate in the United States is only about 20 to 25 percent for first-time marriages. The oft-quoted figure of 50 percent came from projections of what researchers thought the divorce rate would become when states around the nation were passing no-fault divorce laws, and they watched the divorce numbers rising in the 1970s and early 1980s. But the divorce rate has dropped since then and never came close to the projected 50 percent. Among church-goers, the divorce rate is even lower, in the single digits or teens. Feldhahn's research also found that the vast majority of marriages in the United States are happy. (3, 4)

(1) Robert E. Emery, *Marriage, Divorce, and Children's Adjustment, Developmental Clinical Psychology and Psychiatry*, v. 14 (Newbury Park, CA: Sage Publications, 1988).

(2) Reinier Bloem, "Child Psychology Divorce," accessed January 27, 2018, http://www.children-and-divorce.com/child-psychology-divorce.html.

(3) Shaunti Feldhahn, *The Good News About Marriage: Debunking Discouraging Myths about Marriage and Divorce*, First Edition (Colorado Springs, CO: Multnomah Books, 2014), p. 10.

(4) Paul Strand, CBN News Washington Senior Correspondent, "Divorce Shocker: Most Marriages Do Make It," CBN News, U.S., May 6, 2014, accessed January 27, 2018, http://www.cbn.com/cbnnews/us/2014/May/Divorce-Shocker-Most-Marriages-Do-Make-It/?exitmobile=true.

CHAPTER 2:

(1) Czarina Ong, "Young Woman 'Possessed' after Playing with Ouija Board Dies at Church During Exorcism Ritual," Christianity Today, December 1, 2015, accessed January 27, 2018, http://www.christiantoday.com/article/young.woman.possessed.after.playing.with.ouija.board.dies.at.church.during.exorcism.ritual/72171.htm.

(2) Paul Burnell, "Exorcisms on the Rise," National Catholic Register, June 4-10, 2000.

(3) Dan Burke, "Halloween, the Catholic Faith and the Occult: An Interview With Father Jose Antonio Fortea, National Catholic Register October, 31, 2014, accessed January 27, 2018, http://www.ncregister.com/daily-news/halloween-the-catholic-faith-and-the-occult/#ixzz3tE6CFx7a.

(4) Martin Barillas, "Beware of Quija Boards: Life Imitates Art at an Exorcism in Colombia," Spero News, October 31, 2014, accessed January 27, 2018, Ωhttp://www.speroforum.com/a/EOJKJEXXDP38/75298-Beware-of-Ouija-boards-Life-imitates-art-at-an-exorcism-in-Colombia#.Vl-xOPmrSM-.

(5) Mark Woods, "Sales of Ouija Boards Spike, But How Dangerous Are They?" Christian Today, December 6, 2014, accessed January 20, 2017, http://www.christiantoday.com/article/sales.of.ouija.boards.spike.but.how.dangerous.are.they/43834.htm.

CHAPTER 3:

(1) Trailer for Blood Money, a documentary directed by David K. Kyle, exposing the truth behind the abortion industry: https://www.youtube.com/watch?v=cYaTywSDmls&eurl=http%3A%2F%2F

YouTube: Carol Everett: Marketing Abortion (LIFE Today / James Robison): http://www.youtube.com/watch?v=OFXnRQl2Hv4&feature=youtu.be and http://heartsunitedforlife.com/?p=1731.

YouTube: An Abortion Provider Speaks, https://www.youtube.com/watch?v=mXZCOaRVrbg.

(2) Carly Kennelly, "Consumer Reports Ranks Planned Parenthood Condoms Low," KTBX.com, The People You Know; The News You Trust, January 7, 2005, accessed January 27, 2018, http://www.kbtx.com/home/headlines/1339521.html.

(3) Barbara Hollingsworth, "Planned Parenthood Produces Video Promoting Bondage and Sadomasochism to Teens," cnsnews.com, February 16, 2014, accessed January 27, 2018, http://cnsnews.com/news/article/barbara-hollingsworth/planned-parenthood-produces-video-promoting-bondage-and.

(4) Paul E. Rondeau, "Teen Pregnancy Rate Drops 45.7 Percent When Planned Parenthood Leaves Town," The Christian Post: American Life League, January 14, 2014, accessed January 27, 2018,

http://blogs.christianpost.com/american-life-league/teen-pregnancy-rate-drops-45-7-percent-when-planned-parenthood-leaves-town-19621/.

CHAPTER 4:

(1) Bernard Nathanson, Aborting America (New York: Doubleday, 1979), p. 193.

In efforts to keep abortion legal, pro-choice advocates claim that making abortion illegal would bring harm to women because women will abort anyway and may die in the process. The history of abortion in Poland invalidates that claim of harm, a claim which pro-choice advocates say makes abortion a legal "necessity." Is this claim of harm another lie? Poland was occupied for forty-four years by Russia, which legalized state-paid abortion in the first three months of pregnancy. The official state numbers of abortions during those years in Poland average approximately 146,550 annually and drop significantly to 59,417 by 1990, with the advent of the Solidarity Independence Movement and the influence of St. Pope John Paul II. By 1993, abortion was effectively banned in Poland, except in the most exceptional cases, in response to pressure from the Catholic Church, which had been instrumental in the fight against Communism.

What was the result? In 1998, the total number of induced abortions in Poland was 253. One hundred and ninety-nine were done to save the "life and health" of the woman, forty-five for "fetal impairment," and nine for rape or incest.

In summary, a large nation, for four and a half decades, had abortion-on-request, paid for by the state. Certainly, the practice of abortion in Poland had become deeply ingrained. Then came independence and a law that took the total number of abortions down to 0.004 percent of what they had been. And this happened contrary to all predictions by government agencies, the media, the UN, and Planned Parenthood. To perhaps everyone's surprise, 25 percent fewer miscarriages and 30 percent fewer female deaths occurred than when abortion was legal. In the latest annual report, twenty-one women died from pregnancy-related problems, with none listed as dying from illegal abortions.

These are firm statistics, annually reported and heatedly discussed by the Polish parliament, its ministries of health, labor, social welfare and education, as well as by mass media, nongovernmental organizations, and anyone else interested in the problem.

If abortions are again forbidden, will illegal abortions, with all of their alleged tragic consequences, take place? In Poland, the answer was no. (2)

(2) J. C. Wilke, "Clear Evidence: If Forbidden, Abortion Will Not Return to the Back Alley," Life Issues Connector, Life Issues Institute, April, 2000,1,3, accessed January 27, 2018, http://www.abortionfacts.com/facts/12.

CHAPTER 5:

(1) Stanley K. Henshaw, "Unintended pregnancy in the United States," Family Planning Perspectives, 1998, 30(1):24-29 & 46, accessed July 26, 2017, https://www.guttmacher.org/journals/psrh/1998/01/unintended-pregnancy-united-states.

(2) 2006 Guttmacher Institute Report (Guttmacher Institute, formerly the research arm for Planned Parenthood).

(3) Rachel K. Jones, Jacqueline Darroch, and Stanley K. Henshaw, "Contraceptive Use among U.S. Women Having Abortions in 2000–2001," Perspectives on Sexual and Reproductive Health, 34(6) (2002): 294–303, accessed July 26, 2017, https://www.guttmacher.org/journals/psrh/2002/11/contraceptive-use-among-us-women-having-abortions-2000-2001.

(4) Induced Abortion in the United States, January 2017 Fact Sheet, Guttmacher Institute, accessed July 26, 2017, https://www.guttmacher.org/fact-sheet/induced-abortion-united-states.

(5) Jenna Jerman, Rachel K. Jones, and Tsuyoshi Onda, *Characteristics of U.S. Abortion Patients in 2014 and Changes Since 2008* (Guttmacher Institute, May 2016 Report), accessed July 26, 2017, https://www.guttmacher.org/report/characteristics-us-abortion-patients-2014.

(6) Center for Disease Control (CDC) Morbidity and Mortality Weekly Report Abortion Surveillance—United States, 2009, Surveillance Summaries, 61(SS08) (November 23, 2012): 1-44, http://www.cdc.gov/mmwr/preview/mmwrhtml/ss6108a1.htm.

(7) Vincent M. Rue, Cynthia Tellefsen, "Library: The Effects of Abortion on Men: Its Emotional, Psychological and Relational Impact," accessed January 27, 2018, http://www.catholicculture.org/culture/library/view.cfm?id=8089.

See also: "Reclaiming Fatherhood: A Multifaceted Examination of Men Dealing with Abortion," September 8-9, 2008; Site Sponsor: National Office of Post-Abortion Reconciliation and Healing, 1-800-5WE-CARE, http://www.menandabortion.info/10-aftermath.html.

CHAPTER 6:

On Planned Parenthood's website, the organization bolsters its position that motherhood causes more emotional problems than abortion by noting that the American Psychological Association does not recognize the existence of the symptoms of "post-abortion trauma" or "post-abortion syndrome." (6)

The American Psychological Association has admitted that ideology, not science, governs the APA's support for abortion. This admission came in response to a request by a Washington Times columnist for the organization's reaction to a 2005 New Zealand longitudinal study. The study was conducted over twenty-five years by David M. Fergusson, Ph.D., a pro-choice atheist, and his research team. (7) The researchers were so surprised by their findings, which showed that abortion was directly linked to mental illness, that they began reviewing the studies cited by the APA in its claims that abortion was beneficial, or at least non-harmful, to women's mental health. The researchers concluded (1) that the APA's publications defending abortion are based on a small number of studies that had major methodological shortcomings, and (7) that the APA appeared to be consistently ignoring a body of studies that have shown negative effects from abortion.

When asked to comment on the New Zealand study and the pro-choice researchers' criticisms, APA expert, Dr. Nancy Felipe Russo, told the Washington Times that the APA's position on abortion was established on the view that abortion is a civil right and that Dr. Fergusson's study would have no effect on the APA's position because "to pro-choice advocates, mental health effects are not relevant to the legal context of arguments to restrict access to abortion." If evidence doesn't matter, then the APA task force has performed a breech in public responsibility. (8, 9)

(1) Mota et. al., "Associations between Abortion, Mental Disorders and Suicidal Behavior in a Nationally Representative Sample," The Canadian Journal of Psychiatry 55(4) (April 2010): 239-246.

(2) Priscilla Coleman, Ph.D. et. al., "Induced Abortion and Anxiety, Mood, and Substance Abuse Disorders: Isolating the Effects of Abortion in The National Comorbidity Survey," Journal of Psychiatric Research (2008), doi:10.1016/j.jpsychires.2008.10.009, https://archive.org/stream/526009-induced-abortion-and-anxiety-mood-and-substance/526009-induced-abortion-and-anxiety-mood-and-substance_djvu.txt.

(3) Priscilla Coleman, Ph.D., "A Tidal Wave of Published Data: More Than 30 Studies in Last Five Years Show Negative Impact of Abortion on Women," Abortion Is the Unchoice, accessed January 27, 2018, LifeNews.com, accessed January 27, 2018, http://www.lifenews.com/2010/11/12/opi-1006/.

(4) Chicago Tribune, March 11, 1981, p. 8, col. 1.

(5) Steve Aden, "War on Women: Planned Parenthood Denies Info on Abortion Risks," LifeNews.com, July 27, 2012, accessed January 27, 2018, http://www.lifenews.com/2012/07/27/war-on-women-planned-parenthood-denies-info-on-abortion-risks/

(6) "The Emotional Effects of Induced Abortion," accessed July 26, 2017, https://www.plannedparenthood.org/uploads/filer_public/0c/9a/0c9a91c0-3e94-48d8-b110-374da1275df8/abortion_emotional_effects.pdf.

(7) David M. Fergusson, Ph.D. et. al., "Abortion in Young Women and Subsequent Mental Health," Journal of Child Psychology and Psychiatry 47(1) (2006): 16-24.

(8) David C. Reardon, Ph.D., "'Evidence Doesn't Matter'—APA Spokesperson Says of Abortion Complications: Studies Showing Emotional Problems Not Relevant to American Psychological Association's Pro-Choice Advocacy," Elliot Institute (February 15, 2005), accessed January 27, 2018, http://lifeissues.net/writers/rea/rea_06evidencenotmatter.html.

(9) Priscilla Coleman, Ph.D., "Report on Abortion and Mental Health Violates the Methods of Science," APA Task Force Report: A Breech of Public Responsibility (2010), accessed January 27, 2018, http://afterabortion.org/2010/apa-task-force-report-a-breech-of-public-responsibility/.

See also the continually updated research the Elliott Institute website, showing that women are more likely to suffer emotional injury after undergoing abortion: http://afterabortion.org/1999/more-research-on-post-abortion-issues/.

CHAPTER 7:

(1) Marriage Savers by Michael McManus.

CHAPTER 8:

(1) "El Alfarero" ("The Potter") by Nena Leal

(2) Tim Reidy, "CARA on Real Presence," America: the National Catholic Review, October 18, 2010, accessed January 27, 2018, http://americamagazine.org/content/all-things/cara-real-presence.

(3) Mary Gautier, "Knowledge and Belief about the Real Presence," The National Catholic Reporter, Oct. 24, 2011, accessed January 27, 2018, http://ncronline.org/news/catholics-america/knowledge-and-belief-about-real-presence

CHAPTER 9:

(1) Carmen Blanco, "Low Confession Numbers Prompt Creative Outreach by Dioceses, Churches," The National Catholic Reporter, Catholic News Service Washington, August 6, 2009, accessed January 27, 2018, http://ncronline.org/news/faith-parish/low-confession-numbers-prompt-new-efforts.

CHAPTER 11:

(1) Medjugorje is now the third largest pilgrimage site in the world. Parish archivist, Marija Dugandzic, has confirmed that in the thirty years following the start of the alleged apparitions, 27 million Holy Communions were distributed in Medjugorje's St. James Church, and 540,000 visits were registered from cardinals, bishops, priests, and nuns. Five hundred and thirty-two healings were medically documented, 520 men became priests, and 123 women became nuns as a result of pilgrimages there. See Jakob Marschner's Medjugorje Today article from November 3, 2011: "At Least 532 Were Healed in Medjugorje," referenced from: http://www.medjugorjemiracles.com/2011/11/medjugorje-miracles-man-hears-again-532-documented-healings-643-vocations/.

As of this writing, the apparitions in Medjugorje have neither been approved nor condemned by the Church, and the Church almost never approves of apparitions until after they have ended. St. Pope John Paul II the Great was an ardent believer in the authenticity of the alleged Marian apparitions in Medjugorje. This was confirmed by Monsignor Slawomir Oder of Poland, the postulator for the cause of J.P. II's canonization, who meticulously recorded the late pontiff's views in the book, Why He Is A Saint. To Monsignor Maurillo Kreiger, former bishop of Florianopolis in Brazil, John Paul II said, "Medjugorje, Medjugorje, it's the spiritual heart of the world." See pages 191 and 194 of the author's book, Full of Grace: Miraculous Stories of Healing and Conversion through Mary's Intercession. Also see Denis Nolan's Medjugorje and the Church.

Of note: Dr. Theresa Burke, the founder of Rachel's Vineyard, the largest program for post-abortion healing in the world, received her inspiration for her work during an alleged apparition in Medjugorje, as told in person to the author.

(2) Rachel's Vineyard Retreats for post-abortion healing offer hope and healing for the soul for women, men, and couples throughout the United States and abroad in thirty-five countries, ten languages, and over 1200 locations. Information and retreat locations can be found at www.rachelsvineyard.org.

(3) The following is a list of the symptoms of post-abortion syndrome (PAS), a variant of PTSD (Post-traumatic stress disorder). These symptoms will not necessarily appear at the same time, nor is anyone likely to experience all of them. Some may occur immediately after an abortion and others much later. If a person can identify with more than two symptoms, it could be that he or she is experiencing post-abortion syndrome. PAS symptoms include: guilt, anxiety, avoiding children or pregnant women, numbness, sexual dysfunction, depression, thoughts of suicide, anniversary reactions, flashbacks, wanting to get pregnant again, fear of infertility, unable to bond with present or future children, fear that current or future children will die, eating disorders, alcohol and drug use.

Reference: Dr. Paul C. Reisser and Teri K. Reisser, A Solitary Sorrow: Finding Healing & Wholeness After Abortion (Wheaton, H. Shaw Publishers, 1999). Also see: "Post Abortion Syndrome Symptoms," Ramah International, https://ramahinternational.org/post-abortion-syndrome-symptoms/.

(4) Brian Young, "Life Before Roe: a Brief Survey of U.S. Abortion Law Before the 1973 Decision," American Life League, 1995, accessed January 27, 2018, https://www.ewtn.com/library/PROLIFE/LIFBFROE.TXT.

CHAPTER 12:

Two weeks before President Plutarco enforced anticlerical legislation in Mexico on June 14, 1926, he was awarded a medal of merit from the head of Mexico's Scottish Rite of Freemasonry for his actions against Catholics. (3) The new laws included outlawing religious orders, depriving the Catholic Church of property rights, and clergy of civil liberties and the right to vote. (4, 5)

Calles's enforcement was strict and violent. In response, people in strongly Catholic areas, especially the states of Jalisco, Zacatecas, Guanajuato, Colima and Michoacán, began to oppose him. On January, 1, 1927, a war cry went up from the faithful, "¡Viva Cristo Rey!" ("Long live Christ the King!")

During the war, the Mexican government violently persecuted the clergy and tortured and massacred suspected Cristeros and their supporters. The rebels had scarce logistical supplies and relied heavily on the Feminine Brigades of St. Joan of Arc, and on raids into towns, trains and ranches in order to supply themselves with money, horses, ammunition, and food. By contrast, later in the war, the Calles government was supplied with arms and ammunition by the United States government. In at least one battle, American pilots provided air support for the federal army against the Cristero rebels. (6)

By the time the war ended in 1929, about 90,000 people on both sides had died. A truce was negotiated with the assistance of U.S. Ambassador Dwight Morrow in which the Cristeros agreed to lay down their arms. Calles, however, did not abide by the terms of the truce; he had approximately 500 Cristero leaders and 5,000 other Cristeros shot, frequently in their homes in front of their wives and children. Particularly offensive to Catholics after the supposed truce was Calles's insistence on a complete state monopoly on education, suppressing all Catholic education and introducing "socialist" education in its place, saying: "We must enter and take possession of the mind of childhood, the mind of youth." (7)

(1) Fox Quesada, Vicente, and Rob Allyn, Revolution of Hope: The Life, Faith, and Dreams of a Mexican President (New York: Viking, 2007), p. 17.

(2) Kathleen Naab, "The Cristero War: The Story Behind the Cover Up: Historian Gives Evaluation of Film, Explains What Happened in 1920s Mexico," Zenit: The World Seen from Rome, May 30, 2012, accessed July 26, 2017, https://zenit.org/articles/the-cristero-war-the-story-behind-the-cover-up/.

(3) Olivier Lelibre, "The Cristeros: 20th century Mexico's Catholic Uprising," The Angelus, Vol. XXV, No.1, January, 2002.

(4) Anthony James Joes, Resisting Rebellion: The History and Politics of Counterinsurgency, (Kentucky; University Press, 2006), p. 70.

(5) Jim Tuck, "The Cristero Rebellion – Part 1," Mexico Connect, August 1, 1997, accessed January 27, 2018, http://www.mexconnect.com/articles/286-cristero-rebellion-part-1-toward-the-abyss.

(6) Christopher Check, "The Cristeros and the Mexican Martyrs," This Rock, September 2007; p. 17.

(7) Brian Van Hove, S.J., "Blood-Drenched Altars," Faith & Reason, 1994, Eternal Word Network, accessed January 27, 2018, http://www.ewtn.com/library/HOMELIBR/FR94204.TXT.

CHAPTER 13:

Ideal standards for female beauty are subjective, according to time period and culture. In places where Western media has not infiltrated a nation's culture, the thin ideal has not (yet) taken hold of women. Nigeria has businesses dedicated to helping people put on weight, offering places where they can go to do nothing but eat and sleep. In Mauritania, young girls are encouraged to gain weight in order to be more attractive to potential partners. On the island nation of Tonga, where 90 percent of the population is overweight, heaviness is considered a status symbol. In Cape Town, South Africa, two-thirds of teen girls perceive excess weight as a sign of happiness and wealth.

Television was not introduced in the remote provinces of Fiji until the mid-1990s. Over the next three years, teenage girls went from viewing heaviness positively to viewing it negatively, and 74 percent thought of themselves as too fat. Many decided to diet. Globally, rates of eating disorders, such as anorexia and bulimia, are steadily increasing in young girls.

Aspirations for thinness are impacting girls at a surprisingly young age. In various studies, 40 percent of six-year-old girls expressed a desire to be thinner. An overwhelming majority of ten-year-old girls, 81 percent, feared being fat. Half of girls in fifth grade through twelfth grade felt that magazine images made them want to lose weight. (1, 3)

(1) Carolyn Coker Ross, MD, "Why Do Women Hate Their Bodies?" Psych Central: World of Psychology, accessed January 27, 2018, http://psychcentral.com/blog/archives/2012/06/02/why-do-women-hate-their-bodies/.

(2) "Women's Body Image and BMI: A Look at the Evolution of the Female Figure over 100 Years," Body image and BMI: 100 years in the U.S., accessed January 27, 2018, http://www.rehabs.com/explore/womens-body-image-and-bmi/.

CHAPTER 14:

At the "high" end of the beauty business of cosmeceuticals, exclusive clinics in various tourist locations worldwide are offering face lifts and cosmetic procedures using tissues from aborted fetuses and stem cells from human embryos, which are said to rejuvenate the skin. (4) In the Ukraine, women are paid $200-$300 (three month's salary) to carry their pregnancies to a very late stage and to deliver the babies in a kind of forced premature birth. While still alive, the babies are cut open and their organs harvested when they are still as fresh as possible. The parts end up in clinics worldwide offering fetal injections to "eliminate cellulite from their buttocks, thighs, and arms." In Moscow, alone, there are fifty such beauty parlors and cellulite clinics where treatments cost up to $20,000.

At a clinic called the Institute for Regenerative Medicine in Barbados, wealthy American and British women who cannot avail themselves of "high" end beauty clinic treatments at home, due to regulatory restraints, spend $25,000 per session on a "treatment consisting of having liquefied fetal tissues injected into their bodies so they can feel refreshed." (5)

Because beauty products made from fetal and embryonic tissue are not mass-produced and have a very limited shelf life, they are priced high. In the United States, the following products run on the "low" end of fetal cosmeceuticals. The anti-aging cream, Amatokin, produced by Voss Laboratories, costs $190 for one ounce. Four milliliters of ReVive Skincare's Peau Magnifique retails for $1,500. (1) A cream by Neocutis called Journee Bio-Restorative Day Cream with PSP has a price kept confidential from the general public and is sold only through a doctor's office. (6)

(1) Ben Johnson, "Aborted Baby's Heart Was Beating As We Harvested His Brains: Worker in New Planned Parenthood Video," Aug 19, 2015, Life Site News, accessed January 27, 2018, https://www.lifesitenews.com/news/breaking-i-saw-an-aborted-babys-heart-beating-outside-his-body-new-undercov.

(2) Victoria Evans, "Commercial Markets Created by Abortion Profiting from the Fetal Distribution Chain," Licentiate Dissertation Thesis, November 2009, Faculty of Bioethics, Athenaeum Pontificium Regina Apostolor Um, p. 54, accessed January 27, 2018, https://sfarchdiocese.org/documents/2017/10/licentiate_thesis1.pdf.

(3) Jung-yoon Choi, Barbara Demick, "Human Flesh Found in Chinese Health Pills," Los Angeles Times, May 8, 2015, January 27, 2018,

http://latimesblogs.latimes.com/world_now/2012/05/south-koreans-confiscated-pills-human-remains.html.

Laurie Burkitt, with contributions from Min-sun Lee, "South Korea Steps Up Fight Against Human Flesh Pills from China," Wallstreet Journal, May 7, 2012, January 27, 2018, http://blogs.wsj.com/chinarealtime/2012/05/07/south-korea-steps-up-fight-against-human-flesh-pills-from-china/.

"Bizarre Craze Behind Smuggling of Pills Containing the Powdered Flesh of Babies," May 7, 2015, Fox News, January 27, 2018, http://www.foxnews.com/world/2012/05/07/south-korea-finds-smuggled-capsules-containing-human-flesh/.

(4) M.A. Glueck, M.D., R.J. Cihak, M.D., "Fetuses Harvested for Cosmetic Procedures," The Medicine Men, 2006.

(5) B. Clowes, "Special Report: Ukrainian Trafficking in Baby Parts," Human Life International, 270, 2007.

(6) Information available on the Neocutis website: http://www.neocutis.com, January 27, 2018.

(7) The following is excerpted from the Diary of St. Faustina Kowalska: Divine Mercy in My Soul:

Jesus made known to me how very pleasing to Him were prayers of atonement. He said to me, "The prayer of a humble and loving soul disarms the anger of My Father and draws down an ocean of blessings." After the adoration, half way to my cell, I was surrounded by a pack of huge black dogs who were jumping and howling and trying to tear me to pieces. I realized that they were not dogs, but demons. One of them spoke up in a rage, "Because you have snatched so many souls away from us this night, we will tear you to pieces." I answered, "If that is the will of the most merciful God, tear me to pieces, for I have justly deserved it, because I am the most miserable of all sinners, and God is ever holy, just, and infinitely merciful." To these words all the demons answered as one, "Let us flee, for she is not alone; the Almighty is with her!" And they vanished like dust, like the noise of the road, while I continued on my way to my cell undisturbed, finishing my Te Deum and pondering the infinite and unfathomable mercy of God. (Diary, 320)

After I received the last sacraments, there was a definite improvement [in her health]. I remained alone. This lasted for half an hour and then came another attack; but this one was not so strong, as the doctor intervened. I united my sufferings with the sufferings of Jesus and offered them for myself and for the conversion of souls who do not trust in the goodness of God. Suddenly, my cell was filled with black figures full of anger and hatred for me. One of them said, "Be damned, you and He who is within you, for you are beginning to torment us even in hell." As soon as I said, "And the Word was made flesh and dwelt among us," the figures vanished in a sudden whir. (Diary, 323)

CHAPTER 15:

In her book, The Pivot of Civilization, Margaret Sanger, the founder of Planned Parenthood, wrote: "Our failure to segregate morons who are increasing and multiplying demonstrates our foolhardy and extravagant sentimentalism... [Philanthropists] encourage the healthier and more normal sections of the world to shoulder the burden of unthinking and indiscriminate fecundity of others; which brings with it, as I think the reader must agree, a dead weight of human waste. Instead of decreasing and aiming to eliminate the stocks that are most detrimental to the future of the race and the world, it tends to render them to a menacing degree dominant. We are paying for, and even submitting to, the dictates of an ever-increasing, unceasingly spawning class of human beings who never should have been born at all . . ." (4)

Sanger stated in a letter to Dr. Clarence Gamble, heir of the Proctor and Gamble soap company fortune and fellow eugenist, "We should hire three or four colored ministers, preferably with social-service backgrounds and with engaging personalities. The most successful educational approach to the Negro is through a religious appeal. We don't want the word to go out that we want to exterminate the Negro population. And the minister is the man who can straighten out that idea if it ever occurs to any of their more rebellious members." (5)

Analysis of 2010 Census Bureau data shows that 62 percent of Planned Parenthood abortion facilities are within walking distance (two miles) of a census trace that is at least 50 percent African American (2), and 33 percent are within walking distance of a census tract that is at least 50 percent Hispanic (3). Between 2007 and 2010, nearly 36 percent of all abortions in the United States were performed on African American women, even though blacks made up only 12.8 percent of the population. Another 21 percent of abortions were performed on Hispanics, who constitute 17 percent, and an additional 7 percent on other minority races. All told, more than half of all babies killed by abortion between 2007 and 2010 were minorities. (6, 7)

(1) Margaret Sanger (editor), The Woman Rebel, Vol. 1, No. 1, reprinted in Woman and the New Race (New York: Brentanos Publishers, 1922).

(2) Susan E. Enouen, P.E., "New Research Shows that Planned Parenthood Targets Minority Neighborhoods," Life Issues Connector, Life Issues Institute, October 2012, accessed January 27, 2018, http://www.issues4life.org/pdfs/pptargetsblackamerica.pdf.

(3) Documentary: Maafa21: Black Genocide in 21st Century America by Life Dynamics: http://www.maafa21.com.

(4) Margaret Sanger, The Pivot of Civilization, Chapter: "The Cruelty of Charity" (New York: Maxwell Reprint Co., 1970, ©1922), pp. 116, 122 and 189.

(5) Margaret Sanger's December 19, 1939 letter to Dr. Clarence Gamble. Original source: Sophia Smith Collection, Smith College, North Hampton,

Massachusetts. Also described in Linda Gordon's Woman's Body, Woman's Right: A Social History of Birth Control in America (New York: Grossman Publishers, 1976).

(6) Karen Pazol, PhD, Andreea A. Creanga, MD, PhD, Kim D. Burley, Brenda Hayes, MPA, Denise J. Jamieson, MD, Abortion Surveillance-United States, 2010, November 29, 2013 / 62(ss08);1-44.
Centers for Disease Control and Prevention,
http://www.cdc.gov/mmwr/preview/mmwrhtml/ss6208a1.htm?s_cid=ss6208a1_w.

(7) Kirsten Andersen, "Sky-high Abortion Rate Among Blacks, Minorities Only Getting Worse: Latest CDC Data," December 4, 2013, Life Site News, accessed January 27, 2018, http://www.lifesitenews.com/news/sky-high-abortion-rate-among-blacks-minorities-only-getting-worse-latest-cd.

CHAPTER 16:

(1) In 1931, Jesus appeared to St. Faustina, clothed in a white garment with His right hand raised in a gesture of blessing. His left hand was touching His garment in the area of His heart, from where two large rays came forth, one red and the other pale. Jesus said to her: "Paint an image according to the pattern you see, with the signature: Jesus, I trust in You. I promise that the soul that will venerate this image will not perish. I also promise victory over [its] enemies already here on earth, especially at the hour of death. I, myself, will defend it as my own glory (Diary, 47, 48). I am offering people a vessel with which they are to keep coming for graces to the fountain of mercy. That vessel is this image with the signature: 'Jesus, I trust in You' (327). I desire that this image be venerated, first in your chapel, and [then] throughout the world (47).

(2) Elaine Murray Stone, Maximilian Kolbe. Saint of Auschwitz (Paulist Press: New York, 1997).

(3) Fr. Frank Pavone, "We Won't Kill Anybody: Overcoming The Civil Rights Disconnect," LifesiteNews.com, January 3, 2014, accessed January 27, 2018, https://www.lifesitenews.com/blogs/we-wont-kill-anybody-overcoming-the-civil-rights-disconnect.

(4) Johanna Dasteel, and Ben Johnson, "Poll: 50 Percent of All Catholics Support Abortion in 'All Or Most Cases'" LifeSitenews.com, July 25, 2013, accessed accessed January 27, 2018, http://www.lifesitenews.com/news/poll-50-percent-of-all-catholics-support-abortion-in-all-or-most-cases.

CHAPTER 17:

Abortion through artificial contraceptives happens because contraceptives allow for breakthrough ovulation, which means a human being can be created, but the woman's body is made into a hostile environment, so the new life is flushed away and killed. Norplant allows for breakthrough ovulation 50 to 65 percent of the time. Depo-Provera has breakthrough ovulation 40 to 60 percent of the time. The IUD has regular ovulation 100 percent of the time. (2) The new pills of today, with their lower estrogen dose, allow ovulation up to 50 percent of the time. (3) See the documentary 28 Days on the Pill at https://vimeo.com/12090300.

Under the principles of informed consent, The American Medical Association published an article on February 9, 2000, suggesting that women be informed that by taking certain contraceptives, they are potentially creating a life that will not be allowed to live. (14) Currently, women are not being told of "the post-fertilization effects" of oral contraceptives, so by and large, women do not know.

(1) See Patricia Sandoval's Cara a Cara interview, Testimonio Impactante de Un Aborto, accessed January 27, 2018, https://www.youtube.com/watch?v=XlpS4Q-0n5Q. For an interview in English, which tells the story of Patricia Sandoval's life, see https://youtu.be/efskKIAgtGg.

(2) William F. Colliton, Jr., M.D., FACOG, Clinical Professor of Obstetrics and Gynecology, George Washington University Medical Center, "Birth Control Pill: Abortifacient and Contraceptive," American Association of Pro-life Obstetricians and Gynecologists, accessed July 26, 2017, http://aaplog.org/birth-control-pill-abortifacient-and-contraceptive/.

(3) Randy C. Alcorn, Does the Birth Control Pill Cause Abortions? 10th ed. (Eternal Perspective Ministries, 2011).

(4) Dr. Thomas Hilgers, "Norplant," Linacre Quarterly, 1993, pp.64-69.

(5) Study of Abortion Deaths Ad Hoc Commission, "Infant Homicides Through Contraceptives," 1994, Bardstown, KY. Ph: 502-348-3963.

(6) David Sterns, M.D. Gina Sterns, R.N., B.S.N., Pamela Yaksich, "Gambling with Life, How the I.U.D. and 'The Pill' Work," Vital Signs Ministries, January 8, 2005, accessed July 26, 2017, http://www.vitalsignsministries.org/index.php/articles/gambling-with-life/.

(7) J.T. Finn, "'Birth Control' Pills cause early Abortions," Pro-life America: Facts on Abortion, updated April 23, 2005, accessed January 27, 2018, http://www.prolife.com/BIRTHCNT.html.

(8) Walter L. Larimore, MD, Joseph B. Stanford, MD, MSPH, "Postfertilization Effects of Oral Contraceptives and Their Relationship to Informed Consent," The Polycarp Research Institute, reprinted with permission from: "Archives of Family Medicine," February 2000, Vo. 9, No. 2, pp. 126 - 133, American Medical Association, accessed January 27, 2018, http://www.polycarp.org/larimore_stanford.htm. For printable version: http://www.polycarp.org/larimore_stanford.pdf.

(9) World Health Organization Statement, September 2005, "Carcinogenicity of Combined Hormonal Contraceptives and Combined Menopausal Treatment," accessed January 27, 2018, http://www.who.int/reproductivehealth/topics/ageing/cocs_hrt_statement.pdf.

(10) Centers for Disease Control and Prevention, accessed through the Compressed Mortality database, http://wonder.cdc.gov/. Also see, www.thepillkills.org, accessed January 27, 2018.

(11) "Pollution: An Introduction," Directgov.com.uk. The National Archives, accessed January 27, 2018, http://webarchive.nationalarchives.gov.uk/20121015000000/http://www.direct.gov.uk/en/Environmentandgreenerliving/Thewiderenvironment/Pollution/DG_064397.

(12) Theo Stein and Miles Moffeit, "Mutant fish prompt concern: Study focuses on sewage plants," Denver Post, October 3, 2004.

(13) Catholic News Agency: "Medical Association Points Out Prophetic Nature Of Humanae Vitae," Rome, Italy, Jan 6, 2009, accessed January 27, 2018, http://www.catholicnewsagency.com/news/medical_association_points_out_prophetic_nature_of_humanae_vitae/.

(14) "River 'Pollution' Sparks Fertility Fears," BBC News, March 17, 2002, accessed January 27, 2018, http://news.bbc.co.uk/2/hi/uk_news/1877162.stm.

(15) And we read in the Scripture, for God says very clearly: Even if a mother could forget her child - I will not forget you - I have carved you in the palm of my hand. We are carved in the palm of His hand, so close to Him that unborn child has been carved in the hand of God. And that is what strikes me most, the beginning of that sentence, that even if a mother could forget something impossible - but even if she could forget - I will not forget you. And today the greatest means - the greatest destroyer of peace is abortion. And we who are standing here - our parents wanted us. We would not be here if our parents would do that to us. Our children, we want them, we love them, but what of the millions? Many people are very, very concerned with the children in India, with the children in Africa where quite a number die, maybe of malnutrition, of hunger and so on, but millions are dying deliberately by the will of the mother. And this is what is the greatest destroyer of peace today. Because if a mother can kill her own child - what is left for me to kill you and you kill me - there is nothing between. . .

We are fighting abortion by adoption, we have saved thousands of lives, we have sent words to all the clinics, to the hospitals, police stations - please don't destroy the child, we will take the child. . .And we have a tremendous demand from families who have no children, that is the blessing of God for us. And also, we are doing another thing which is very beautiful - we are teaching our beggars, our leprosy patients, our slum dwellers, our people of the street, natural family planning.

And in Calcutta alone in six years - it is all in Calcutta - we have had 61,273 babies less from the families who would have had, but because they practice this natural way of abstaining, of self-control, out of love for each other. We teach them the temperature meter which is very beautiful, very simple, and our poor people understand. And you know what they have told me? Our family is healthy, our family is united, and we can have a baby whenever we want. So clear - those people in the street, those beggars - and I think that if our people can do like that how much more you and all the others who can know the ways and means without destroying the life that God has created in us.

Taken from the official website of the Nobel Prize: http://www.nobelprize.org/nobel_prizes/peace/laureates/1979/teresa-lecture.html.

CHAPTER 18:

Factors that influence the youth to have sex earlier or later in life:

- The more that teenagers are satisfied with their mother–child relationship, the less likely they are to be sexually experienced (8). Conversely, poor communication with parents about sex and parental substance abuse are also linked with risky sexual behaviors. (8)
- Teenagers are most likely to seek sexual information from their friends (61 percent) and least likely to seek information from their parents (32 percent). Youths who resist engaging in sexual activity tend to have friends who are also abstinent. They also tend to have strong personal beliefs in abstinence and the perception of negative parental reactions. (8)
- Youths who are sexually active tend to believe that most of their friends are sexually active, as well; that rewards outweigh the costs of sexual involvement; that sex overall is rewarding; and that it is all right for unmarried adolescents over age sixteen to engage in intercourse. (8)
- Teens who watch a lot of television with sexual content are more likely to initiate intercourse in the following year. (10)
- Television in which characters talk about sex affects teens just as much as television that actually shows sexual activity. (10)
- Teens from low-income families may have sex earlier than those from wealthier families. In a U.S. study of nearly 1,000 low-income families in three cities, one in four children between the ages of eleven and sixteen reported having had sex, with their first sexual intercourse experience occurring at the average age of 12.77. (2005) (7) The national average for first time sex is higher at about seventeen.

1) Philomena's story is known only because three separate people, completely unknown to each other, received the same details of her life through private revelations. One of the revelations received an official Imprimatur (stamp of approval) from the Vatican in the same year it occurred. The revelation was

locutions in Philomena's own voice, given to Mother Luisa di Gesu in August, 1833. See Genevieve Cunningham, "St. Philomena the Wonder-Worker: Her Story in Her Own Words," August 10, 2016, accessed July 26, 2017, https://www.catholiccompany.com/getfed/st-philomena-wonder-worker/.

(2) "Patroness: St. Philomena, Patroness and Protectress of the Living Rosary," Universal Living Rosary Association, accessed January 27, 2018, http://www.philomena.org/patroness.asp.

(3) According to the Durex 2005 Global Sex Survey of 317,000 people from forty-one countries, the world's largest ever survey on sexual attitudes and behavior, the global average age in 2015 for first time sex was 17.3, and the trend was for people to lose their virginity earlier, with sixteen to twenty year olds becoming sexually active by 16.3 years. January 27, 2018, http://www.data360.org/pdf/20070416064139.Global%20Sex%20Survey.pdf.

(4) "NSFG - Key Statistics from the National Survey of Family Growth," accessed January 27, 2018, http://www.cdc.gov/nchs/nsfg/key_statistics.htm.

(5) U.S. Bureau of the Census, America's Families and Living Arrangements (Washington, DC: U.S. Government Printing Office, 2009).

(6) Gladys Martinez, Casey E. Copen, and Joyce C. Abma, Teenagers in the United States: Sexual Activity, Contraceptive Use, And Childbearing, 2006-2010 National Survey of Family Growth, Vital and Health Statistics, 2011, Series 23, No. 31; DHHS publication no. (PHS) 2012-1983 (Hyattsville, Maryland, Washington, DC: U.S. Department of Health and Human Services, Centers for Disease Control and Prevention, National Center for Health Statistics).

(7) "Low-Income Kids Report First Sexual Intercourse at 12 Years Old in New ISU Study - News Service - Iowa State University," accessed January 27, 2018, http://www.news.iastate.edu/news/2009/aug/teensex.

(8) Factsheet on Adolescent Sexual Behavior: II. Socio-psychological Factors. Advocates for Youth, 1997.

(9) Rebecca L. Collins, Marc N. Elliott, Sandra H. Berry, David E. Kanouse, Dale Kunkel, Sarah B. Hunter, Angela Miu, "Does Watching Sex on Television Influence Teens' Sexual Activity?" Document #: RB-9068, Rand Corporation, 2004. Online version, accessed January 27, 2018: http://www.rand.org/pubs/research_briefs/RB9068.html.

CHAPTER 19:

1) YouTube: Testimonio: El aborto en Primera Persona por Patricia Sandoval, published on March 31, 2015 by Fundación Jaime Guzman, accessed January 27, 2018, https://www.youtube.com/watch?v=0wAlHFBGerA.

2) The following is a list of the symptoms of post-abortion syndrome (PAS), a variant of PTSD (Post-traumatic stress disorder). These symptoms will not necessarily appear at the same time, nor is anyone likely to experience all of them.

Some may occur immediately after an abortion and others much later. If a person can identify with more than two symptoms, it could be that he or she is experiencing post-abortion syndrome. PAS symptoms include: guilt, anxiety, avoiding children or pregnant women, numbness, sexual dysfunction, depression, thoughts of suicide, anniversary reactions, flashbacks, wanting to get pregnant again, fear of infertility, unable to bond with present or future children, fear that current or future children will die, eating disorders, alcohol and drug use.

Reference: Dr. Paul C. Reisser and Teri K. Reisser, A Solitary Sorrow: Finding Healing & Wholeness After Abortion (Wheaton, H. Shaw Publishers, 1999). Also see: "Post Abortion Syndrome Symptoms, Ramah International, https://ramahinternational.org/post-abortion-syndrome-symptoms/.

3) YouTube: Dark Secrets: Finding Healing after Abortion, published by the Diocese of Oakland, January 27, 2018, https://www.youtube.com/watch?v=pRV-SPiH29g.

4) YouTube: "A Video That Changes Lives and Souls in 15 Minutes: The Incredible Story of Patricia Sandoval," https://youtu.be/efskKIAgtGg.

5) "Transfigured" DVD, available at QueenofPeaceMedia.com. Astrid Bennet Gutierrez, EWTN host, says of this video: "Patricia Sandoval's astonishing and compelling testimony is convincing youth throughout the world of the sanctity of life and sacredness of sexuality. Sit down and watch this story with your young people and you'll help spare them a lifetime of regret."

6) Steven Ertelt, "Ex Staffers Ready to Expose Planned Parenthood to Congress," LifeNews.com, December 14, 2011, January 27, 2018, http://www.lifenews.com/2011/12/14/ex-staffers-ready-to-expose-planned-parenthood-to-congress/.

(7) Pope Francis, "General Audience: On the Passion Suffered by Children," Zenit: The World Seen from Rome, Vatican City, April 08, 2015, accessed January 27, 2018, http://www.zenit.org/en/articles/general-audience-on-the-passion-suffered-by-children.

CHAPTER 20:

(1) YouTube: Cardinal Arinze on Pro-Abortion Politicians, published by Catholic News Agency, April 9, 2008, accessed January 27, 2018, https://www.youtube.com/watch?v=kv3MRyKfEHA.

CHAPTER 21:

1) See www.PatriciaSandoval.com and www.QueenofPeaceMedia.com/patricia-sandoval.

Queen of Peace
MEDIA
.com